LOVE, FREDDIE

LOVE, FREDDIE

FREDDIE MERCURY'S SECRET LIFE AND LOVE

LESLEY-ANN JONES

First published in 2025 by Lesley-Ann Jones,
in partnership with Whitefox Publishing Ltd

www.lesleyannjones.com
www.wearewhitefox.com

EU GPSR Authorised Representative
LOGOS EUROPE, 9 rue Nicolas Poussin, 17000, LA ROCHELLE, France
E-mail: Contact@logoseurope.eu

ISBN 978-1-916797-96-3
Also available as an eBook
ISBN 978-1-916797-97-0

Edited by Nicola Bigwood
Designed and typeset by seagulls.net
Cover design by Gunjan Ahlawat
Project management by Whitefox Publishing
Printed and bound by CPI Group (UK) Ltd, Croydon CR0 4YY

'Wonderful, kind and moving. Thoughtful, delicate and dignified, just as he was. A faithful, respectful rendering of Freddie Mercury's real life.'

"B."

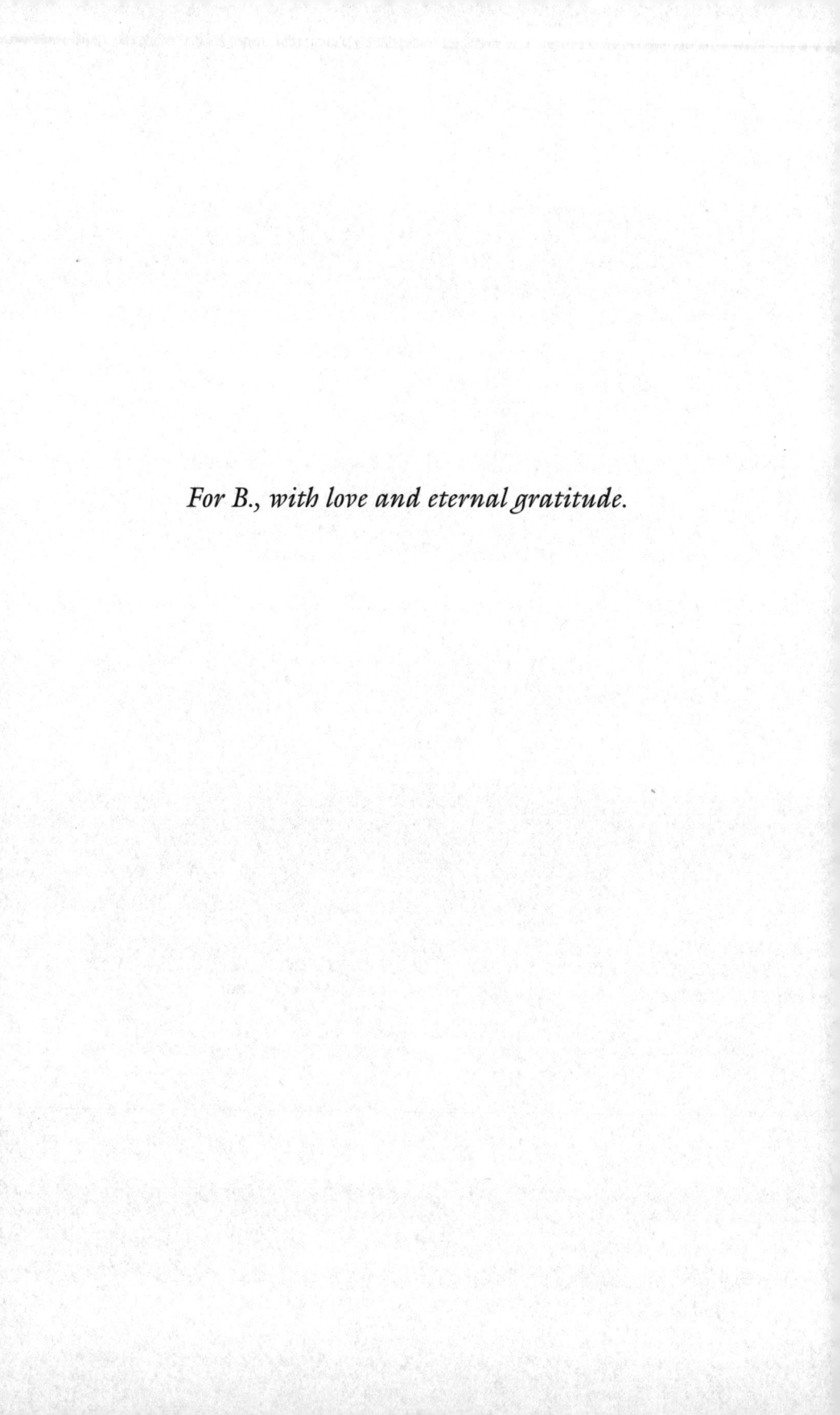

For B., with love and eternal gratitude.

Come to me in the silence of the night;
Come in the speaking silence of a dream;
Come with soft rounded cheeks and eyes as bright
As sunlight on a stream;
Come back in tears,
O memory, hope, love of finished years.

Oh dream how sweet, too sweet, too bitter sweet,
Whose wakening should have been in Paradise,
Where souls brimfull of love abide and meet;
Where thirsting longing eyes
Watch the slow door
That opening, letting in, lets out no more.

Yet come to me in dreams, that I may live
My very life again tho' cold in death:
Come back to me in dreams, that I may give
Pulse for pulse, breath for breath:
Speak low, lean low,
As long ago, my love, how long ago.

Christina Rossetti (1830–1894)

IN MEMORIAM

Farrokh Bulsara : Frederick/Freddie/Fred Bulsara :
Freddie Mercury
5 September 1946–24 November 1991

• • •

Boomanshaw Rustomji : Bomi Bulsara, Freddie's father
14 December 1908–26 December 2003

Jer Bomi Bulsara : Jer Bulsara, Freddie's mother
16 October 1922–13 November 2016

Maria de Montserrat Viviana Concepción Caballé i Folch :
Montserrat Caballé
12 April 1933–6 October 2018

Ursula Ledersteger : Barbara Valentin
15 December 1940–22 February 2002

Michael Edward Chester Smith :
Michael David Rock : Mick Rock
21 November 1948–18 November 2021

Robert Andrew 'Andy' Peebles
13 December 1948–22 March 2025

Joseph 'Joe' Fannelli, 12 April 1954–2 June 1993

David Minns, 4 February 1954–May 2007

James 'Jim' Hutton, 4 January 1949–1 January 2010

Anthony Philip Swern : Phil 'The Collector' Swern
30 June 1948–31 August 2024

Peter Waters Dingley : Johnnie Walker
30 March 1945–31 December 2024

*The work that one does is a way of
keeping a diary.*

Pablo Picasso

*If liberty means anything at all,
it means the right to tell people what
they do not want to hear.*

George Orwell

*The best people possess a feeling for beauty,
the courage to take risks, the discipline to
tell the truth, the capacity for sacrifice.
Ironically, their virtues make them vulnerable;
they are often wounded, sometimes destroyed.*

Ernest Hemingway

CONTENTS

CHAPTER 1

TOUCHING THE SUN

15 December 2021: a Wednesday. Waking early, I shuffled to the kitchen to make tea, carried my cup back to bed, snuggled down with my phone and immersed myself in headlines before getting up to work. Which was not, at that time, the easiest thing to focus on.

The world was in the grip of Covid-19. The UK's first national lockdown had been imposed on 23 March the previous year, then lifted two months later. Further restrictions were introduced during 2020 in response to an alarming surge in cases. Most of the rules were relaxed during the Delta-variant-driven third wave in mid-2021. Now, ten days before Christmas, we found ourselves facing deadly Omicron, the variant that the UK's Health Security Agency was calling 'probably the most significant threat' of the pandemic to date as they warned of 'staggering growth' over the next few days. That wave was to persist into spring 2022. By then, Covid would have claimed sixteen million lives.

Boris Johnson, the British Prime Minister at that time, suffered a humiliating rebellion against measures to slow the speed of Omicron. Much was made of reports that more than a million of us could be isolating on Christmas Day. Professor Chris Whitty, England's Chief Medical Officer, warned that Omicron was spreading 'unbelievably fast'. The day before, 14 December, 59,610 cases had been confirmed. Health chiefs, however, believed the true number of infections to be infinitely higher. From Geneva, the World Health Organization stated that the coronavirus variant was spreading across the planet at an unprecedented rate.

In other news, scientists revealed that the critical ice shelf in western Antarctica known as the Thwaites Glacier could break apart within three to five years, leading to huge rises in sea levels. It was also confirmed that space agency NASA's Parker solar probe had flown through the unexplored atmosphere they call 'the corona' and had touched the sun. This had in fact taken place the previous April; but the extraordinary feat could not be confirmed until several months later, once crucial data had been returned to Earth.

Did this awesome occurrence dominate headlines, broaden our perspective and dazzle the world with some desperately needed hope? It barely got a look-in. The media were in meltdown over a raucous gathering at Conservative Party HQ the previous day, which was exposed when someone leaked video footage of senior Number Ten staff living it up at an illegal Christmas party. Cue mass fury. The government appeared to be thumbing its nose at the little people by not following its own rules. The consequences, for many, were catastrophic; though nowhere near as dire as for the droves who had died and would continue to expire in isolation, in hospitals and in nursing homes, separated from loved ones and denied a dignified farewell.

Something else happened that day to fix the date and those events in my mind, so firmly that I doubt I will ever forget them. It was the arrival in my inbox, at 11:55, of an email marked 'To the attention of Lesley-Ann Jones about her book'. Little did

I know that this would be the first of an avalanche of missives about Freddie Mercury that would land over the next three and a half years, delivering a story so unprecedented and unlikely that at one point I questioned my sanity for believing it.

Having researched and written three complete, stand-alone studies of Freddie, published as four original volumes by a single publisher, Hodder & Stoughton, between 1997 and 2021 – biographies that necessitated lengthy, complicated journeys to his birthplace, Zanzibar, off the East African mainland, and to St Peter's school in Panchgani, India, where he boarded between the ages of eight and sixteen – you might expect my knowledge of the Queen frontman's life and career to be far-reaching. Yet everything I knew faded to near insignificance when set beside the abundance of revelations volunteered by my anonymous correspondent, whose first unsolicited communication ran to a staggering twenty-six thousand words.

'I wanted to write to you for years (for almost fifteen years and the first edition of your book),' the writer began. 'I hesitated a long time and I thought it through before making a decision. Because Freddie wanted his privacy to remain private; because it's still so hard and very painful; and because he would have been furious with me and would have hated that I do it. But you are Freddie's biographer. Because you did a great work in your last book about him, I think some facts should be brought to your attention about his childhood, his music, his polygamous bisexuality, about Phillimore Gardens and Freddie the private man, and about Freddie's last will. You hear it here first, and you have the right to use it as you see fit. I ask for nothing in return … except the truth, for him.

'I'm not a writer,' they went on. 'As I haven't spoken English since decades, I cannot speak it fluently anymore (it's not the language of my mother)' – in other words, it was not their mother tongue.

'So please excuse me for spelling/grammar/conjugation/ syntax errors and dull writing. Merry Christmas and Best Wishes to you, your family and all your loved ones.

'B.'

. . .

Was it a hoax? Were these the wild imaginings of some disgruntled troll or hater? Published authors are accustomed to receiving eccentric correspondence. So I didn't respond immediately. I printed out the forty-one-page email, shoved it in my bag and wandered down the road to my local café. I'd get back to it that night once I'd had a chance to digest it and make notes. If true, its revelations were mind-blowing. There could even be consequences. I intended to reply, as I needed to find out who had sent it. I wanted to re-read and absorb the contents before I did.

I felt I should explain to the writer that their primary suggestion – the point, in effect, of them having contacted me – was not feasible. It would be impossible to update *Love of My Life*,[1] my latest book about Freddie, without proof that these incredible disclosures were genuine. I would have to know their identity before I could take things further. I would also need written permission to publish. Agents, editors and lawyers would have to be involved. The revelations were likely to cause a global sensation. Why wouldn't they? On the world stage, Queen are still huge. Freddie's untimely death guaranteed him immortality comparable to that of James Dean, Marilyn Monroe, Elvis Presley and others whose legends transcend time. There was the risk of upsetting and infuriating certain individuals who might take exception, or even attempt legal action. Should I leave well alone or publish and be damned? I already knew the answer. 'If you were as close to Freddie as your email suggests,' I went on, 'I would move mountains and risk everything I own to make it happen. Proof and evidence are key. If, for example, you were [Freddie's former fiancée] Mary Austin, that would be proof enough. But perhaps you are somebody even closer?'

I thanked the writer for their kindness, typed reciprocal Christmas wishes, and bid them a 'safe and sane' New Year. People were saying such things to each other during the Covid years. No one was taking anything for granted.

Two days later, I received two further emails within hours of each other. Their first landed at 08:43. The second dropped in just after noon.

'I'm not Mary [Austin],' the first assured me. 'I have the greatest respect for her, and for the love and peace she gave [Freddie]. Of course it would be easier, for you, and for me, if she talked. But she has chosen to remain silent these past thirty years, despite everything she has been through. I admire her for that, and I respect her decision.'

They also had the greatest respect, my correspondent wrote, for Queen's bassist John Deacon and drummer Roger Taylor. But, the writer stressed, they were neither of them. Nor were they Queen producer Reinhold Mack, nor one of Mack's children with his wife, Ingrid, in case I should leap to that conclusion:

in some ways an obvious assumption to make, given that the couple's third son, John Frederick, is the godson of both Freddie and John Deacon, and also that Freddie named him. They were not a relative of any of the aforementioned either. One of 'Freddie's so-called "friends"', then, to borrow the writer's punctuation? Not a chance. Regardless of their identity, why were they writing to me?

'Who else but you?' they responded. 'There are a few errors in your book, yes, but I know that you wrote it to the absolute best of your knowledge and according to information given to you by other people. It's a serious work, and I thank you for it. That is why I contacted you. Because there are facts that should be brought to your attention. There's still a lot to say about the forty-five years of [Freddie's] life. Yes, I could have gone to your friend David Wigg, who I have nothing against. He might seem the obvious choice. He's the journalist Freddie trusted the most. Freddie granted him more interviews than anybody else. Long and substantial interviews, too, not fifteen-minute throwaways. But things changed over the final six years of Freddie's life. He never told David nor any other journalist that he was HIV positive. Nor did he tell them when he developed full-blown AIDS. So no, I couldn't have gone to David Wigg. That would not have made sense.

'You are the only one who tried to find out who [Freddie] was beyond the lines of coke, the shots of vodka and the sordid nights,' they would later add. 'You are the only one who didn't take a fact over a short period of time and apply it to his whole life. The dark years lasted only between 1983 and 1985. He was promiscuous before that, it's true, but in a totally different emotional state. Freddie wanted his privacy to remain private. I have crossed the line by talking to you. Time after time, all those so-called "friends", one after the other, stabbed him in the back. All those books, articles in the press, documentaries that depict him in certain ways … for years and decades, I protected my heart and my mind against all these attacks.

'He was not perfect. Nobody is. I knew his dark side, but I also knew his brilliantly bright side. I know why he had these bright and dark sides too. Why am I talking? Warts and all? Yes, but without lies. It's better. That's why I step across the line. For him, not for me.'

• • •

That was how our relationship began. There were nights when I could barely sleep, so restless was I to receive the next instalment. Before long, our conversation turned to Queen's controversial blockbuster film.

On 24 October 2018 (2 November in the US), twenty-seven years after Freddie's death at the age of forty-five, Queen and their associates released their motion picture *Bohemian Rhapsody*. It starred Rami Malek as Freddie and Lucy Boynton as Mary Austin, who was presented as his longtime friend and former fiancée. Gwilym Lee portrayed guitarist Brian May, Ben Hardy their drummer Roger Taylor, and Joe Mazzello the band's bassist John Deacon. Focusing on the life of their lead singer, the film charted Queen's career from their formation in 1970 to their triumphant appearance in Bob Geldof's and Midge Ure's fundraising extravaganza *Live Aid* at London's old Wembley Stadium, on 13 July 1985. Produced by Regency Enterprises, GK Films and Queen Films and distributed by 20th Century Fox, *Bohemian Rhapsody* broke box-office records worldwide. It grossed more than $910.8 million (£735 million) against a modest production budget of around $50 million (£40 million). It became the sixth-highest-grossing movie globally during 2018 and was that year's biggest-selling biographical and drama film, only ceding its crown five years later to *Oppenheimer*, starring Cillian Murphy as J. Robert Oppenheimer, the father of the atomic bomb. At the 91st Academy Awards in 2019, *Bohemian Rhapsody* won four Oscars: for Best Actor (Rami Malek), Best Film Editing, Best Sound Editing and Best Sound Mixing. Nominated for Best Picture alongside *Green Book*, *Black Panther*, *BlacKkKlansman*, *The Favourite*, *Roma*, *A Star Is Born* and *Vice*, it lost to *Green Book*. It also took Best Motion Picture – Drama at the 76th Golden Globe Awards; was nominated for the Producers Guild of America award for Best Theatrical Motion Picture; and claimed the BAFTA Award for Best British Film. To go with his golden gong, Rami Malek scooped the Golden Globe, Screen Actors Guild and BAFTA awards for Best Actor. In addition to its colossal clean-up, *Bohemian Rhapsody* became the UK's fastest-selling digital download film of all time, shifting 265,000 downloads over only eight days.

For those in the know, however, the film fell short. Professional critics denounced it as 'middle-of-the-road', 'a bit of a mess', 'sanitised', 'ridiculous' and 'royally embarrassing'. It was jeered as 'terrible, 'self-indulgent' and 'revisionist', and even called 'an act of brazen myth-making'. Its creators were accused of having played 'fast and loose with the truth'. One journalist scoffed that the producers had 'made a saleable PG-13 movie out of an R-rated rock life' in order to put bums on seats. The rub? It seemed the size of it. The internet was almost broken at one point by people falling over themselves to chart the picture's multiple errors and shortcuts. Such as? Ignoring the crucial first eighteen years of Freddie's existence, spent in Africa and India – which had been, despite the subsequent rock superstardom that he achieved with Queen, arguably the richest, most colourful, most adventurous and most tragic of his life. Then there were the blue eyes: Freddie's were a shade of brown so deep that in certain lights they were often mistaken for black. As my correspondent would later remark:

'The pale blue eyes were a bad mistake. He said so much with his eyes: his approval, his disapproval, his encouragement, his support. Joy, happiness, tenderness and, later on, some kind of melancholy. His gaze had an incredible power. Whatever he wanted to express with it, no one could challenge it. Definitely not me. I also noticed in the movie that his jaw does not fit with his powerful voice. The way he sits in front of the piano is wrong. And his arms and hands: where are they! He spoke not only with his hands but with his whole arms, all the time, even during quiet or very serious conversations. Only during press conferences or filmed interviews did he control his arms and hands. The rest of the time, he spoke with these wonderful, passionate arm gestures. Where is his sense of humour? His jokes? His funny games? His daily joy (and I don't mean just at parties)? I barely recognise Freddie in this film.'

As for presenting him under his original name, Farrokh Bulsara, and having him change that only after he had met his future Queen bandmates: that didn't happen. The name 'Freddie' had been coined by fellow pupils years earlier while he was still at boarding school in India, thousands of miles from home. And one of the film's pivotal characters, a record company executive by the name of Ray Foster, who is played by *Wayne's World* star Mike Myers, never existed in real life.

The film features an actor playing the late Capital Radio DJ Kenny Everett, a friend of Freddie's, who debuts the band's signature track 'Bohemian Rhapsody' on his London-wide radio show.[2] It was not 'Ev', however, but BBC Radio 1's 'Diddy' David Hamilton who did the honours, being the first presenter to play that track live on air. David did so on his national programme, featuring it as his Record of the Week.

What else? Bassist John Deacon never recorded vocals on any of the band's albums, although he did sometimes sing back-up on stage during gigs. Some of Queen's songs are featured in the wrong chronological order: for example, 'We Will Rock You' and 'Fat-Bottomed Girls'. The film introduces Jim Hutton, later a boyfriend of Freddie's, as a waiter at one of Mercury's house parties. But Jim was working at the Savoy as a hairdresser when the two first met. It was not Freddie's 'former fiancée' Mary Austin who persuaded Freddie to 'reunite' with the band and take part in *Live Aid*: they had only recently concluded their *The Works* tour, and had not called it a day. Nor was it Freddie who talked the rest of the band into 'doing' *Live Aid*. That privilege went to their manager, Jim 'Miami' Beach, played by Tom Hollander, who relayed a demand masquerading as a request from Bob Geldof. Freddie was as yet unaware that he was infected with HIV before the Wembley concert on 13 July 1985. So he did not, as we see on screen, announce that devastating news to the rest of the band ahead of their performance. 'The movie could not ignore the AIDS element, of course,' my pen friend told me. 'They had no choice but to address it. But Freddie developed full-blown AIDS in 1989, not 1985. To make that claim totally changes the actual history of the last six years of his life.'

Freddie did not take his new boyfriend Jim to see his parents at their home before the *Live Aid* concert. The film states, in a title card at the end, that Freddie remained friends with Mary and continued in a relationship with Jim until his death. But Freddie and Mary never ended their partnership. They each remained the other's Significant Other until the day Freddie died. Jim, as some of us had suspected, had been no more than a convenience, a live-in sex partner at a time when, thanks to AIDS, Freddie was no longer able to play the field. The film also neglects to deliver his full 1980s Munich experience, the episode that constituted his final, fatal fling before he relinquished hedonistic living and sought refuge, too late to save himself, in a more coddled and civilised domestic existence. And – *humongous* mistake – it ignores completely the Austrian-born German actress Barbara Valentin, despite the fact that they all knew her to have been a major figure in Freddie's life. The pair were once so close that they purchased a flat together.

To sum up, this discomfiting piece dangles from a timeline so excruciatingly at odds with reality that it comes across at times as quite ridiculous. It mangles the truth in the name of entertainment? Ain't that Hollywood? Some of its history-rewriting is understandable: it is impossible to cram a forty-five-year life into a two-and-a-bit-hours-long biopic. But the way in which it hinges on a character who is a substantial reinvention of the man it purports to celebrate is unforgivable. It is also a monumental cliché. But ain't that Queen? Their original fans have always known and accepted this about them. Those who had followed them since the seventies overlooked and forgave the film's errors, omissions and additions as 'creative licence' and 'tongue-in-cheek', just as they had long embraced the band's curiosities and eccentricities. They had taken Queen to their hearts for what they were, adoring them for their differences. Their very cliché-ness was what rendered them unique. In short, Queen fans were fine with the film, enjoyed it at face value, fell in love with the music all over again, and took its shortcuts and shortcomings with lashings of salt.

Many other filmgoers emerged scathed, with an unpleasant taste in their mouths, together with the uneasy feeling 'that something essential and elemental is missing' – as Peter Travers put it in *Rolling Stone*. Not that he could have known so when he wrote them, but the journalist's words were the understatement of the century.

• • •

'Not once does he laugh in it,' my correspondent reminded me. 'Not once does he look happy. The movie attracted a whole new generation of fans who not only cannot know Freddie Bulsara, they can't even know Freddie Mercury – because this film presents a version of him so far removed from the truth. Even worse, certain people then began to rewrite Freddie's whole story, so that it fitted with the image they had made of him in the movie.'

This film does not depict Freddie Mercury, they insisted: 'Still less Freddie Bulsara. The only truth in the picture is the soundtrack. Ten years for that!'

A bit harsh? The *only* truth?

'In their defence,' the writer conceded, 'I know that the band and their management were caught in a glue trap. There were issues with producers and directors, disagreements during the shoot, many tensions, delays, contract breaches, and of course they were legally and financially obliged to release the movie within a contractually agreed timeframe. This was the first time since their days with the Sheffield brothers that the band didn't watch their backs enough.' They were referring to Norman and Barry Sheffield, co-founders and co-owners of London's Trident recording studios, who extended Queen an early break that came at a price and set them back at the beginning of their career.

'Freddie would have been appalled by the movie,' was their conclusion. 'It would have made his hair stand on end. Had Freddie still been alive, there would have been a totally different outcome. He would have been fully involved at every step of the creative process. As was his habit, he would have controlled everything down to the smallest detail. Things would have been done *his* way, otherwise it would never have been released. Though I do believe it would never have seen the light of day, because Freddie would probably have got bored very quickly, would have changed his mind about doing it, and would have decided to pull out of the whole thing before it ever got off the ground.'

They proceeded to pronounce 'regrettable' the many Freddie birthday tributes, the band's 2020 'official' fiftieth birthday celebration, the events commemorating the anniversaries of his death – 'How can one celebrate a death? I have never understood that' – and the sad demise the previous month of Mick Rock. The photographer who 'shot the seventies' had been Freddie's loyal friend for many years, had known everything there was to know about him, and had kept for life his most carefully guarded secrets. Rock's death brought up, they admitted, 'a lot of emotional stuff for me'.

What about Freddie's bandmates?

'I make a distinction between "the Queen Machine" and the four Queen members,' they responded. 'The business as opposed to the band itself. I will never say that Roger Taylor or John Deacon exploited Freddie's death. John has always had the same attitude: that of "last one in". He would give his point of view or opinion but held back whenever it came to a vote. That in itself is a way of taking part. Tellingly, he has not spoken publicly about Freddie for almost twenty-five years.'

Whenever Roger talks about Freddie, they added, 'he is always very respectful. There is never innuendo or ambiguity. You have to remember that while Queen were Freddie, Roger, John, Brian and no one else, and while the four of them were the only decision-makers, Queen as an entity was almost exclusively Freddie, right from the very start. It was he who created Queen. Yes, there was the earlier band called Smile that featured Roger and Brian, but Queen was something quite different from them. Their ambition, aim and vision were all Freddie's. He never gave up, even when they were immersed in their problems with the Sheffield brothers, deeply in debt, and at other challenging times. Freddie was the ultimate decision-maker. Roger, John and Brian had to submit to Freddie's decisions – which were rarely questioned, even when the other three did not agree. They knew that Freddie had a vision beyond their own. While the Queen sound is largely Roger and Brian, it was Freddie who made it Queen. Maybe this is one of the reasons, among others, why John left the scene after Freddie's death.'

. . .

In August 2021, Brian May began alluding in interviews to a possible sequel to *Bohemian Rhapsody*. He and Roger Taylor were 'in discussions', he said. Which came as no surprise. Few studios or production companies would refrain from chasing a follow-up to a film that had proved a global sensation and made a handful of people so rich that they will never be able to spend the money it made for them. Brian did admit that it might take 'years' to get the screenplay right. It had taken 'years', after all, to nail down their erratic storyline for *Bohemian Rhapsody*. How to top that? What if the only way would be to betray Freddie's faith in them, break their promise to him and reveal his final and most extraordinary secret to the world?

I find it hard to believe that they would be capable of such a thing. But could rumours of this proposed new film be the straw to break the camel's back – the thing that prompted this as yet unknown insider to track me down and propose that I reveal all on their behalf? I wondered. To begin with, at least. But as I was to discover over the next three and a half years, the situation was far more complicated than that.

. . .

'I'm aware that I am contradicting myself by saying all this to you,' said my correspondent. 'Freddie wanted his privacy to remain private, yet here I am, talking to you. Why? Because of a movie that is full of fabrication. Because of the so-called "friends" who stabbed him in the back. Because of all the books, articles and documentaries that brim with discrepancies and depict him falsely, as someone other than who he really was. I have protected myself for decades against the many cruel attacks and self-serving injustices. But now I find I can remain silent no longer. I have no wish, no desire, no aspiration to come out of the shadows, talk about myself, be interviewed by the press, be photographed or appear on television. I will never in my lifetime share the things that I treasure most: the photos, videos, notes, letters, gifts and everything else that Freddie gave me. I know how selfish this makes me. But I am not a public woman ...'

A-*ha*. The first indication of the sex of my correspondent.

'I am shy, an introvert, private, aloof and silent,' *she* said. 'Outwardly, I am very different from him. I wear no costume. I have no profile. I maintain no social media accounts. I have lived anonymously for forty-five years, and I am more than happy as I am. My lifestyle will not change as a result of what I am telling you, whether or not the information is made public. I have no intention of opening Pandora's box. One of the many precious things Freddie taught me is that if you want your secret to remain secret, you just have to keep it in your heart and not tell it to anyone ... except Mic, who was my cat at that time.'

'... *the many precious things Freddie taught me* ...' were the words that changed everything. Pennies poured. I was suddenly aware that I could see her face. I understood. I knew precisely, or at least I had an idea – impossible though it seemed – who I was dealing with. The heart skips in such moments. I really did hold my breath. I should sit down, I flapped, but I was in fact seated at my desk. Did I dare ask the question? Would she deny it? Might my prying inflame and drive the poor woman away?

She pre-empted me.

'Emotionally, I am not able to go further. You have the right, my permission and authorisation to reveal this truth. You can quote me and do whatever else you need to do. I ask for nothing. I need neither money nor recognition. No other biographer has written anything that warrants a response from me. You are the only one. I am aware that I am putting you in a delicate and awkward position. The last thing I want is to get you into trouble. I can't tell you how difficult this has been for me.

'I know I should have found the courage to write to you years ago. I am truly and deeply sorry that I did not. I cannot offer any reasonable explanation. All I can say is, I am here now.'

• • •

Maybe one day, at the age of sixty or sixty-five, she would muse to me a year or so down the line, Freddie would have got round to writing his memoirs.

'Who knows? I think that he probably would have done it. Part of him wanted the world to know the truth about him, because he hated lies and betrayals more than anything. Those things were what hurt and angered him the most. Because he was virtually incapable of dishonesty, he readily believed that others were as honest as he was. But at the end, he was used, abused and betrayed behind his back. He hated that people saw only his outrageous side. It upset him terribly when people were attracted only to his fame and fortune, and would depict him as a superficial, arrogant and silly person when in reality he was quite the opposite. Underneath the outrageous character he was a very shy and private man. Behind the shyness lurked a great depth of heart and soul that only a handful of people knew. He would probably have reached a point beyond which he could no longer tolerate lies and betrayals. He would have exploded, because that was his way, and would at last have gone public with his own truth. I do think that he would have done it one day. It was only a matter of time.'

. . .

She and I remained close. We established trust, a bond and a mutual understanding. We came to regard each other as friends. At the time of writing, we have known each other for more than three years. Because I have promised never to disclose her name, I will refer to her throughout as 'B.' I must state for the record that at no point did she offer me money to write it, nor would I have accepted anything from her. I wish to make clear that I have written Freddie's true story unbribed, uncompromised and completely of my own free will. She wishes to make clear that she will make no money from either the sale of the book or any subsequent adaptation of it.

She sent me a handwritten letter, the text of which follows, and a copy of which appears at the centre of this book.

. . .

'Freddie Mercury was and is my father. We had a very close and loving relationship from the moment I was born and throughout the final fifteen years of his life. He adored me and was devoted to me. The circumstances of my birth may seem, by most people's standards, unusual and even outrageous. That should come as no surprise. It never detracted from his commitment to love and look after me. He cherished me like a treasured possession. I was, naturally, devastated by his death.

'Shortly before he died, he gave me a collection of private notebooks that he had been writing since 1976, before I came into the world. They revealed, in at times excruciating detail, the story of Freddie's whole life. They were written in his own handwriting, in ballpoint pen, in his own words. He entrusted to me, his only child and his next of kin, the written record of his private thoughts, memories and feelings about everything he had experienced. His gift to me was our secret. Although those who lived with him and shared his life knew of the existence of the notebooks, none of them knew, after his death, what had become of them. His family, fellow band members, closest friends, associates and management have had no idea until now that he gave them to me as a present.

'Mary Austin – the wonderful woman who was to all intents and purposes his wife until death parted them – knew absolutely everything about him, including all his undisclosed secrets. The others – his real, true friends whom he could count on fewer than the fingers of one hand; the band; the great army of so-called friends, employees and hired help, those with whom he had working relationships (journalists, designers, film makers, roadies, fan club staff); the even greater army of so-called personal this or that (personal assistant, personal film maker, personal designer, personal photographer ...); wider acquaintances and everyone else – knew only what Freddie wanted them to know. Which wasn't much.

'Freddie was an intensely private man. He gave so few interviews that he was famous for it. Because of this it has been easy, since his death, for many people to exploit and betray him. To twist his words, to rewrite his story, to speculate and make up this theory or that about his life, in order to equate him to the image of the Freddie Mercury that they seek to portray. Their versions of Freddie are far removed from the man he really was. They have done this for their own profit and ego. Freddie would have been deeply wounded by it all. After more than three decades of lies, speculation and distortion, it is time to let Freddie speak.

'I had read everything that Lesley-Ann Jones had ever written about my father when I wrote to her towards the end of 2021, with the intention of offering her the responsibility of sharing his true story. I had been meaning to contact her for years, having read so much of her work: not only about Freddie, but also about other artists. I was struck by her obvious pursuit of the truth, and by how closely she came to capturing "the real Freddie". Her book *Love of My Life: The Lives and Loves of Freddie Mercury*, published in 2021, portrayed him more accurately than anything I had ever read. So much of what has been written and committed to film about him by so-called friends, lovers, employees and colleagues has been at best a gross distortion of the truth, at worst an exercise in exploitation. Those who have been aware of my existence kept his greatest secret out of loyalty to Freddie. That I choose to reveal myself in my own mid-life is my decision and mine alone. I have not, at any point, been coerced into doing this.

'Lesley-Ann and I talked intensely for many months from late 2021. We continue to communicate to this day. Our long discussions have been very moving, at times unbearable and heart-breaking. I revealed to her who my father was. I told her the truth about his childhood, his life, and everything that built the infant, the boy, the teenager, the young man, the grown man, the Dad he was to me, the stage persona and the Mercury mask that he created. I explained to her how he compartmentalised his life, and of course talked at length about our precious time together.

'Lesley-Ann flew to Montreux in May 2023. I do not live there, but the city was chosen because of Freddie's attachment to the place. She made the journey to meet me and my family there; to see Freddie's seventeen notebooks, cards, private notes, letters, bank statements and other relevant documents; to view photos and private videos, and to listen to audio. She tried for a long time to persuade me to publish some of my photographs. It is by no means her fault that I decided not to agree to this. Although I understand very well the importance of illustrating a book, I had to decline to publish the records of our time together. They are from a father to his daughter and only child. They are records of my Dad and the grandfather of my children. We cherish them, they are private, and we want them to remain private. None of these personal items will ever be exhibited to the public. Nor will they ever come up for auction. It is, however, my legal right to share everything I learned from my father's notebooks. It is also my right to destroy the notebooks, should I ever see fit to do so. Freddie's fans, the lovers of his music and the millions who honour his memory must respect this. I hope and pray that they will. If they cannot, that will prove that I was right to keep our mementoes to myself.

'The life I live with my husband and our family in another country is intensely private. We want things to stay that way. We cherish our peaceful and anonymous life, and we want nothing to disturb it. Nobody needs to know who I am. I will have nothing more to say beyond what I have revealed in this book. There will be no further interviews other than those that I have given to Lesley-Ann. I owe it to my father to cherish privacy as one of the most precious privileges in life. As he himself said, it was the thing he regretted giving away so readily. The one thing he wished that he could get back.

'Here, then, for the first and only time, is Freddie Mercury's true story. I have chosen to entrust it to my dear friend Lesley-Ann Jones. Every syllable that you read here was revealed to me by Freddie himself.

'B.'

CHAPTER 2

MY DEAREST TRÉSOR

Time is the last illusion. It slips through our fingers like mercury. We cannot hold it. Though we may squander it, we can never command it, nor can its swagger be stalled. It stands still, stops clocks, halts hearts and lingers on hands only in fiction. It cannot be fast-forwarded nor rewound. That it dances to its own irrefutable beat of truth, Freddie knew better than most. His time on Earth was cut short. He sang Time's truth but was denied its blessing. It waits for no one. It did not wait for him. Not that he was consumed with regret. The only thing for which he longed at the conclusion of his life was more time with his beloved only child.[1]

He called her 'my dearest Trésor', and 'my little Froggie'. These endearments are easily explained. 'Trésor' is French for 'treasure'. 'Froggie' alludes to cuisses de grenouilles or frogs' legs, a classic Gallic delicacy. Her mother and Freddie's paramour, his daughter reveals, was French. But who *was* she?

• • •

Freddie had a one-night stand? Show me the rock star. Casual sex might as well be part of the job description. That he got a girl pregnant should come as no surprise, given his known history of relationships with women. What makes him unique among his kind is that he didn't deny it, leg it, throw money at it or instruct lawyers to force the unfortunate female to abort – all of which, in such circles, are the more common reactions. He stuck around. He made a commitment. He didn't merely acknowledge paternity; he jumped for joy and would have crawled over broken glass to get to it. He then threw himself into impending fatherhood and celebrated the arrival of his baby daughter as the greatest achievement of his life. He was, when she was born, thirty years old. When he died in November 1991, he was forty-five. His only child was not yet fifteen. For the entirety of his fame as Queen's frontman, but unbeknown to his legions of adoring fans around the world, he was a devoted, hands-on dad. His secret daughter was the absolute love of his life. She took precedence over all others, even his precious longtime love Mary Austin. Not only that, but Freddie has grandchildren. If only he had lived to know and love them. But they know him. Raised on recordings of their grandfather reading bedtime stories to their mother when she was a little girl, it is the memory of their 'Papy' that they cherish, not the legend of a global rock superstar. Freddie's secret family life, documented by his own hand in private journals long believed to have been lost or destroyed, rewrites almost everything we thought we knew about him.

· · ·

Although she had not spelled it out, she did not deny who she was when I asked her outright. I had been warming to the idea that my new pen pal could be Rory Taylor, the doctor daughter of drummer Roger.[2] The only thing I had to go on was a smattering of medical references in the emails I received. Then, during the early hours of 14 January 2022, I was jolted awake by the realisation as to who she had to be. Desperate to ask, I held back, for fear of scaring her off. Yet again, curiosity got the better of me. At 11:35 that morning, I wrote her this:

'I am increasingly convinced that you must be Freddie's own child ... simply from mentions you have made about him not having been around to help you grow up, references to you having been protected, the fact that there is no mention of you in his will, why Freddie would have given you his personal effects otherwise, etc. The godchildren we know about, but you have never been discussed. Other members of Freddie's "entourage" must surely know of your existence. [Jim] Beach and [John] Libson (the executors) will know, as presumably you have been taken care of financially ... You mentioned that your mother's native tongue is/was not English (Who was she? What happened to her?). If true, it is amazing that it has never leaked out. But be warned, someone in the know will make it known. Peter Freestone, who, they say, "knows everything about Freddie that there is to know", would not have known something like that? I wonder. You know that my mind is doing overtime night and day on this.'

Her response was not what I might have expected.

'I could have chosen never to contact you. I could have burned them [Freddie's notebooks, entrusted to her just before he died] or simply have waited for decades more before doing anything with them. Like Catherine Camus [daughter of the French-Algerian writer and philosopher Albert Camus, who died in 1960], who published the correspondence between her father and his mistress nearly fifty-eight years after his death.'

She was reminding me that there was no rush. Though in a way, there really was. Wait another generation and Freddie's true story would have significantly less impact, because many of those who mattered in the scheme – his fellow band members, his original fans and followers – would have died.

'You could indeed [have waited, and have published much later],' I replied. 'It is an interesting comparison that you make with Camus. His influence has waned greatly. The publication of said correspondence was not as incendiary as it might have been, had it been shared much earlier. But rock 'n' roll is a curious world. Just as John Lennon's "40/80" – the fortieth anniversary of his death that fell during the year when he would have turned eighty years old – is now considered to have been the last great Lennon year (and was the year when my book on the former Beatle was published), there comes the moment for all rock stars when their worth begins to wane. Gen Zs "get" Freddie. But I do not see the music lasting much beyond the deaths of the remaining members of Queen … two of whom have been solely responsible for keeping it alive.'

We tip-toed around the periphery in this manner for the rest of the month. I was beside myself to know more. She was reluctant to allow me to reveal her identity. She got cold feet. We signed off several times, resolving never to write to one other again. We even said goodbye. But a flame had been lit and was refusing to be extinguished. Desire to tell the true story burned in us both. She admitted that she was terrified of exposing her nearest and dearest to unwanted intrusion and disruption. I agreed never to reveal her identity or location, nor to publish her name or her circumstances. I promised that her secrets would always be safe with me. We left it at that … each of us knowing, I think, that there was never going to be a final farewell.

• • •

Ten days and several extensive emails later, she messaged me again one morning soon after 7 a.m.

'You know who I am,' she wrote. 'You more or less guessed it. Of course members of his entourage – the true family, the real friends – know of my existence, because Freddie was the reason why we were all connected to each other. Emotionally, I am not able to go further, because of the promises I made and because of how difficult and hard it is to re-live all of this. I have never got over losing him. I probably never will. I know you understand, and I thank you.'

• • •

Her life did not begin with some exquisitely romantic love story. It commenced, she confessed, 'with one of those moments they say are as old as time: an act of adultery. The families of my mother and her husband were the kind in which divorce and abortion were unthinkable. Affairs were swept under the carpet and illegitimate, adulterine children were concealed. Private business was dealt with behind closed doors. Discretion was paramount and absolute. If mistakes were made, responsibility must be taken for the consequences.'

Freddie, her mother and her mother's husband had been close friends for years before her conception.

'My mother and stepfather remained married after I arrived. I have to say that they did stay together until my mother died, some years later, and they seemed very happy together. They also maintained their friendship with Freddie: probably because of me. It can't have been easy for my stepfather to stay friends with a man who had slept with his wife during his absence, nor for him to accept their child with open arms. But he was a very resilient man, my stepfather. I so admired him.'

When Freddie returned from the Australian leg of Queen's *A Night at the Opera* tour in late April 1976, he was confronted by his boyfriend of the moment, David Minns.

'Minns was pestering him about Freddie's fiancée, Mary Austin, and their relationship,' B. shares from Freddie's diary entries. 'Freddie was uneasy. He felt confused, and in need of moral support. My mother, meanwhile, had recently suffered a miscarriage and was feeling sad and depressed. At the end of March, her husband went away on business for two or three months. It was in this context that she and Freddie got together, and wound up finding love and comfort in each other's arms. No test had to be taken because there was no doubt about paternity.[3] The father could not have been my stepfather. He was simply not there.'

To her mother, in the most Catholic sense, her marriage was everything.

'Apart from this affair with Freddie,' comments B., 'there were never any others. She was a devoted Roman Catholic and a devoted wife. *Almost*. It is important to say here that she never blamed Freddie for what happened between them. She always blamed herself, for her "weakness". She also blamed me. I was a black stain on her marriage and a daily visual reminder of the mistake she had made.'

But Freddie never saw their liaison as a mistake:

'He did feel guilty, however. Not because of my birth: he was over the moon about becoming a dad and couldn't have been more excited. It was because I wasn't going to be born into the perfect family set-up: mum, dad, siblings, pets, in a beautiful house with a garden. That was the kind of life he had always envisaged for himself and his children, should he ever be lucky enough to have any.'

Why didn't her mother seek a termination?

'Because of her religious beliefs,' B. explains. 'Also, it was the 1970s. Such a thing, in those days, was unthinkable.'

Medical abortion under strict restrictions had been legal in the UK only since October 1967. For B.'s mother, it was not an option.

'The three of them sat down to some stormy and difficult discussions before my birth. Thank goodness they were all intelligent enough to do things properly and peacefully. I was born in February 1977 while Freddie was on tour in America.'

Why, I asked her, is Freddie's name not recorded on her birth certificate?

'Because my mother was married to another man. In 1977, the official father of a child was automatically taken to be the mother's husband.'

Queen had departed for their *A Day at the Races* US tour the previous month, where they performed forty dates across North America between January and March before returning to Europe for gigs in Sweden, Denmark, West Germany, the Netherlands,

Switzerland and the UK. For their finale, they played two nights at London's Earl's Court at the beginning of June.

'Freddie was torn,' says B. 'He knew that he would be thousands of miles away on my mother's due date, so he wouldn't be able to see me for several weeks. He coped with that by recording his thoughts and feelings in his notebooks. He set out his thoughts day by day, night by night, even hour by hour, for posterity. He wrote down his secret history and his most personal feelings and reflections in a series of large, good-quality notebooks.'

The collection comprises seventeen journals, four of which are bound in dark-blue cloth. The remaining thirteen have full-grain stitched leather covers. Five are black, two dark blue, two saffron yellow, two red and two pine green. Their thick, horizontally lined paper pages have rounded corners. Each book has 192 pages. Freddie used ballpoint or rollerball pens to write in them, sometimes in black ink, at other times blue. Only occasionally does he resort to pencil. He wrote between 160 and 180 words on each page, and he filled every page, no gaps. Some of the books have twenty-eight lines per page, while others have thirty. At a conservative estimate, Freddie wrote around 555,000 words – more than half a million, which equates to at least five and a half published volumes' worth – over a period of a little under fifteen years. Only Mary Austin, B.'s stepfather, her mother and her nanny knew that Freddie had given them to her.

His first entry in his original journal was made on Sunday, 20 June 1976 – a leap year – two days after Queen released their John Deacon-penned single 'You're My Best Friend' from their 1975 album *A Night at the Opera*. The band were getting ready for a short UK tour that September, which would include their biggest concert to date, in Hyde Park on the eighteenth of that month. Which also happened to be the anniversary of the death of Freddie's late idol, Jimi Hendrix.

'He started to keep a journal as soon as he knew that my mother was pregnant and that he was going to be a father,' B. explains, 'because he had no idea how things would develop, nor how he was going to deal with it all. His life was complicated enough as it was at that time, thanks to the situation with my parents, his relationship with Mary, and a confusing, increasingly violent period with David Minns, during which Minns was leaning on him to end things with her in order to be with him. Now, to top the lot, an unplanned pregnancy and pending fatherhood. He put pen to paper to clear his head, unravel it all and try to work out how to proceed. The long, difficult discussions with my stepfather continued. Their friendship was of course jeopardised by the infidelity and was in danger of being destroyed. Freddie had to work out how to get through all that without too much damage. My stepfather made certain stipulations. They decided together to make the best of things, and to create an unconventional family: one with a mother, two fathers and what would eventually be an assortment of children, all of whom would be treated exactly the same.'

Freddie first set eyes on his beautiful baby daughter in mid-March 1977, as soon as he could get there after the band returned from the American leg of their *A Day at the Races* tour. There is video footage of father and child's first encounter, the baby placed in Freddie's arms by her nanny, Maria.

'There are things about my very early years that I know in great detail because I have watched the videos and read the notebooks,' she says, 'but of which, of course, I have no memories of my own.'

Maria shared with her charge her priceless eye-witness accounts. The beloved nanny, who had long been part of the family, continued to live with Freddie's daughter until her death in 2023 at the age of ninety-six.

'She witnessed almost everything about the situation, even before my birth,' B. reveals. 'She was present throughout my infanthood and childhood, was involved in all the organisation, in the relationship between Freddie, my mother and my stepfather, in all the comings and goings, the visits, the phone calls, the subterfuge and strategies that were necessary to prevent people from making connections between Freddie and me. In all the airports, planes and hotels, the cars, the gigs, the waiting … the endless waiting. She became even more important in my life after my siblings were born, and still more so later on, after Freddie became ill. She gave me love, affection and attention and was a real Italian Mamma, the primary maternal figure in my life – much more so than my biological mother. She witnessed the births of my own children, and watched them grow too. Whenever she had something to say about me, everybody listened to her. She was a wonderful and extraordinary human being.

'Once I was here and Freddie was officially a father, he wrote copiously in his journal about my development and the times that we spent together. He didn't want to forget a single thing. He also wrote to relieve the complexity of the situation, and in order to be able to deal with its delicacy. He wrote because he was deeply damaged by his own childhood and teenage years, and because he didn't want me to suffer or feel the same things as he had. He needed me to know that he loved me unconditionally, and that I was always in his heart and at the forefront of his mind – even when we could not be together and could only talk on the phone.

'Most of his material memories of his childhood and teenage years had been left behind in Zanzibar when he and his family fled the country in 1964, during the genocide. He lost almost everything he had ever owned. The family had to abandon all their furniture, most of their clothes and almost all of their precious personal effects. Because of this, by the time I came along, Freddie was in the habit of keeping absolutely everything. Having so few possessions from his own childhood, what amounted to little more than a few notes, photos, and bits and pieces, he was determined to keep a comprehensive record of mine.

'He wrote me all his memories of his childhood. He told me his life story in great detail, including everything that had made him who he was. He didn't hold back. He described every aspect of his past. It seems likely to me now that he was also using his writings as a form of self-analysis.'

In his notebooks, Freddie confides his innermost thoughts and feelings in raw detail.

'They are not confessions,' his daughter says. 'They are truly his confidences, without a single concession to himself. And yes, some people will be surprised and probably not happy with some of his revelations. Because of everything he told me, I don't believe that he wrote the notebooks for publication, or that he ever wanted anyone but me to see them. He wrote them privately, keeping them hidden away at the flat in Phillimore Gardens where he and Mary continued their loving relationship after they had officially "broken up". Just before he died, he gave them to me. If, one day, he decided to write his memoirs, he might have referred to his notebooks to help him. But that was not the reason why he wrote them.

'He forbade me to read some of his writings until I had turned twenty-five. He did that in order to protect me, he said. I didn't burn the notebooks when he died, because I had made this promise to him. I was going to destroy them, but my step-father told me that I should perhaps wait until my twenty-fifth birthday before making up my mind. Once destroyed, I could never have got them back.'

Regarding her mother, she admits, there is not much to say:

'Things could have been much better between us, but she screwed up. She was cold towards me, and barely at all mater-nal. I stopped trying to figure out why when my stepfather said he didn't understand it either. I realised I'd never get a satisfac-tory answer. It's possible that she didn't know herself. I must admit, I rarely asked her any questions. What had happened, had happened. Everyone involved just decided to make the best of it. My compensation, strangely, was that my stepfather adored me.

'Nothing was ever swept under the carpet. They never sought to hide the truth from me. Freddie never avoided ques-tions and always had an age-appropriate answer for me. There was no monumental moment of revelation. They didn't sit me down one day, take deep breaths or knock back a stiff drink and say, "We have something to tell you." I was slowly made aware of the complexity of the situation. Because of that, it always felt natural to me. Later on, of course, I had his notebooks to refer to. I also heard the whole story verbally, from Freddie himself.'

The family appears to have managed a potentially explosive situation with care, compassion and discretion, despite the huge strain it must have placed on all of them.

'I lived in England for the first year of my life,' B. informs us. 'Then we moved to Switzerland – not to Montreux (where Queen purchased Mountain Studios in 1979) but not far from there; nowhere is far from anywhere in that country – until the end of summer 1985. From then until early September 1991, our main residence was in London. I never counted the many trips I made between Switzerland, England, Germany, Italy and everywhere else. I travelled so often, they used to say of me that I'd been born with a suitcase in my hand. I travelled luxuriously, exclusively, by private plane and chauffeur-driven car rather than scheduled flights, bus, taxi or tube. Freddie was always welcome at our family homes in London, Switzerland and the South of France,' she says. 'He had his own room at each residence, both to make things easier in terms of organisation and to ensure absolute privacy. Because, had we tried to do all this while staying in hotels, we would all too soon have been spotted and exposed.'

The three parents were intelligent enough to do things properly and peacefully, she adds: 'Privacy was of paramount importance to both Freddie and my stepfather. They each imposed their conditions, but there was never any official confidentiality agreement. They were well aware that if they didn't come to an understanding between themselves, or respect the wishes of all three equally, they would wind up in court and things would have been much worse for everybody. Together they did, or tried to, make the best of a peculiar situation. They did so primarily for my sake, and also for their family. To my knowledge there was only ever one heated discussion in all the years, and that was in early 1985. The Monster in Freddie was starting to crack. He had gone off the rails, was incredibly miserable, and felt very bad about everything.'

Freddie's role and place in the triangle were never disputed. Nor was anything ever hidden from their daughter.

'He never avoided my questions,' she insists. 'Not even the most sensitive ones. He always took into account my capacity to understand. I was slowly made aware of how things were. Everything relating to my upbringing was discussed and agreed upon. Education, which schools I should attend, rules regarding what I should and shouldn't be allowed to do at whatever age, conditions regarding phone calls between Freddie and me, where we should meet, where I would be taken on holiday and so on: everything about me and my life was decided by committee. As were arrangements regarding how I should be protected. Which couldn't always have been easy for them. But they deployed every possible subterfuge and strategy to prevent anyone who had nothing to do with it from making connections between us. This applied especially in the case of Freddie's employees, and also in his business relationships. And they succeeded. Only those who needed to know of my existence were told about me. I was enrolled in schools where the teachers and auxiliary staff were accustomed to receiving the offspring of "celebrities" and "personalities", and who were well-versed in discretion regarding the families of their pupils and students. Nevertheless, I had to change schools frequently, and not only when we moved house. It was all part of the plan to keep me secret. Though I have to say, I never felt hidden or that I was anything to be ashamed of. The opposite.'

Her most significant lessons, says B., were taught to her by Freddie.

'I think the most important thing he ever taught me was tolerance. Of different skin colours, religions, the many cultures, social classes and sexualities in the world. Thanks to him, I respect all people as living beings and know that I must never hurt anyone deliberately. Freddie was convinced that, with love and tolerance, we could have a much better world. As he saw it, those qualities lead to respect, honesty and truth. We can live without happiness, but we cannot live without love. Love, of course, is the thing that brings happiness. It might seem a strange thing to say, but his fatherly love taught me what motherly love is about.'

In effect, she says, 'I had two fathers. I called Freddie "Dad" and I addressed my stepfather as "Pa". He never differentiated between his own children and me. My round-the-clock Italian nanny, Maria – who was much, much more to me than a nanny – had worked for my stepfather's family long before I was born. She had been his nanny when he was a child, and was a trusted, cherished member of the family. My stepfather never disowned me. He assumed responsibility for me right from the start. Because of Freddie's lifestyle, performing all over the world and spending long periods recording in the studio with the band, I had no choice but to live with my mother and step-father, knowing that he would come to us as often as he could. Such arrangements were complicated and costly. But money was never a problem, because my stepfather was as wealthy as Freddie. They were sensible and grown-up about everything. As Freddie had his rooms in our houses, I didn't go to him, he came to me. Yes, I was protected from the world of showbiz and all that goes with it. But it was never the case that I was prevented from enjoying a proper, open and loving relationship with my dad because they were constantly having to conceal me from journalists and photographers. I enjoyed the closest imaginable relationship with Dad from my birth for as long as he lived. We adored each other.'

During his lifetime, B. stresses, she never felt his absence.

'Of course I would have preferred him to be there with me every morning when I woke up, and every day when I got home from school,' she says.

'Had he been with me every birthday and every Christmas Day, I would have loved that too. But that was the life I had, and the life he had. We just had to put up with what we couldn't have. Ours was not that dissimilar from the life of a lot of my friends, whose parents were separated or divorced or whose fathers were often absent for business reasons. They didn't get to see their dads much more than I saw mine, most of the time. Some kids were sent away to boarding school or to their grandparents or other relatives. That never happened to me. Anyway, such a thing was never a possibility.'

She enjoyed, B. insists, an ordinary and happy childhood.

'Unusual, strange and odd by most people's standards, yes, I accept that. Very privileged, also. But happy all the same. We have to remember that children do not analyse. They accept love, affection and attention wherever they find it, never questioning the source. I never felt uneasy about my situation, nor did I feel that there was anything strange about it. Not at the time. My relationship with my dad was probably really intense by most father–daughter standards. But I loved it. Never a second was wasted. Whenever he was there, he was totally there, one hundred per cent. He was there just for me. In most families, you can be with your children and have a million things to do or think about, so you are not really present for them exclusively. But not Freddie. When he was with me, it was as though there were no one else in the room. Even when we could only speak over the phone, he was completely attentive and really listened to me. He was interested in everything I had to say. He never once said to me, "Wait a minute," or "Not now!" When I hear myself saying such things to my own children, I remember how my dad was with me, and I feel ashamed.'

She speaks at length and so fondly of a Freddie the world never knew. The Freddie who fed his baby in her highchair from a little pot with a spoon and with all the patience in the world, his face wreathed in delighted and loving smiles. Of the Freddie who would sit for hours helping her with words when she was learning to read. Of him making her say her recitations, of them painting with four hands and playing four-hand piano, building sandcastles, playing with the dolls' house, staging pretend tea parties with dolls and teddies and a beautiful porcelain toy tea set; of sledding in the snow and decorating the snowman in winter, and playing together in the pool and in the garden during summer; of singing duets together, and dancing – 'I don't know who crushed whose feet more'; of mad moments flipping pancakes with their cats; of her fourteen birthdays and their fourteen Christmas celebrations; of him letting her sleep peacefully in his arms in front of the many cartoons they used to watch; of the times he would help her to put on her shoes before taking her to the opera; and, after hour upon hour spent playing in the water, of him taking a brush and untangling her hair with infinite patience. Left to their own devices, they were like any other father and daughter: walking and talking endlessly, playing spirited games of chess, or simply sitting together silently on the terraces of cafés, admiring the view and basking in the sun. They had all the time in the world, until it ran out on them.

'He would write me little messages and cards at the slightest opportunity. To whom else,' she says, 'could he begin a card with "My Trésor", "My Dearest Trésor", "My Little Angel" or "My Little Froggie"? To whom else could he sign those cards from "Dad", "Daddy" or "Your Papa"? And to whom else could he have written that I was "the light of his life", that he was so proud of me, that I filled his life with joy, that he missed me and always had me in his heart? I should never forget that he loved me, he would say. I was "the best thing he ever did in his life", and "the greatest gift he had ever received".'

• • •

She would not trade their endless one-to-one discussions, she says, for anything in the world.

'During periods when we couldn't see each other, we had our daily evening phone calls almost without fail. I can think of only two or three occasions when the call couldn't happen. He was always so desperate not to miss it that sometimes, for example during Queen's *The Works* tour in 1985 when they were travelling in Brazil, New Zealand, Australia and Japan, he would forget the time difference and call me when it was Europe's middle of the night.

'Whenever he was about to go away on tour, we would sit and examine a globe together so that I could see exactly where he was going. He'd also give me a map with his itinerary, so that I would always know where he was. Because his visits necessitated extensive arrangements, not least to keep them secret from all those who didn't need to know about me, I almost always knew when he was coming to me. Except for the strange period when Queen were recording their *The Works* album at the Record Plant studios in Los Angeles and at Musicland in Munich, between August 1983 and January 1984. There was a lot of tension between the band members at that time. Whenever Freddie had had enough and walked out of the studios for a couple of days, he would always come to see me. He'd pitch up unannounced, and what a great surprise that would be. The day before, neither he nor I would know that he was coming. But then, surprise, when I got home from school, there he would be.

'It was very easy to talk to my dad. He never raised his voice. He always encouraged me to speak openly to him about absolutely anything, and always to let everything out. No topic was off limits. I could even use swear words if I felt the need. He never stopped me until everything was out in the open. At the end of the conversation, he might tell me that some of the words I'd used were inappropriate or that he didn't want to hear them leave my mouth again. But he was always very attentive to what I was feeling, and so caring, thoughtful and protective. He would sit and listen patiently to whatever I had to say, even though my rambling on must have bored him rigid at times. If it did, he never showed it. Because he had always told me that I could talk to him openly about absolutely anything, when I got my first "boyfriend", the first thing I did was rush to tell my dad! His response was funny. "Oh, *God*," he moaned, "I wasn't expecting *that* to happen so quickly!" But as always, he was wonderful. Sometimes, I really did give him a very hard time.'

The education he gave her, says B., was based on discussion.

'He opened my mind, developed my curiosity, and led and guided me to intense reflection. Our long conversations, even when they were only over the phone, are more valuable to me than all the presents he ever showered me with. We'd spend hours and hours talking about whatever came up. If he forbade something, he would always explain his reasons for that. Whenever the law was laid down, I had to obey him because I knew exactly *why* I had to. Freddie was very strict. He was rigid in his principles and sometimes tough, but I always knew why he had to be. He would prepare me carefully, in a very funny way, and his reasoning was filled with tenderness and kindness. Had he lived longer, of course, there would have come a time when he would have set the kind of limits that I would not have wanted to comply with. I would have rebelled against him. He tolerated my childish insolence and cheek, but I did know my boundaries. I knew I shouldn't disobey him or be disrespectful. He hated that; it really infuriated him.

'When I reached my teens, the word "No" became a trigger for me. So conflict between us would probably have been inevitable for a while. But I was always aware, because he never let me forget them, that his three main principles were truth, honesty and respect.'

She was a precocious child, she confesses.

'Because of that, I was never in a class with children my own age. The classes I was assigned to, and the friends I made, were always two, three or even more years older than me. I recall an occasion when a group of my older friends and I wanted to go to a Mötley Crüe concert. That would have been during the autumn of 1989. I was not yet thirteen years old, while the friends I was planning to go with were already between fifteen and seventeen.'

She refers to the Crüe's 1989–1990 *Feelgood* world tour, during which they trekked across North America, Europe, Australia and Japan in support of their *Dr. Feelgood* album.

Her friends and she were big fans, she recalls.

'My mother didn't want me to go, because I was obviously too young. As I had never been close to her and didn't have a particularly good relationship with her, I was rebelling against her. I was all too aware that she favoured and took better care of her other children. So I didn't ask permission. I simply informed her that I was going to a gig with some friends and that I wouldn't be home until late. Just like that. So of course she objected, as any mother would. On this occasion, Freddie sided with *her*. He didn't want me to go either! That made me mad. I was pretty angry in general about a lot of things at that time. It was because I knew, inside, that something was very wrong. I remember noticing that spring that my dad had lost quite a lot of weight, and that his skin and hair had changed. Sometimes, when he laughed, a shadow would appear in his eyes. Just for a split second, and I had no idea what it could mean. There was also an aura of melancholy around him that was quite unsettling. I knew that something was going on, but I didn't know what. No one said anything to me, and I couldn't bring myself to ask. Dad had always noticed whenever something was troubling me, but at that time I was hiding behind my anger as a kind of protest. Because I was aggrieved about so many things, I got away with it. I knew he didn't want me to go to the gig, but he didn't say explicitly that he forbade me to go. So I played on words, and I defied him. I simply said that I was going to a friend's house to do homework together, and left out the part about the gig. When I didn't come home at the time they were expecting me, my mother called my friend's parents, who informed her that we were at the concert. That was when the bomb went off. They contacted Freddie immediately to let him know. I knew very well what his reaction would be, because I shouldn't have done it. He was furious, and he sent for me. When I was standing right in front of him, he gave me a look so stern, it could have frozen your blood. He said, very calmly, that he should slap me for what I had done. He never did so, because he would never have done such a thing. He didn't believe in physical punishment. But it was never necessary, because just that look of his was enough. I stood there getting more and more upset. He spoke very calmly without raising his voice. We had a very long discussion about what I had done, but mostly about the gig.'

Not that Freddie spelled out to his daughter why he didn't want her to go to it: 'Not the real, true reason. He recognised the quality of the band's music, and he acknowledged their theatricality. So why the "No"? Looking back, I think he was only freaked out that I was a fan of a band who would do, backstage, even more outrageous, scandalous and indecent things than he and Queen ever did. At the end of our discussion, he said, still very calmly, that I should never disrespect him again. Everything that needed to be said had been said. We would speak of it no more. I am amazed now by how easy it was to talk to him, and by the fact that he never raised his voice. In that respect, he was so very far removed from the Big Star Mercury persona.'

Freddie taught his daughter to believe in herself: 'To follow my feelings and instincts. He helped me to listen to my gut, and to know that whatever I felt deeply inside could not be wrong. He said I had to experiment, and to try things for myself. That I had to make my own mistakes, and even to be disobedient – but not too much and not too often! He said it was the only way that I would learn. He encouraged me to have no fear of falling, because he would always be there to support me and to help me get back up. He certainly has been. Even though he died decades ago, his notebooks have ensured that he has always been there for me. Those precious books have provided me with all the answers, and so much comfort besides. It's as if he antic-ipated all that I was going to need over the years to come, once he'd left me, and went out of his way to still be here for me. I also have the advantage of a huge amount of private audio and video recordings; even though they now feel very strange to watch, because I am older than Dad was when he died.'

• • •

Freddie was Zoroastrian.[4] The circumstances of his daughter's birth dictate that she cannot be recognised as a member of that faith herself.

'My mother and stepfather were both Catholic,' she says, 'so I was baptised and received into the Christian faith. But Freddie paid a great deal of attention to my religious education, especially my Zoroastrian education. He would say to me that there is no god but God, and that I could deal directly with him. He taught me that the heart is the most incredible thing, because it allowed me to feel totally Christian and totally Zoroastrian at the same time. Similarly, I could be both completely British and from another part of the world and a different nationality at the same time. Not just half and half, or a bit of this and a bit of that. It made absolute sense to him, because that is how his heart was. That was how he loved.'

He was a personification, in other words, of the principle that love divided is undiminished.

'My mother and stepfather are no longer with us,' she informs us. 'My mother died some years ago, and we lost my beloved stepfather, like so many others, at the beginning of the Covid pandemic.'

When she was eighteen years old, she lost her boyfriend and his brother in a car crash. There were two other passengers in the vehicle, both cherished friends of hers. Both survived. One walked away virtually unscathed. The other was seriously injured and was forced to endure thirty months of rehabilitation, learning to eat, walk and write again from scratch. Although she, mercifully, was not in the accident herself, the tragedy scarred her because it happened so soon after losing her father.

'For ten years after Freddie's death, from when I was fifteen until I turned twenty-five, I was no more than a ghost of myself,' she reveals. 'I learned to live with it eventually, but I have waited and waited to get over it. Now that I am nearly fifty years old, I am beginning to think that day will never come.'

• • •

Freddie wrote his journals in a very personal style.

'That is why I have pointed out lies, misunderstandings and interpretations, and have told you his truth without quoting him word for word,' she says. 'Except for some occasional extracts from statements he had made in published interviews, I think he wrote the earliest notebooks like diaries, as a kind of reminder to himself for the future. These have subsequent annotations. Later on, he would write in a very conversational way about his day-to-day life, his memories, his thoughts – on just about everything. There are stories about, and the inspiration behind, some of his songs, and what he was getting at when he wrote them. The more recent volumes, he wrote directly to me. He knew that he would not be around to keep reminding me of what mattered to him, his story, his childhood, his distant past, and all the things that made him who he was. He knew there may come a time when we would no longer be able to have our long discussions; when he would not be around to help me grow up, nor to tell me the many things he couldn't yet tell me because I was too young to hear and understand such things. He wrote so that I would never doubt him or forget who he really was – because he knew that after his death, the vultures would descend. Some of them had already taken flight. So he revisited his life for me, his remorse and his regrets for me, without ever seeking to make excuses for himself. He did all this with a most disarming and touching lucidity.'

She treads carefully – aware that there could be people who might seek to destroy her with counter claims and objections, or who could even try to obtain the notebooks for themselves.

They will never get them, she declares.

'If anyone ever came for them, or if I found myself challenged legally for their ownership, I would simply burn them. Why? Because Freddie gave them to *me*.

'I feel today that part of him *did* want the world to know the truth about him, but not before the appropriate time. He also needed a safeguard. He was well aware that if he left the notebooks in the hands of his management, for example, his gay life might be censored. Had he left them at his home, Garden Lodge, certain friends or members of his household might have removed them – as happened with some of Freddie's photos, tapes and videos – and they might not only be exploited for financial gain, but the "warts and all" element would be deleted, so that large parts of his truth would be lost.'

Freddie even writes in one of the notebooks, she says, about his final resting place: 'He names three possible locations and gives the reasons on which those choices were based, before settling on one.'

Garden Lodge, Montreux, India and Zanzibar were not on the list, she discloses: 'It would have surprised me, had they been there. The place he wrote about in the notebooks as his preference was NOT unexpected, because he was very traditional and conventional.'

I inform her that I know exactly where his remains were laid to rest, and that I've visited the site several times in the past. On one occasion, I saw Mary Austin there, I tell her. B. asks me to promise never to reveal its location to her.

'Anyway, I have my own lovely Freddie "mausoleum",' she says. 'I don't need to go to such a morbid place. He is at peace, and that's all that matters.'

• • •

Freddie's diaries shed fascinating new light on his relationships, especially with those who went on to publish personal accounts of their years in his orbit. Inevitably, his words contradict some of the revelations in various books, particularly the reminiscences of Jim Hutton: the man painted as his 'partner', 'boyfriend', 'husband' and 'live-in lover' from the mid-1980s until Freddie's death in 1991; and of Peter Freestone, the assistant famously referred to, and celebrated around the world as, 'Freddie's best friend' and 'the man who knew him best'. Did Freddie feel threatened by the possibility that some of his close associates might rewrite his life after his death, casting themselves more favourably and of greater importance than they really were? He does not dwell on anticipation of future compromise. Nor does he state anywhere that it had been fear that had prompted him to put pen to paper. He doesn't even explain why he entrusted his journals into the care of one of the only two loved ones whom he knew beyond doubt would never betray him. There is a sense that he was aware, all along, that the world was not ready for who he really was. Perhaps he believed that a time would come when diversity would be tolerated. When it would be safe to share his story and his truth.

Freddie will have known, just as we all know, that time plays tricks on the memory. Recollections will always vary, but what he wrote about members of his entourage is unequivocal. Both Jim Hutton and Peter Freestone have been called out by scholars and Freddie fans alike for inaccuracies and contradictions in their memoirs. Such criticism aside, I wish to say in their defence that both were never less than accommodating and helpful to me. Each of them always treated me with kindness and respect.

Jim is now deceased. Benign, friendly Peter remains on the outer edge of the inner circle. He has continued to act as a kind of spokesman for Freddie over the past thirty-three years, as part of the bi-annual Mercury celebrations in Montreux; acting as an accuracy consultant on the *Bohemian Rhapsody* feature film; providing voice-overs for the Montreux Freddie Tours; and co-hosting Freddie-related soirées at the home of the late Claude Nobs, a close friend of Freddie's and founder of the world-renowned Montreux Jazz Festival.

• • •

The few who knew that Freddie had a child know who they are. Others will know she is telling the truth when she refers to the small pigmentation on his face, just below his left eye. She doesn't mean the scar under his right eye nor the one on his right cheek-bone, both of which he sustained during boxing bouts at school.

This pigmentation, she says, 'could not be seen in videos or in photos, in the bright light of day, under stage lights or on a film set. It went undetected by the camera's flash. When he wore make-up or whenever he had a tan, it was virtually invisible. It was also often hidden by his dark under-eye circles. You could only see it when you were so close to him that you were right in his face and he in yours, and only if he wasn't made-up or too tanned. If I were not who I say I am, how would I know that about him?'

• • •

Freddie's daughter came to know her father's deepest inner feelings, and got to know his most private self, only after he had died: 'And that was only by reading his journals again and again,' she confides. 'There are people who spent so much more time with him face to face than I did. But that doesn't mean they truly knew him; still less that they knew him better than I do. Some of them barely knew the real Freddie at all. That's blatantly obvious, from much of what they have written and said since his death.'

But what about his early life? His birth in Zanzibar, his infancy, and the long, distant years spent at boarding school in India? I had travelled extensively to explore such destinations, in search of the truth. Was the Freddie I found in those places really him?

CHAPTER 3

ORIGINS

'Those who have said that Freddie wanted to erase and cancel his past, or even that, if he'd had the choice, he would have chosen to begin his life in London at the age of eighteen, missed the point completely,' says his daughter.

'They have no idea of what he lived through in Zanzibar during the genocide, nor of what he and his family endured throughout the ensuing months. They don't know how appalling he would have found their words. But they should know, so I am here to tell them how deeply hurt he would have been by their assumptions.'

• • •

Farrokh Bulsara was born on 5 September 1946 at the Government Hospital on the south side of Stone Town, the largest city and historic capital of Zanzibar, an archipelago off the coast of East Africa. Now the main public facility and known as Mnazi Mmoja Hospital, it serves the entire population, facing the many challenges of a government-run medical centre in a developing country. It is as overrun today as it was almost eighty years ago, with many patients travelling great distances to be treated there. The Bulsaras' firstborn happened to arrive on the Parsee New Year's Day.

'In our calendar,' says B., 'days begin "at sunrise", which is fixed at 6 a.m. The New Year's Day was actually 4 September 1946: from sunrise that morning until just before sunrise on 5 September. As he was delivered before sunrise on the fifth, they were able to say that he was born on New Year's Day, the day of our God and the day when we wish each other "Farrokh Fravardin". Hence his given name, Farrokh. The word translates as auspicious, blessed, fortunate and happy. "Fravardin" is the name for the first month of the Shenshai Calendar (Parsees do not have the same calendar as that of Zoroastrians from Iran; there are actually three calendars used by Zoroastrians around the world); it is also the name of the nineteenth day of each month. This one is difficult to explain. It has to do with guardian angels, and the spirit guide that every being has, protecting it as it helps it to grow and develop.'

Formerly the centre of the East African slave trade, Zanzibar had a long history of international business. Its islands were a cauldron of African, Arab, Indian and Persian cultures. After becoming a protectorate in 1890, the territory remained under British control during that first post-Second World War year of Freddie's birth. His parents, Jer and Bomi, both hailed from a long-established Parsee community in the Indian city known during the British Era as Bulsar – hence the adopted family name. Since renamed Valsad, it lies on the west coast of the state of Gujarat, a few miles inland of the Arabian Sea and 130 miles north of Mumbai, formerly Bombay. As I wrote in *Love of My Life*, 'It is often attested that Freddie spent most of his childhood in Zanzibar. He did not. He spent only the first eight years of his life there.' As soon as he turned five, his parents enrolled him at

St Joseph's Convent Missionary School, where he was taught by Anglican nuns. The building, which still stands and which I have visited, has cellars believed to have been used to house slaves. The facility is known today at Skuli Ya Sekondari Tumekuja. Freddie was a pupil there for three years.

'The house of his childhood years was in the centre of Stone Town at the corner of a narrow street and Shangani Main Road, which is known today as Kenyatta Road,' his daughter shares from Freddie's diaries. 'Theirs was, he says, a typical Zanzibari Stone Town home. He describes it as a very beautiful house, with a wooden balcony, ornamental carvings and a roof terrace. It was decorated throughout with Persian rugs. Freddie's mum filled her vases with fresh flowers every Sunday. On special days, she would garland the door and the living room with scented blooms. They had a special table for framed photographs of their late relatives, at which Jer would perform Loban, a Zoroastrian ritual, every Sunday. This involves burning loban, a frankincense-like resin, in a metal bowl, for purification and Divine grace. It has a perfume that lifts the soul.

'The shops in the streets below sold precious jewellery from the Gulf, Persian rugs, carved ivory, earthenware, copper trays, sculptures, carved wooden furniture, hammered-silver trinkets and all manner of beautiful things. Freddie would feast his eyes on those treasures. One of the local shops he loved sold magazines from overseas, as well as all kinds of books, including colouring books for children, and stationery for Europeans. Every two or three months, cargo ships delivered loads of imported items that were otherwise unavailable in Zanzibar. Because they are so popular in the West, and have been adapted so many times for film and television, people tend to think that the stories of Freddie's childhood were the Middle-Eastern folk tales in *One Thousand and One Nights*. But that's incorrect. The main source of his childhood stories was *The Shahnameh*.'[1]

Because he did not have many toys, much of Freddie's childhood play depended heavily on his imagination.

'Freddie loved and often played with the electric train set his dad had brought him home from one of his trips,' says B. 'And his mum bought him books: *The Shahnameh*, *Aesop's Fables*, and Beatrix Potter's *The Tale of Peter Rabbit*. He spent long hours reading and re-reading the stories in these three books and trying to reproduce their beautiful illustrations. That was how, at a very young age, he began to learn to draw. The first works of art he ever saw were the beautifully carved wooden doors of Stone Town. An old neighbour taught him all the different styles, what their patterns meant, and how to "read" a door.'

Zanzibar in those days, she recounts, 'was a place of innocence and beauty. There would come a time when Freddie would long to go back to the place it had once been. His life there had been so simple but so charmed. Together with his little friends, Ahmed, Ibrahim and Mustapha, he would play for hours in Stone Town's streets. Those three boys were very dear to him. They were the brothers he never had.'

As Freddie said, his early childhood could not have been happier.

'Those children enjoyed such a carefree existence. They stuffed themselves with pawpaws, bananas, yellow mangoes and coconuts until their stomachs ached. They played with donkeys and chickens, imitated the shriek of bushbabies when they went out looking for them, and would sing and dance under the watchful eyes of their mothers and nannies. They would be joined on the open-air benches by neighbours who sat around chatting in clashing languages: kiUnguja, Arabic, Gujarati and English. Stone Town thrummed with sound and life. When the big rains came, everyone would dance in the streets, clapping their hands, stamping their feet and singing the joy of the rainfall.

'Some of those Stone Town streets were so narrow, not even the little donkey carriages could pass through them. Even the sunlight would be blocked out. One narrow lane led to the Cable & Wireless building down on the seafront, and to Freddie's favourite childhood beach, at Ras Shangani Point: an area of land on the west of the island, but still part of Stone Town, that juts into the Zanzibar Channel. That beach extends from the old Cable & Wireless building, which is today the Serena Hotel, to what used to be the Jubilee Gardens but which is now known as Forodhani Park. It was there that Freddie learned to swim. He loved to play in the clear, shallow water there. He spent a great deal of his early years larking with his friends on that pure white sand and splashing about in the waves. He sometimes went with his parents to the Sultan's Palace, where they would stand and watch the inspection of the guard. After that, they would walk over to the Jubilee Gardens in front of the Beit al-Ajaib, the House of Wonders, where his dad, Bomi, worked as a civil servant. They would sit on the beach and relax, looking out over the sparkling turquoise sea. Freddie loved playing and laughing there with his dad. He would also run around on the sand collecting beautiful shells for his mother. He was always looking for little ways to show how much he adored her, because there was no one like his mum.

Years later, he would take her precious emeralds, and pearls from Japan, instead of seashells. Even though they were very strict about manners, politeness, behaviour and respect, especially for elders, Freddie's parents were very loving and devoted people. Bomi was an extremely thoughtful, loyal and honest man, who was very good to his family. He supported and encouraged his son unfailingly. He cared deeply for both of his children and was always concerned with how they were feeling.'

Freddie's mother, B. says, taught him the basic prayers that he was expected to say each night before he went to bed.

'The two of them would sit and pray together. Both his mum and dad taught him to read Gujarati, so that he could follow the small prayer book they had given him.'

Later on, he received an English translation too. Despite posthumous claims that he spoke no language other than English, B. confirms that her father also spoke Gujarati fluently: 'It was his mother tongue, after all,' she says, 'and the language of his early childhood. He spoke it with his parents, who also spoke English. They raised him to be bilingual, and also to be proud of his Parsee and Zoroastrian roots.'[2] They would tell their son stories about their religion, and about Parsee history and culture. Having attended Parsee schools in India, Bomi and Jer were both traditional and religious. Strict believers in the laws of purity, they observed the rituals closely. Freddie started going with them to the Agiary, the Zoroastrian fire temple on the outskirts of Stone Town, when he was little more than a toddler. Not only was he fascinated by the singing: the prayers, always sung in a spirited way, were the most extraordinary sound he had ever heard. The music got under his skin, and it grew on him. The family visited both the Agiary and its beautiful rose gardens regularly. Freddie found the contrast between the "city of stone" and the luxurious surroundings of the Agiary very striking. From there, they would move on to spend the day at the Parsee Club nearby.'

That sacred place, built in 1895 and gifted to the Parsee community, where the eternal flame once burned, is now a ruin. Although Zanzibar's Zoroastrian community had thrived for hundreds of years, the majority fled in 1964 at the start of the revolution. Their former fire temple fell into disrepair. Community representatives from London visited years later and removed the scriptures, altar offerings, holy images, books and paintings, to carry them back to England for conservation. The dilapidated building, known today in Swahili as Shamba ya Parisi – the Temple of the Parsees – is privately owned and used for storage. Its once flourishing rose garden is now a wasteland, though its cemetery remains. Ancient tombstones lean into the overgrowing grass, their inscriptions carved in both English and Gujarati.

Freddie's Navjote initiation into the faith took place at the Agiary when he was seven years old. Even though he was so young, he took the ceremony very seriously. He was taught to practise the rituals and what was expected of him on the day, B. explains:

'His mum hung lights and garlands of flowers in the backyard, and prepared wonderful delicacies for their guests. Parsees are partial to celebrations, and during Freddie's childhood there seemed always to be some occasion or other to mark. It was almost a case of any excuse to party and spread joy. Birthdays, navjotes, marriages, the eighteen-day Muktad festival' – as the

Fravardigan festival or festival of the fravashis, equivalent to the Christian All Souls, is popularly known – 'the coming of the rains, anything and everything was celebrated. Birthdays were extra special. For his own, Freddie bathed in milk and flowers while his mother prepared special dishes. Little wonder that, as an adult, he always made such a big deal of his birthdays. That was what he'd been used to as a child. From a very young age he understood the importance of celebration and why parties mattered. Religion was also important to him: not just his own, but the faiths and customs of others. He and his family respected and celebrated the festive days of friends who were not of his faith. As well as the monthly Zoroastrian celebration, the feast days of Anglicans, Protestants, Roman Catholics and others were observed. Freddie had such an enquiring mind, even as a little boy. He said he was always asking questions about the many cultures and religions in Zanzibar. He loved his few years at the missionary school.'

But good secondary education was not available there at that time. Embassy employees, British subjects working for the government and stationed in Zanzibar, and non-natives did not put their children into secondary school in Zanzibar because the educational standard was too low. While other children were enrolled at schools on the mainland, Freddie was despatched to India at the tender age of eight. In Panchgani, a hill station in the 'Western Ghats' of the Sahyadri Mountains, he was educated at St Peter's Church of England School.

That was where his wondrous childhood ended, his daughter explains: 'Bomi and Jer firmly believed they were doing the right thing, and that it would be good for him. They sat him down for a difficult talk and informed their only son that they were sending him far away to live at a school. They had to tell him he would hardly see them for the next two years. They also told him a little of what his life at boarding school would be like, although what could they really say? Nothing could have prepared him for the horrors that awaited him. Freddie was devastated and heartbroken. He couldn't understand why they would do this to him. He packed a few little things, including prints of photos of his parents and sister that they'd had taken only a few weeks earlier. He packed his copy of *The Shahnameh*, and his prayer book. But he was made to leave his beloved teddy bear behind, because St Peter's did not allow toys. As he prepared for his journey, Freddie was traumatised. He couldn't bear the thought of leaving home. From that day on, he was never able to pack properly for a trip, nor could he bring himself to say the word "goodbye". For the rest of his life, he would find those things painful, if not impossible.'

On the eve of Freddie's departure for India, his father presented him with his own stamp album, in which he had preserved the many postage stamps he had collected during his years spent travelling.

'There were stamps that had belonged to Bomi's father before him, as well as those he had collected from the mail he received at work,' says B. 'Freddie carried it carefully with him all the way to St Peter's. He would cherish it all his life, and never let it go. He saved the Zanzibar stamps from the letters he received from his parents. Bomi would also send him stamps that he continued to collect himself and bought others especially for him. That album was hugely important to Freddie. It was a tangible and very personal piece of home.'

Only after the Bombay-bound ship had set sail did the full horror of his situation engulf him. It dawned on Freddie that he was being sent away for a really long time. He was travelling with other children, the sons of friends of his parents, so he was not entirely alone and at the mercy of the crew for the duration of the arduous journey. Even so, the experience damaged him profoundly. He went so far as to say that it destroyed the world he had known and loved hitherto. On his arrival in Bombay, he was met by relatives, who took care of him until it was time to make the long onward rail journey to Panchgani.

'It's often stated that the journey by boat lasted eight weeks or sixty days,' says B. 'In *The Untold Story*, Rudi Dolezal's and Hannes Rossacher's 2000 documentary about Freddie that was produced by Queen's manager Jim Beach, and which was re-released six years later as *Lover of Life, Singer of Songs*, it was suggested that the voyage, during Freddie's childhood, had taken eight weeks. Mary Austin later said, "I think it took six weeks." The fact that she said "*I think*" is important.

'The passage between Zanzibar and Bombay, confirmed Freddie in his notebooks, actually took between ten and fifteen days. There were only one or two runs per month, made by the SS *Karanja* and her sister ship the SS *Kampala*.'

Those colonial ocean liners had been built at the Govan shipyard on Glasgow's River Clyde by Alexander Stephen & Sons, the *Kampala* in 1947 and the *Karanja* one year later. Operated by the British India Steam Navigation Company, they connected Bombay with Pakistan, Kenya, Tanzania, Mozambique and South Africa, calling at Zanzibar and the Seychelles en route. There were first-, second- and third-class cabins, dining rooms and other public rooms. Rudolph A. Furtado, whose father, Mr Louis J. Furtado, once worked as a cargo supervisor for the line and who had also sailed on the *Karanja*, recalled the entertainment on board: a live orchestra, movies, tombola, quizzes, wooden horse-racing and a games room with table tennis, most of the ping-pong balls ending up over the side of the ship. First-class passengers also enjoyed a cocktail lounge, afternoon teas, a card room, dancing and a library. According to former fellow pupil Subhash Gudka, who attended St Peter's between 1958 and 1962 and who sometimes made the journey with Freddie, 'There were about sixty of us East Africa students travelling to India to study then. For the school year,' he told the *Hindustan Times* in 2018, 'we'd take the same ship to India, Freddie boarding at Zanzibar and me at Mombasa. I'd join him in First Class.'

What a culture shock Bombay must have been to those small schoolboys from another world. How frightened they must have been, as well as filled with wonder when they arrived in that city for the first time, sailing towards the great Gateway of India and its architectural neighbour the Taj Mahal Palace, the finest hotel in the East. The vessels on which they voyaged would later be acquired by the Shipping Corporation of India, when they were renamed. The *Kampala* was scrapped in 1971, the *Karanja* in 1988.

'So yes,' B. continues, 'from the day that Freddie left his parents in Stone Town to the day he arrived at St Peter's School in Panchgani, the whole journey took more than five weeks. But the time actually spent at sea was no more than ten to fifteen days. Once in Bombay, Freddie's relatives there took care of him, and saw him on his way to the school in Panchgani.

'Again, it's really important to spell this out. The shocking "eight weeks at sea" so often stated (the origin of that statement is unknown) is completely incorrect. It also gives a really poor impression of Bomi and Jer as parents, that they would find it acceptable to abandon their eight-year-old child to the care of strangers on board a large ship for two whole months. It was not the case. Freddie travelled – with the children of friends of his parents – for no more than two weeks on the ship. Which is still, admittedly, too long for an unaccompanied minor. Such a thing seems inconceivable today. But in those days – the mid-1950s – and in that part of the world, it was just the norm. The eldest of the boys looked after the youngest of the boys. It was just the way that things were done.'

* * *

It became apparent soon after his arrival that he was going to have to learn the hard way.

St Peter's life at that time – remember that we are talking seven decades ago, and there is no suggestion whatsoever that its regime is brutal today – hinged on discipline, deprivation and punishment.

'The upheaval for Freddie was cataclysmic,' says B. 'It destroyed everything his life had been until then. No aspect of his previous existence remained. He came to believe that boarding school was the very worst thing on Earth to which anyone can subject a child. He was determined that, when he fathered his own children, under no circumstances would they ever be sent away to be educated. Fending for himself at such a young age overwhelmed him. He felt utterly lost. He became prone to bursting into tears without warning, which he was unable to control. All too soon aware that he had to rely on himself because he had no one else to depend on, he became withdrawn. So desperate was he not to show his true feelings in case he was ridiculed or punished, he built a façade and perfected the art of pretence. During waking hours he projected a rough and tough personality that was completely at odds with who he really was. He did as he was told, pretending that everything was fine. In his bed alone at night, however, he would cry silently, longing for sleep that rarely came. If he managed to nod off, it was only ever for about three hours. Because much-needed rest eluded him, Freddie was exhausted all the time. Surrounded by hundreds of other boys, he felt totally alone.'

His 'personal space', as Freddie described it, was furnished with nothing more than a narrow single bed and a tiny closet. His confinement depressed him and his emotions grew numb, until he could no longer feel.

On many levels, his daughter shares from the pages of Freddie's journals, the Great Pretender with whom he would later become synonymous was born right there at St Peter's School, years before he first heard the song.

There were pockets of consolation and salvation. Freddie loved to draw, for example, to appease his overactive imagination. But because paper supplies were rationed and he would soon use up his meagre share, he learned to create his alternative universe in his head.

On the subject of 'alternative universes', these became very important to Freddie during his years away from home.

I was fascinated by Roger Taylor's declaration, at the launch of Queen's reworked debut album *Queen* at London's Ham Yard Hotel in October 2024, that he was 'horrified' by how religious so many of Freddie's lyrics are. 'Freddie was not religious in the slightest way, so God knows what he had been reading!' said Taylor. But as he himself had admitted earlier, he and his bandmates suspected there was far more to Freddie than they ever knew.

'Roger said they were very close as a group, but even *they* didn't know a lot of things about Freddie because he was quite a mystery, on the TV programme *Good Morning Britain* one week after Freddie's death in 1991,' says B. 'But the subject had been discussed as early as 1977, in an interview with Tim Lott in *Sounds* magazine on 4 June:

'"Lott: Brian has admitted that after five years, he hardly knows the lead singer.

'"Freddie: It's true to a certain extent. I want my privacy, and I feel I've given a lot for it. Sometimes you do want to hide. I do keep myself to myself."'

Far from being irreligious, then, Freddie prayed fervently to God as a young child, and continued to do so until the very end of his life.

'He spent a lot of time praying in bed,' says B. 'It comforted him. He found in prayer the warmth of the Parsees, along with the sense of security he had always taken for granted back home in Zanzibar. That connection to his family kept him sane. His mum, dad, sister and wider family were the most important things in his life. He missed them so much and was desperate to go home and see them. He longed to feel his mother's arms around him, enfolding him and keeping him safe, and to listen again to his father's wonderful stories. Whenever he was able to snatch some sleep, he would dream only of them. There they would all be, down on the beach, laughing and playing together and having fun. It all seemed so real that when he woke up and realised it had only been a dream, he would be inconsolable.'

Freddie would remain tormented for life by his parents' decision to send him away.

'He knew the reasons, of course – that a decent secondary education was not available in Zanzibar in those days,' B. reminds us. 'He knew they had believed they were doing their best for their beloved son. They had chosen a boarding school in India specifically because they had family in that country, who would be responsible for him in their absence. But he never really understood how they could have let him go so easily. A part of him never accepted what they had done. He was convinced that they loved him. He never doubted that. But he couldn't get past his feelings of abandonment and rejection. He was consumed by separation anxiety that would never leave him. He even wondered whether their decision had been his fault. Alone in a strange environment, he had no one to turn to. No one to complain to about his searing homesickness. No one to give him affection, attention or moral support, all of which he needed so badly. Those feelings of abandonment, loneliness, anxiety and extreme sadness haunted him all his life. A little boy as shy and as sensitive as Freddie should never have been sent away to boarding school.'

It was, she says, the deepest wound in his life, and the one that would never heal.

'It hurt him for the rest of his days. Because he was never able to face the issue in adulthood, he never found the means to overcome it.'

The irony was that this worst of all wounds was what drew Freddie towards music. He used it to fill the void, thus leading him into a life he could never have imagined.

'All he wanted, he said, was to make music, make people happy with it, and make up for the happiness he himself had been denied during the Panchgani years,' says B. 'Most of his songs are about love and happiness. He had blamed his parents for their terrible decision. He also knew that without his privileged education and artistic knowledge, the man would probably never have become the artist.'

On his private pages, Freddie does not beat about the bush. His outpourings are so searing and raw, they might as well be blood-stained. The reader is left in no doubt that his boarding school years were profoundly unhappy. He had merely endured them, but had never enjoyed them. Although he did cultivate a handful of well-chosen friends, he was never pro-active or assertive within that friendship group. Interaction with his peers did not come naturally. Freddie tended to linger in the background, never saying very much. He didn't get along that well with some of his fellow pupils because they had perceived his vulnerability and weakness, and would sometimes take advantage of it.

'It made some of them cruel towards him,' says B. 'A few called him "Bucky" on account of his prominent teeth. It was a nickname he couldn't stand. Those particular boys taunted, teased and ridiculed him relentlessly. Some were even violent, forcing Freddie to learn to defend himself. They would bully him in the dormitory, the bathroom, even the toilet. He could never escape them, no matter where he went, and he really suffered because of it. To endure that kind of treatment week in, week out, month after month was, he said, akin to Chinese water torture. This kind of thing was supposedly the norm in boarding schools in those days. But it was something that Freddie had never known, couldn't have expected and was by no means prepared for. Until St Peter's, when Freddie was among friends, he had only ever known love, friendship, fun, support and joyfulness. Learning how to be independent, to fly with his own wings and not to rely on anybody else, came hard to him.'

Freddie's first two years at St Peter's were tough. Aware that this was now his world and that he had no choice, he decided that he had best get on with it. A keen student, he did well across the board in all his subjects. He even won the Junior All-Rounder trophy, for general studies, elocution, dramatics, sports and extra-curricular pursuits. Away from the classroom, he spent most of his time alone. It was during those lonely hours that he would lose himself in his own private creation, a safe and secret imaginary world. He began to conjure the fantasy land of Rhye, its roots in the stories of his childhood. He didn't fashion it as a song to begin with, nor even as a piece of music. Those things came later. It was merely his own little realm, into which he could retreat and find relief.

'There are many interpretations of "The Seven Seas of Rhye",' B. acknowledges. 'Unfortunately, they tend not to be correct. It's ironic that his song about an imaginary place to which he could escape in his head when things got too much eventually became Queen's first proper hit. His boarding school having been very strict, he had learned to be satisfied with the smallest mercies. Perhaps this was the most significant of them all.'

Something that irked Freddie terribly, and which was both pointless and downright cruel, was the school's strict rule of silence during his time there. Boys were instructed not to speak to one another except during breaks or games. Thus were those young children, whose very development depended on communication and interaction, forced to sit and eat their meals in silence, to take baths without talking, even to play and watch movies without being able to chat among themselves. Again, there is no suggestion that any such practice persists today. What did the school imagine itself to be at that time, a silent monastic order?

'And if a boy disobeyed,' reports B., 'he would be punished. Punishment was routine, for everything and nothing. It made Freddie miserable.'

Freddie would be well known in later life for his bird-like appetite. Few who knew him in adulthood ever knew the real reason why. He had experienced trauma while at boarding school thanks to a particularly brutal practice: 'In Freddie's day, if you didn't finish your food, you were deprived of the next meal,' explains B. 'He never got over this. Anxiety inhibited his ability to eat. He learned to manage on far less food than his body needed. The long-term effect was that, as a grown man, he had a very poor appetite. He also hated food waste. Much later, after he had assumed the guise of Freddie Mercury, he contradicted that stance by allowing himself the luxury of not having to finish everything on his plate.'

This was by no means the only cruel practice to which he was subjected.

'His first two years at St Peter's School were horrible,' she reveals. 'They were very unhappy and unpleasant for him. The school's laws and rules in those days were almost military. Its schedule allowed the boys very little free time. One minute this little boy was being pampered and showered with love at home, and the next he was alone in a big school thousands of miles away, with no one to console or hug him when he needed it. He missed his family very much. He was punished frequently for minor misdemeanours. He couldn't even call his parents to be comforted, because they did not have access to the telephone. That episode of his life, that terrible lack of personal contact, was probably the reason why, in later life, he would become so dependent on the telephone. Certainly he called me virtually every day, to pass the time of day, ask me what I'd been doing, what I had read, watched, listened to, what I had played, what I wanted to do, whether I was loving what I was doing, whether I had slept well, eaten well, whether everything had gone well enough at school, and whether or not I'd been teased. It was as though he was reliving his own childhood through me; should I say, the warm, loving, affectionate childhood he wished he had experienced himself. As with all children, his childhood and school years had had a huge impact on Freddie's life. He spoiled me regularly and lovingly because he had not been lovingly spoiled himself.'

From all that he told her and from everything he wrote, she is able to state with accuracy that Freddie endured an awful childhood.

'It was because those first two years at St Peter's were so terrible for him that he soothed himself with dreams and created the fantasy land of Rhye,' she reveals. 'There were eight songs about Rhye that together make up what could be considered Freddie's first opera.

'Contradicting much speculation, those eight songs are "My Fairy King" from 1973's debut album *Queen*; the unfinished version of "The Seven Seas of Rhye" (debut album) that he finishes on *Queen II* as "Seven Seas of Rhye"; "Nevermore" (on *Queen II*), "Funny How Love Is" (*Queen II*), "Lily of the Valley" (on 1974's *Sheer Heart Attack*), and three other songs that were never recorded – because Freddie discarded them very early during the writing of *Queen II,* when they adopted the black-and-white concept for the album.'

• • •

'Freddie started to get better, or more accurately, to feel less bad, during his third year at St Peter's,' B. reports. 'But he was still teased, ridiculed and humiliated by some of the other boys. That persecution lasted, as did the bullying, until the end of his days at the school. He came to enjoy the company of his small group of well-chosen friends, but always stayed in the background and never spoke much.'

During the school holidays, when he did not go all the way home to Zanzibar because the journey was too arduous and the cost prohibitive, Freddie stayed with his aunt Sheroo Khory in Bombay. It was she who facilitated Freddie's first piano lessons.

'And at the age of twelve,' B. confirms, 'he began taking music lessons at St Peter's. When he left the school four years later at sixteen, he had passed his Grade IV exams in both Theory and Practical. It was without question the learning and practising of music that lifted his gloom and helped him to be happy,' she says. 'He knew instinctively that music would save him. It also changed him. From the moment he made that discovery, the only things he cared about were his music, art and literature. He as good as dropped everything else. During the spring of 1961, he joined the band the Hectics, and worked hard in search of the happiness the music brought him.'

It was on 10 April 1961, the year Freddie would turn fifteen, that he wrote home to inform his parents that he had joined a band. In correspondence preserved by his now late mother, Jer, revealed in the documentary *Freddie Mercury: the Untold Story* and shared widely in the mainstream and on social media, the young teenager enthused about his progress on the piano and told them that 'Bruce Murray had the idea to form a band and asked me if I wanted to be in it. We will call ourselves the Hectics. And apart from Bruce and myself, Victory Rana, Derrick Branche and Farang Irani will be in the band. Tomorrow we will meet for our first rehearsal. I'm very excited about this. Love, Farrokh.'

But less than a year later, despite the band's popularity and prowess, relationships within it were not as rosy as they may have looked. Freddie's letter home on 15 March 1962 spells it out:

'Dear Mum and Dad, as I write this letter to you, I'm so angry because a terrible injustice has happened to me. Let me tell you: we were all in the dormitory at Lawrence Villa, with Victory, Farang, Derrick and all the other boys. Suddenly, Bruce started to hit me. "Let's box, Bucky!" he said. And although I said, "No!", he just started. Within just a few moments, against my will, there was a boxing match going on and I was in the middle of it. The boys were all screaming and shouting and throwing pillows at us.

Because of the noise, Mr Davis suddenly entered the dormitory and stopped the fight. Bruce lied and said I was the one who started the fight, and that he was just defending himself. All the boys backed him up, so Mr Bason, the Principal,[3] decided I had to be punished. And what a terrible punishment they picked for me. I had to go to the barber's shop and have my hair cut really short. I hated Bruce for that. You know how much I love my hair. It'll never be the same again. I'm so upset and angry.'

It seems that other members of the band were sometimes just as inclined as other pupils to tease and humiliate him when they were not playing music together. Could their behaviour have been provoked by envy of Freddie's superior musical talent? For as teacher Mr Joseph L. Davis pointed out in the documentary, 'Remove the piano and there was nothing left of the Hectics.' The general bullying that he endured while at school frustrated Freddie. 'The result was that he began to fight more and more frequently,' says B. 'Against the humiliation, bullying and contempt of his so-called "friends", music was his escape. He thought they were his friends, so he couldn't understand them. Loyalty and trust mattered hugely to him. He would never let a friend down. But it was as though there were not a jot of loyalty among the rest of them. Still, he said, he learned to live with the humiliation, and put on a happy face. This was the reason why he did not maintain contact with any of those boys after he left the school. They weren't nice to him, and his memories of those years with them, apart from the music they shared, were miserable. Except for his conversations with Mary, he never talked about those boys or those years with his adult friends or any members of his staff.'

In my book *Love of My Life*, Freddie's childhood friend Gita Choksi, née Bharucha, who had attended neighbouring Kimmins Girls' School in 'Panchi' (as they called it) and was part of the pack who followed the Hectics, remembers an encounter with the band's former guitarist, Derrick Branche. Derrick had moved to Australia and had become an actor, appearing in the 1980s British television series *The Jewel in the Crown* and in the 1985 feature film *My Beautiful Laundrette*. 'Derrick told me that he had been terribly excited to get tickets for a Queen concert in London, at Earl's Court,' she told me. 'He couldn't wait to see our old schoolfriend afterwards. He went backstage with his companions after the concert, explained to the security people who he was, and they allowed them into the dressing room area to wait for Freddie. When eventually Freddie came in, he spotted Derrick, looked down his nose, didn't say a word, then turned around and walked back out. "Only five minutes earlier," Derrick said to me, "I was telling my friends how Freddie and I were not only at school together but in a band together, and how thrilled I was that I was about to see him again. He recognised me, I know he did. But he ignored me. And in that moment, he made me out to be a liar."' There may be three sides to every story – his, hers and the truth. But given Freddie's sad recollections in his diaries about his experiences, his reaction that night makes clear that the hurt had not healed.

Other than for activities organised between the local boys' and girls' schools, male and female pupils got to interact with each other only occasionally, usually no more than a couple of times a month, when, accompanied by a school official, they would be allowed off the premises for a few hours. The only other time when they were allowed to see each other was during school holidays.

Although Jer and Bomi wrote regularly to their son, postal deliveries within India were infrequent. Freddie would sometimes wait two months or more for a reply to a letter he had written home. He was always so delighted to receive mail that he would rush to sit and write a response almost immediately, always reassuring his parents that he was fine and telling them that they must not worry about him. All of which was far from the truth, but his parents had no way of knowing otherwise. In the moment, at least, even if most of the time he was miserable, his elation at having heard from them at last was real.

'His mum and dad never knew how bad and unhappy their son really felt,' reveals B. 'But anyway, pupils were not allowed to express their sadness or homesickness in letters home to their parents' – probably for fear that families would withdraw their miserable sons, thus threatening the establishment's budget and, ultimately, its existence.

Freddie, we know, had loved music from a very young age. Fascinated by Parsee songs and prayer music, he had loved to experiment at home with his own singing voice. At St Peter's, he joined the choir. That was the beginning of his musical training. He and his fellow choristers practised almost daily after class and also took part in Sunday church services. Freddie learned quickly. He soon got the hang of hymnal structure and harmonious singing. A strong sense of melody, he later said, was already running in his veins.

Both boarding school and life in India exposed Freddie to rich cultural diversity, but also to extensive poverty and deprivation.

When pupils were allowed off campus once or twice a month, and would come across beggars, lepers, disabled people without feet, they took such tragic things to be just a fact of life in India.

'During the holidays, however,' says B., 'things were different. Freddie's eyes were opened. He came to understand how privileged he was.'

On one of his stays with Aunt Sheroo in Bombay, Freddie happened to discover the Towers of Silence and their significance – where Parsees lay out the bodies of their dead to be consumed by birds of prey. Although there were no Towers of Silence in Zanzibar, there was, as we know, a graveyard beside the Agiary.

'That discovery came as quite a shock to Freddie,' says B. 'He had not known that such places existed, and he was repulsed. But eventually he came to understand it as part of the circle of life. We eat to live on Earth, and we must eat with the consciousness of sacrificed life, whether that be the life of an animal or a plant. At the end of our lives here on Earth, we in turn become food for other living beings, because we have to move on to the World of Thoughts. I think that all Parsees must be shocked when they first discover the existence of the Towers of Silence. But at the same time, we are taught the reasons for them, and of course about the World of Thoughts. Once it all makes sense, the practicalities seem less shocking.'

Freddie did also have good experiences during his school holidays – such as when his auntie taught him to play chess, says B.

'She had all the time and patience in the world for him. She opened his eyes to a world he had never seen before, and to the things that really matter. Whenever he went to stay with her, he would be surrounded by family and felt happy and secure. But when he had to pack his things and return to boarding school, it was a terrible wrench to his heart. The same aunt taught him to appreciate music across the genres and, as previously mentioned, arranged his first piano lessons. Freddie was hooked! He played with enormous enthusiasm all the songs he could get his hands on. He started transposing them from one key to another and changing their structure. He began doing this, and found that he had the knack for it, when he was still quite young. His auntie also encouraged him to draw and paint. All these things became important forms of self-expression to him.'

During his teens, Freddie continued to visit Aunt Sheroo during the holidays, but also went to stay with other relatives. He would occasionally remain at school during half-terms and longer breaks, and would sometimes make excursions with a small circle of friends, both boys and girls. The group would trek together to the highest points in the Panchgani region, to admire the views.

'Freddie's favourite outing,' says B., 'was to a place from where you could see the Krishna River. He and his friends would sit there together in silence, just looking out, as if over the entire spread of Heaven.

'Fans travel vast distances to reach the locations of Freddie's childhood, hoping to feast their eyes on the places and sites he once saw,' she remarks. 'Unfortunately, if they go looking for his favourite view over the Krishna River, all they will see today is the Dhom Lake: the eleven-mile-long expanse of water that engulfed the ancient landscape he so loved.'[4]

Freddie enjoyed the softer, more sensitive company of his female acquaintances. He developed strong romantic feelings towards some of them, and for one in particular, whom he mentions in the diaries but does not name. Unfortunately, he was gauche and unsure in her company. He had no idea what to say or do, still less how to be cool and at ease when he was around her. Despite his painful shyness, their friendship flourished, until they became quite inseparable. After going through puberty, Freddie found that he had developed the typical form, walk, gestures, fine hands and distinctive facial looks of Persians.

'These gave him a pronounced effeminate appearance, of which he was acutely aware,' reveals B. 'It was accentuated by his shyness. He found himself bullied all the more because of it. Other kids tended to laugh at him, but he couldn't work out why. Should I say, he knew why, but couldn't fathom it. What on Earth was wrong with the way he was? He had been taught from a very young age that Ahura Mazda, the Creator in Zoroastrianism, is both masculine and feminine. He also knew that there is strict equality between man and woman in the same entity. That he grew to personify this himself felt completely natural to him. But it caused fellow schoolboys to mock and reject him in the cruellest fashion. This was, he said, incredibly difficult indeed to deal with.'

Boarding schools, inevitably, were places of sexual exploration. Wrenched from their families and bunched together in an enclosed environment, chaps would be chaps.

'The older boys would teach the younger boys how to masturbate,' explains B., preparing herself to deliver the devastating revelation as to why Freddie's exemplary academic record fell off a cliff.

It was in early 1961, she says, when Freddie was still only fourteen, that things went badly wrong. Freddie describes in his notebooks what befell him in bald language devoid of emotion.

'After having caught him during a collective self-pleasuring session with a group of other boys, one of the schoolmasters started taking Freddie into his quarters to sexually abuse him. This became a regular occurrence. When the man first touched Freddie intimately, he didn't react. He was paralysed. Maybe his abuser read that as encouragement and consent, Freddie wondered. The teacher forced him to bend over. The next step was very painful. Freddie was horrified, and absolutely terrified. His abuser was hasty. He did what he had come to do then left him without a word, showing no concern whatsoever for the boy or his feelings. The abuse went on for many months, all the way to the end of that school year, when the master abruptly left the school. Freddie couldn't speak to anyone about it. But he knew that everyone else there knew about it. The mockery and the bullying naturally increased.' There is no suggestion that any such abusers or abuse exist at the modern-day St Peter's School.

It was around this time, noted Freddie, that he took up boxing, in a conscious effort to defend and protect himself. He also continued to invest his emotional energy in music. Endless practice helped him to deal with the horror of the rapes to which he had been subjected. He didn't know what else he could do, other than pour all his efforts into overcoming the nightmare and try his best to be happy.

'He worked very hard in search of the happiness and elation that music gave him,' says B. 'Music became his whole world. Whenever he could get out of the classroom to practise on the school's piano, he would rush straight there. The rest of the time, he would practise finger exercises on the edge of his desk or on the side of his bed. He soon began writing his own music and dedicated every spare moment to it. It was clear to him that music would be his salvation, and that it would come to dominate his future. Because it made him feel well and whole, he pursued it relentlessly.'

Despite his best efforts, Freddie found that he could no longer focus his mind on anything other than music and art. He began to fail in every other subject at which he had previously excelled. Although he still enjoyed history and literature, he was so obsessed with music, art and his inner life that there was no room or time for anything else. He was desperate to return home.

During one particular school-holiday stay, his aunt couldn't help noticing that there was something different about her nephew. Instinct told her that something was very wrong. She informed his parents immediately, and cross-examined Freddie as to what was going on. He couldn't answer, nor could he look her in the eye. Overcome by the guilt of his failings, the shame he felt for having let down his parents who had made such sacrifices to educate him, and a revulsion that what had happened might be his fault, he felt paralysed. He couldn't confess to his aunt.

'He knew instinctively that something in him was broken, and that it always would be,' explains B. 'His rapist destroyed something in Freddie that he would never get back: his natural ability for emotional connection.'

He tried to block out his misery by immersing himself in rehearsing and performing with the Hectics.

'The band practised as much as they could,' says B. 'When they were not rehearsing music, they were talking about music. Their conversation was dominated by how to play certain songs, how to improve their stage act – which was limited, as they had only rudimentary equipment. Freddie, of course, had tons of ideas. He decided he needed a stage name, fearing that "Farrokh" wasn't rock 'n' roll enough. He discussed various options with the band, and "Freddie" was born.

'Despite many years of speculation,' she says, 'the truth is that he did not start to call himself Freddie, nor did his classmates address him by that name, until he joined the Hectics. Even then, he was still Farrokh outside the band. So even in his early teens, he was already making a distinction between the performer and the real person, with a separate name for each. He would become Freddie full-time only when he landed in England. But it would take his parents a decade to accept that their son Farrokh was now Freddie, and that they too were going to have to address him by that name.'

The damaged young teen's dual identity was now established. Because he enjoyed nothing more than playing and performing with the band – in which he could be someone other than his real tormented self – he morphed slowly but surely into Freddie.

'He had felt so lonely for such a long time, even with so many people around him, what difference could this make? That feeling of being alone in the middle of a crowd, he said, continued to plague him decades later.

'I find the many discrepancies in the testimonies of some of Freddie's so-called schoolmates very strange,' B. goes on. 'Some recall that he was clearly gay from a relatively young age, while others insist that he gave no such impression, and that the possibility of such a thing never occurred to them. We have those who remember that he called everybody "darling", and those who have never mentioned that at all. In fact, Freddie began to address people as "darling" only after he arrived in London. It was Western, it was England, it was the Swinging Sixties, and it was the fashion. He adopted it easily. It very quickly became part of his trademark, his personality. But he had never used it before landing in the UK.' Gita Bharucha, Freddie's friend at the neighbouring girls' school, insists that she was unaware of any homosexual tendencies brewing in Freddie. There were, she says, 'None at all. I swear … There was an art teacher at St Peter's called Mrs Blossom Smith. I knew her daughter, Janice Smith. Years later, she said to me, "Mum always felt there was something different with Bucky."' Gita did ask Janice what she meant. 'But we didn't take it further,' she told me in an interview for *Love of My Life*.

'One of the fallacies often reported is that Freddie failed his academic exams at St Peter's because of confusion over his sexuality,' says B. 'That's totally wrong. He simply did not experience that kind of confusion. Again, he had been aware from a very early age that Mazda is both masculine and feminine, and was comfortable with the strict equality between men and women in the same entity. He awoke to it in himself, recognising that he, too, was bisexual. What was difficult for him was the way that others regarded, judged and rejected his bisexuality. He was very comfortable with it. Why couldn't others be?

'And I have thought to myself,' B. continues, her frustration mounting, 'weren't some of them the same boys who tried to see him again, backstage after Queen gigs, once Freddie had become hugely famous? Once the success and the money had kicked in?

For what reason? A pseudo-friendship based on mockery, bullying, humiliation and abuse, in which Freddie had been their
victim? Who could blame him for ignoring them, for figuratively
wiping them off the face of the Earth?'

. . .

The phoenix depicted in the school emblem was one of the few
positive memories that Freddie took away with him from St Peter's.
Also known as the firebird, the mythical creature obtains new life
by dying in a blaze of flames before arising from its own ashes. To
Freddie, it was also a symbol of the eternal flame, the most important element of the Zoroastrian religion. The phoenix would later
inspire him to create the crest of the band with whom he would go
on to achieve worldwide fame and musical domination.

. . .

Freddie's parents were mortified by their son's misery and were
desperate to know what was wrong with him. He couldn't tell
them. Just as he had been unable to confide in his aunt, despite
the love and attention she lavished on him, he couldn't bring
himself to tell them what had happened to him. All that Jer and
Bomi could do was remove him from the school. Home Freddie
went to Zanzibar, weeping with relief.

He never forgave those schoolfriends who had bullied him.
Nor did he forget how abominably some of them had treated
him. He dropped them, refusing to maintain contact with them.
Good riddance. Other than on the pages of his notebooks and to

Mary, Roger and one other person – the man destined to become B.'s stepfather and Freddie's enduring friend – he never opened up to a single other friend or employee about his unhappy years at St Peter's.

'Dad never told me that he had opened up to my stepfather,' says B. 'I discovered this only after Dad's death, when my stepfather told me during a conversation that these were topics he and Freddie had talked about.'

By his own admission, those days were gone. Talking about them was never going to change what had happened.

Freddie had mixed feelings on the long sea voyage home. While he was desperately sorry to leave beautiful India, a wonderful country and culture that would always remain dear to him, he could not have been more relieved about his deliverance from the harshest of school days. Rare moments of true friendship and respect had been clouded by constant treachery. Music, his only consolation, now had centre-stage importance in his life. He had achieved resilience by building an inner world into which he could escape whenever he needed to. He had learned how to fend for himself. But at the age of sixteen, he had no idea what to do with all this. Nor did he have a clue as to what he would do next. All he knew in that moment was that he could have exploded with excitement, apprehension and pent-up emotion as the ship approached port, where his mum, dad and sister would be waiting for him. The many years away from his loved ones vanished like foam on the waves. The past no longer mattered, because Freddie was home for good.

• • •

Back in Zanzibar, Freddie was at the loosest of ends. Prospects were limited. He had no idea what he might find to do for a living. His expensive boarding school education had qualified him for nothing. Was he supposed to become a docker, unloading heavy cargo from ships and operating huge machinery, or toil as a picker on the plantations? He was fearful and confused.

'Yet the moment he felt the warm sand between his toes again,' says B., 'he knew he was home, and that there was nowhere he would rather be.'

But Zanzibar was no longer as Freddie had left it. When the winds of change blow, according to an old Chinese proverb, some build walls while others build windmills. His dear friend Ahmed was no longer there waiting for him, having left the island for good some years earlier when his family returned home to Oman. Ibrahim and Mustapha attended school on the mainland, so were able to get together with Freddie only during the holidays. Sensing that their days together were numbered, Freddie cherished those final carefree moments as though his life depended on them.

'They played on the beach, just as they had done as little boys,' recounts B. 'They swam together endlessly, and watched the boats go by. They'd sit talking and listening to Western records. They would spend all their free time together, walking around at night listening to taarab' – a type of music heavily influenced by Indian and Arabian musical traditions that was popular at the time in coastal East Africa – 'and they went to the movies. Sometimes they would lie on the roof together and look down on life in the labyrinthine streets of Stone Town under the cloudless, starry sky. They would talk about their life in Zanzibar, comparing it to the barely imaginable lifestyles they caught glimpses of in those glossy magazines from overseas.

'You wrote in your last book,' B. reminds me, 'about Zanzibar's "Project Mercury" being one of the reasons why Freddie chose his name.' This five-year, US$400-million-dollar operation was launched by NASA in October 1958 to test the viability of manned and unmanned space travel in preparation for expeditions to the moon. A satellite-tracking station was constructed in Zanzibar in 1960. Freddie was one of the many Zanzibari teenagers who took to memorising the satellite launch schedules. They would gather on the beach at night, lie on the sand gazing up at the stars, and await the overhead passing of the American spaceship. More than sixty years later, parts of that disused space station still stand. Locals refer to them as 'the Americani buildings'. 'You were right,' affirms B., 'Project Mercury *was* behind his choice of name. As for the band name Queen, that was inspired by an imported glossy British magazine called *Queen* that Freddie used to read in Zanzibar. Along with *The Lady*, it was one of the few British publications available there. He discovered England via those magazines, and along with it the distinctively royal and aristocratic styles that appealed to him so much. As for the Queen crest: the phoenix within it, the symbol of rebirth: that is *him*. Having been born in Zanzibar, he said he experienced his first rebirth in Panchgani. He was born again back in Zanzibar, then again after the genocide, and yet again in England. Years later, he explained, his disease would be a kind of rebirth experience too. Perhaps now you can understand why removing even the smallest event from the life of Freddie Bulsara would mean that Freddie Mercury could not have existed.'

· · ·

The three friends' lives were not so different from those of any other teenagers, in terms of preoccupations and ambitions. But Freddie felt restless. He was filled with vigour but lacked hope for a future on that remote tropical island. He was also disappointed. The jovial group of their childhood had come together again, but things were not the same without Ahmed. Nor were they children any longer. Nevertheless, Freddie longed to go back and pick up where they had left off. At the end of the holidays when his friends went back to school, he found himself alone again. He would have to do without his friends for several more months. What else could he do but fantasise about what else might be out there for him? The posters and pictures clipped from magazines that he'd stuck to the wall behind his bed reminded him that a whole other world awaited him.

'We can only wonder what his life would have been like had he continued in inadequate schooling in Zanzibar, where there was no decent secondary education, against the backdrop of a dense and complicated community and social tensions in those days,' says his daughter. 'His father worked for the British government, so Freddie could not work in the family business as did the sons of shopkeepers or traders. Without a proper education, what could he have done? Would he have worked in those docks or on those plantations for a few shillings a week from the age of thirteen or fourteen, as most Zanzibari boys did in those days? Might he have been enlisted into one of the revolutionary movements that raged there? Would he have found the strength to resist indoctrination? Would he have rallied with independence movements, and would he then have turned against his family and their loved ones? Might he even have been one of the countless victims of the genocide?'

Things had changed in sinister ways. The atmosphere of Stone Town, once thrumming with joy, music and happiness, was now tense. A sense of foreboding prevailed. It had been that way since the death of Zanzibar's longest-serving sultan, Khalīfa ibn Harūb, in October 1960. The well-respected leader who had calmed the region during times of political crisis was no longer around to steady the ship. In 1963, Zanzibar regained its independence, becoming a member of the British Commonwealth.

'When many colonies started gaining independence,' says B., 'Freddie's parents began to think about leaving the island. Things came to a head in 1963. Their children, both British Protected Persons (BPPs), were effectively stateless, living as they did in a territory controlled or once controlled by the British Empire. As such, they could hold a British passport and receive consular assistance and protection from UK diplomatic posts. Bomi had a British passport too. In the past, with growing tensions in an India in favour of independence, Bomi had taken a position in Zanzibar when the opportunity arose – not because Zanzibar Protectorate was an especially attractive proposition to a British civil servant, but because it boasted a strong Parsee community, and some of his family were still there. Realising that independence was coming to Zanzibar, the Bulsaras had to decide very quickly whether to choose British or Zanzibari nationality. They started to think very seriously about relocating to the UK.'

Eleven months after he returned to his birthplace, the eruptions of the night of 11 January 1964 etched themselves so deeply into Freddie's memory that he would never be free of them.

'He was haunted for the rest of his life,' says B., 'by all that he saw and lived [through] during those days of terror.

'It was the school holidays between the monsoons and the hottest time of the year,' she recounts. 'Freddie, Ibrahim and Mustapha spent the evening together on the beach until quite late into the night. It was a festive day, just before Ramadan. They returned home to sleep. When Freddie awoke, the horror had already begun. Aggressive announcements against "imperialists", Asians and Europeans were broadcast on the radio. Born and raised in India, Bomi and Jer were considered Asian. Bomi also worked for the "imperialist government", which made them personae non gratae. They were terrified. People were running for their lives in the streets. Homes and shops were burning. Men with weapons were on the rampage, shooting and setting fire to everything. Freddie, his parents and sister cowered inside their home. Even though all their windows were shuttered, they were deafened by mass shouting and screaming. From their roof terrace they could see dense plumes of smoke rising in the sky. They watched in horror as Arab friends and neighbours were dragged from their homes. Some were publicly executed, decapitated in the middle of the street. Hundreds more were slaughtered on the beaches. Arab and Asian women were raped. Their homes were looted and their shops were burned down. Overnight, as Freddie described it, your friend became your enemy. Madness took possession of their minds.

'A curfew having been imposed, the streets were soon deserted. Rumours about evacuation to safety did the rounds, but no official word came. Hundreds of British citizens remained stranded on the island. They were warned to keep calm and stay patient, and were instructed to stay indoors, but to be ready to leave at a moment's notice. Freddie, his mum, dad and sister packed very few belongings. They had to choose what to take and what to leave behind, which must have been traumatic for them.'

Their anxiety mounted as they waited. In such moments, as Freddie described it, people are headless chickens, they have no idea what to do or how to behave. To attempt to do anything at all seemed futile. Food was running out. The clean water supply would be cut off. While they recognised that mutual support was vital, suspicion was rife.

'Then came the announcement that the evacuation was about to begin,' B. relates. 'The Bulsaras had to leave their home immediately. Where would they go? They had family living in Dar es Salaam on the mainland, but that was never a possibility as far as Bomi was concerned. His travels had taken him to Mombasa in Kenya and Aden (Yemen). He had felt for himself the winds of independence. Tanganyika, Colonial Kenya, Colonial Aden and other British Protectorates had already gained full independence. Their only viable option was the UK.'

Freddie, Ibrahim and Mustapha had parted in the street that night, laughing and joking as always. It was the last time they ever saw each other. Freddie never found out what had become of his friends. He had no idea whether either or both had managed, like him, to flee. He carried the heartbreak of losing them, his only loyal friends, for the rest of his life.

'He could never leave it behind and move on,' B. tells us. 'If he wanted to erase the horror of his past, he would also have to erase the many moments of pure happiness he had spent with the boys. It all went hand in hand. He tried in vain to understand why the genocide had happened. Thousands of people had been slaughtered just for having been in the wrong place at the wrong time. Had his boyhood brothers died too? He owned not so much as a photograph of them. He had nothing whatsoever to remember them by. All he had were the snapshots in his mind, of happy days from a distant life. With the passing years, their faces faded slowly from his memory.'

CHAPTER 4

AND NO RELIGION, TOO

Freddie had grown up in India, B. reflects.

'India nourished him, both artistically and as a human being, with its stories of the Maharajas, the system of castes in which everyone knows his place and never questions it, and its melting pot of races, cultures, religions and ethnic groups living side by side since time immemorial. All the aromas, perfumes and colours Freddie liked best were those of India. He adored the Parsees' vibrant and lavish festivities. In the old days, Queen were often called "the most debauched party-givers in rock". Most people don't realise that their wilder celebrations were inspired by and worthy of the most legendary extravagances of the Maharajas, whose fantastic celebrations featured unlimited wine and food, snakes, and naked women painted to look as though they were clothed (even their bracelets were drawings!). Such things would shock and enchant the British officials in attendance.'

It was during his years in India, Freddie confided to his daughter, that he found himself questioning life more deeply than ever before. If there is only one God, he wondered, then why were there so many different religions? Why so many conflicting rituals and practices? Perhaps, he concluded, they were all nothing more than interpretations of the same thing.

'At St Peter's, he learned to practise his family's religion in his own way,' she says. 'He went to Sunday Mass, as did all the boys. And when he read the Bible, he found the words of Jesus that changed his life: "When you pray, do not be like the hypocrites, for they love to pray standing in the synagogues and on the street corners to be seen by men … but when you pray, go into your room, close the door and pray to your Father who is unseen.""[1]

Freddie understood Jesus's meaning: that prayer should be a private time between God and the worshipper. Jesus was not suggesting that it was wrong to pray with others, but that prayers should be sincere, and offered for the right reasons.

'You wrote the following in your book,' she reminded me: '"In the sacred Zoroastrian text the Vendidad, it is stated: The man that lies with mankind as man lies with womankind, or as a woman lies with mankind, is a man that is a Daeva (demon). This man is a worshipper of the Daevas, a male paramour of the Daevas. For Parsees, homosexuality is not only sinful, but a form, unimaginably, of devil-worship."

'But Freddie's research into his own faith had revealed to him that none of the Avestan texts except the Gathas had actually been composed by Zarathustra. They were all written by individuals of whom we know nothing, not even their names or their functions. Many of these texts were probably written more than a thousand years *after* Zarathustra's lifetime, or they belonged to pre-Zoroastrian religions: the very religions that Zarathustra himself had rejected and against which he had fought. This discovery was a revelation. For Freddie, it opened up a whole new horizon. From that day on, he followed only Zarathustra's words along with his own beliefs and practices. He distanced himself from codified and organised rituals.'

The core tenet of the religion, and Freddie's primary take-away from it, was Zarathustra's greatest principle: that the aim of existence is to lead a happy and joyful life on Earth, and to go contentedly into the World of Thoughts, the spiritual world, at the end of one's Earthly life. He agreed with the requirement of every individual to contribute to the improvement of the world, so that every living being, whether human, animal or plant, may live a life of peace and plenty. He understood that the key to this happiness is the creation of a society based on righteousness, serenity, progress and prosperity. He also knew that happiness and inner peace cannot be attained unless everyone invests in the happiness of all fellow beings. He agreed with the premise that throughout our lives, we all – every man and woman – have free will to choose the kind of life we wish to live. He accepted that the opposing forces of good and evil exert their influences equally. Because freedom of choice forms the basis of the teaching of the Gathas, each individual is responsible for their own happiness or misery.

Freddie meditated often and deeply over the questions posed by Zarathustra in the Gathas. The prophet's basic principles, of goodness, generosity and helping others, and of honesty, loyalty, enjoyment of life and personal achievement, were the standards that guided Freddie throughout his life. In the Gathas, B. explains, 'there is no demon, no devil, no hell. There are neither orders nor commandments. Neither salvation nor sin. Nor do the Gathas ever talk about bisexuality or homosexuality. The first principle is that happiness belongs to he who makes others happy. Every individual must do what is right for him, and what is appropriate according to his own conscience. It's very simple:

the forces that drive people towards happiness are good. The forces that prevent them from reaching it are bad. Good and evil arise only out of human thought. Unfortunately, few people outside the community know any of this. Zoroastrianism is often misinterpreted and is also practised erroneously.'

Freddie was not only a believer. As we know, he remained faithful all his life. No longer a slave to rules and rituals, he practised his religion privately in his own way. It will surprise some to learn that he spent his life looking for Asha: righteousness; Vohu manah: goodness of thought; Khashatra: self-dominance; Armaiti: serenity; Haurvatat: evolution towards perfection; and Ameretat: eternity beyond time. He did succeed, his daughter reassures us, in finding these things. Throughout his life and at the point of his death, he was perfectly at peace with himself about his faith and his religion.

'He probably practised Zarathustra's principles more strictly than most Zoroastrians,' muses B. 'All in the privacy of his own room.'

• • •

When his little girl was old enough, Freddie took it upon himself to teach her the most important Zoroastrian prayers and their meaning, as well as the daily devotions, prayers of repentance, and the many manners, customs and traditions of the faith.

'Not that he followed all of them himself,' she makes clear, 'but it mattered to him to hand down to me absolutely everything that had been part of his story and his life. He gave me the sacred shirt and kusti – the cord that is worn around the waist by Parsees – and taught me their meaning. He gave me the book of Gathas, the daily prayer book, and another containing the Zoroastrian Catechism. And he instructed me in the Zoroastrian vision: that nobody, not even a priest or a prophet, can intervene in the salvation of the soul. It is for you yourself to look to the purity of your own thoughts, words and deeds. You must think nothing but the right thing, speak nothing but the truth, do nothing but that which is proper, and do your duty towards all living things.'

It is true, his daughter agrees, that Freddie never spoke publicly about religion. Nor did he discuss his personal beliefs with most of his friends and acquaintances:

'But as I have said, he did pay a great deal of attention to my religious education, specifically my Zoroastrian education. He truly believed that God is the great architect of the existence of all that we see in the world, and that there is no god but God, whatever path or name he takes. The irony, for me, as I explained, is that I am not recognised as Zoroastrian because I am illegitimate. But my father taught me his own faith, assuring me that I have the right to feel both Christian and Zoroastrian at the same time. I can do this, he said, because there is only one God.'

Freddie was upset by some of the rituals and laws created by various leaders, she says, because they threatened the future of both Parsees and Zoroastrianism: 'Laws pertaining to who is Zoroastrian and who is not; to patrilineality: some refuse to accept children who have only a Zoroastrian father; to identity, conversion, marriage and the rest: for him, such things made it all too exclusive. Freddie's wish was for Parsees to live more openly. He couldn't understand why a religion that is so generous towards others could be so closed and rigid regarding its definition of itself, and who can or cannot be Zoroastrian. He feared that the influence of orthodox leaders would lead to the religion's extinction.'

When Freddie was born, his daughter tells us, his birth was celebrated as a great blessing in the faith because he was a male child. This meant not only that his family name would continue, but that the Parsee community would too.

'The Panchayat, which is the council that makes rules and maintains Zoroastrian family and social values, defines very strictly who counts as Parsee,' she says. 'Only those with a Parsee father – and in India, only those who have both a Parsee father and mother – make the grade. When a Parsee woman chooses to marry a non-Parsee man, the Panchayat states that she is no longer a Parsee, and will not be permitted to take part in special events. But a man who takes a non-Parsee wife remains Parsee all his life. This perplexed Freddie enormously. He couldn't understand it. Parsees, after all, built schools for girls. They were the first in India to give their daughters a good education. Many Parsee women work and are financially independent of their husbands. Freddie's mother, Jer, worked, and that was normal. But a woman could be considered Parsee only if both her father and mother were Parsee, and only if she took a Parsee husband. To Freddie, this was wrong. He was feminist all his life, and he was proud of that. As he said, women carry the children, so they carry the world. We do the most magical thing in all creation: we give birth. To him, this miracle placed women way above men. He never wavered on this. He said that the journey, the way forward, the future, was far more important than the traditions of the past. His views caused a major rift between him and his parents. The many contradictions in Parsee life on important subjects, not only the status of women, troubled him. This reinforced his conviction that he should practise his religion quietly in his own way, according to his own private views.'

Freddie was sometimes castigated by members of his community for not speaking up about his religion. Given that virtually everything he commented on made headlines, wasn't he right to keep his views and beliefs to himself?

'The Parsee community is closely knit,' says B. 'They don't promote Zoroastrianism, nor do they attempt to convert people to follow it. The life that Parsees lead is based on joy, happiness, truth, honesty, respect, loyalty, philanthropy, generosity, the enjoyment of life, personal achievement and family values – with all our hearts and not in the name of a god, a prophet or anybody else. Because my father chose to deal directly with God, and to follow Zarathustra's words alongside his own beliefs and practices – *rejecting* codified, organised rituals – he was dismissed as "not really religious". Even by his own family! But nothing could have been further from the truth. He often mentioned or alluded to God and religion in his lyrics. Some of these references were explicit, such as in the songs "Jesus" (on their debut album *Queen*) and "All God's People" (on the album *Innuendo*).

'He also believed strongly that everyone is entitled to believe what they want to believe. Freddie's faith happened to be Zoroastrianism: a minority religion in every place in which he had ever lived. He just wanted to maintain his beliefs quietly, wherever he happened to be, and to avoid the kind of religious debate that can so often be misunderstood and lead to persecution.

'A number of people have said and written that Freddie was not a believer; that he only sought a god at the end of his life in order to be absolved of his "sins". It's not true. Freddie believed profoundly. He never turned away from God. Because he didn't marry a Zoroastrian woman or produce a son, he failed to satisfy the Zoroastrian expectations placed upon him at birth. But he honoured the faith and its values in so many other ways. With his great generosity, his desire to make everyone happy, with the universality of his thoughts and feelings, the energy he put into his work as an entertainer, with his music – which he regarded as a universal language – his principles, and his respect and love for family. He could not have been prouder of his roots. He favoured Parsee style and taste. The homes of Parsees tend to be richly furnished and decorated with beautiful fabrics and flowers in every room and lit with lamps and candles. He loved all that and did the same. He relished the Parsee sense of occasion and celebration. Tradition demands that we must celebrate life every month if we can, in a colourful place decorated with flowers, fruit and gorgeous fabrics, and soundtracked by wonderful music. Women adorn themselves with their finest jewels. Birthday parties, navjotes, weddings and religious festivals always involve dinners and all kinds of entertaining and are great occasions. All his adult life, Freddie loved to throw big parties and spoil his guests. The same spirit, that generosity and inclination to spread joy, fuelled his exuberant stage performances.'

Freddie and parties, she reflects, was a very strange thing: 'He threw many parties himself, to which he always invited a lot of people, but was rarely if ever invited back. He gave generously to his friends but received few gifts himself. That didn't stop him.

The pleasure that he derived from giving was far greater than anything he would have experienced from receiving. Prosperity is a blessing among Parsees, and Freddie often said how much he loved success and money. Which is not to say that Parsees are greedy. We believe that money is for buying things. The ambition is not to amass more and more money simply for the sake of having it, but in order to give it away. You only have to look at the role of Parsees in India's development. When they built hospitals, schools, institutions, facilities, roads and bridges, they did it for everyone, not exclusively for their own community. Their generosity is for the benefit of all. Despite being a minority group, they play a huge and important role. It is something to be proud of, which Freddie was.'

CHAPTER 5

EXODUS

Having grabbed what they could, and hobbling along with as many bags and suitcases as the four of them could carry, Freddie and his family left quietly but hurriedly without bidding friends and loved ones farewell. Bomi took risks, yanked strings and pulled in favours to get his family off the island to safety. Freddie realised only much later that his father would have stopped at nothing and would even have given his life to save his wife and children.

One of the boats that evacuated British civilians during the Zanzibar genocide was the Royal Navy anti-submarine frigate HMS *Rhyl*. Its sister ships during that tense operation were HMS *Owen* and the stores ship RFA *Hebe*.

'I have long suspected that Freddie was inspired by the sound and rhythm of the name of the ship that carried them to freedom to rechristen as *Rhye* the wonderful fantasy land he had conjured from the Oxus River in Greater Iran. Because we know that the name came after the creation of the realm,' says B.

Only the sultan, his family and a handful of associates were evacuated on 12 January 1964. The authorities dithered to begin with over the removal of British nationals, taking the view that such a complex operation was largely unnecessary. 'Freddie's family and many others lived for several days not knowing what to do, with no idea whether or not they would be evacuated, while madness raged all around them,' says B.

'They were ordered to remain indoors, to shutter their windows and to wait patiently and calmly. That's not easy to do in such circumstances.

'The Bulsaras were evacuated after a few days. They found refuge with relatives. But I don't know whether that was in India or in Tanganyika, as at that time they had family in both countries. From what Freddie said and wrote, I think it was in India, but he didn't specify that destination in his notebooks. The period between their evacuation and the day they obtained the keys to their own house in England was nine months. Freddie never really talked about it, except to allude to a feeling that the four of them were deracinated: uprooted and cast adrift. When he was sent away to India, his roots, his home, were in Zanzibar. Later on, wherever he found himself in the world, his roots, his home, were in London. But during those precarious nine months, that period of deracination scared him.'

His inability to pack and say his goodbyes echoed Freddie's experience when he was sent away to boarding school.

'The nightmares he suffered from that day forward contributed to his already chronic inability to sleep,' says B. 'He never got over the terror he felt when his family were forced to leave Zanzibar. He lived the rest of his life with an open wound.'

Revolutionaries overthrew the sultanate and established a republic. In April 1964, the presidents of Zanzibar and mainland Tanganyika united the two countries to form Tanzania. Months after the Bulsaras had left, Freddie's father learned that their house, along with hundreds of others on the island, had been looted and possessed by the incoming government. Land, residential properties and private clubs were nationalised. Many citizens were imprisoned. Thousands of others disappeared. Decades after the revolution, life on Zanzibar had not recovered. Poverty and hunger prevailed. Draconian laws and forced labour were imposed. Even though he was heartbroken at having had to flee his beloved homeland in such circumstances, Freddie was eventually able to express gratitude towards his parents for having got their family out of there alive. Had they stayed, he knew, they would not have lived to tell the tale.

'This terrible history is a part of Freddie's story that very few people know,' says B. 'He never spoke about it publicly. He discussed it only with his three closest friends: Mary, Roger and the man who would become my stepfather. These were the same trusted people in whom he confided about his childhood, his teenage years, what had happened to him at boarding school, the genocide, his religion and his Parsee roots. All these experiences and more had made him desperately insecure. It was this insecurity that engendered his quest to become a performer.'

Freddie and his family landed in England on Monday, 4 May 1964. Queen Elizabeth II was on the throne and was celebrating, with her husband, Prince Philip, Duke of Edinburgh, the recent arrival of Prince Edward, their third son and youngest child. Alec Douglas-Home was the Conservative Prime Minister, but would be ousted by Harold Wilson and the Labour Party later that year. Three days after the Bulsaras' arrival, Labour would win a landslide victory in the London local elections. *Top of the Pops* had first aired on television four months earlier, West Ham United had just beaten Preston North End at Wembley Stadium to take the FA Cup, and Bob Dylan performed that very night at the Royal Festival Hall.

The family found that exotic-looking people were not welcomed with open arms.

'Life was difficult for them for quite a long time,' B. goes on. 'This, too, affected Freddie deeply. Zanzibar and India had given him his best years, but also his most unbearable memories. The atrocities that he kept hidden became scars that were engraved on his soul. By saying nothing about his background or his past, he avoided being regarded as an alien. By behaving outrageously, ever the actor, he managed to protect and conceal his private self. People saw the armour and not the man; much less the helpless child who never overcame his fear of being left alone.'

His appetite whetted by features and photographs he had seen in magazines, Freddie had long dreamed of travelling to England. He had even imagined meeting Her Majesty the Queen herself, and expected to do so. But when he arrived in the UK, nothing was as he had anticipated. The drab little West London houses where they were taken in, and the modest semi on Gladstone Avenue, Feltham that would become their permanent home, were a million miles from the majestic mansions and fine residences of his preoccupation. He sulked at first with bitter disappointment, though he soon snapped out of it. He knew how lucky they were to have survived, and to have been given a second chance. He told himself that things happen for a reason, that life is pre-destined, and that harsh lessons make us who we are. His father having been able to lay his hands on some savings prior to departure, they had a little money with which to get started. Many others, he knew, had not been so fortunate. The Bulsaras' relatives in London found them temporary accommodation. The Parsee community helped too. Bomi and Jer had their hands full, complying with immigration requirements, finding a permanent home for their family, getting themselves jobs and securing places at schools for their children. Freddie enrolled at Isleworth Polytechnic and Hounslow Borough College that September, choosing a two-year art foundation course. At the age of twenty and armed with an Art A level, he progressed to Ealing Art College, part of Ealing Technical College and School of Art.

'While Freddie was very excited by this completely fresh start,' says B., 'his parents were apprehensive. They were judged by their appearance and were mostly dismissed as foreigners. Some people treated them with contempt. Freddie witnessed all this, but he wasn't put off by it. He had been toughened by everything that had happened to him. His whole world had collapsed three times, and he had learned about life in the hardest ways imaginable. But he had survived. He knew he had a future in London. He was determined to throw himself into it wholeheartedly, and make the absolute best of what came his way.'

Freddie pulled on his costume, perfected his Persian Popinjay and assumed the role of the Great Pretender.

'No one would ever be allowed to disrespect him again,' says B. 'He was no longer the foreigner. Freddie now belonged. He changed his appearance to reflect the changes he felt inside. He couldn't put his finger on it, nor could he have articulated it at that stage, he said. But he knew he had to go his own way and do his own thing. He spent a great deal of time painting pictures and improvising music, visualising his future and raring to make music of his own. He also started staying out all night with his friends. His mother had no idea what was going on, so naturally she was worried. Freddie and Jer argued constantly about it. She didn't like what her son was turning into. She just wanted him to get a degree in a serious field and prepare for a respectable profession. At that point, Freddie said, he felt smothered by his mum. He describes having felt as though she was trying to cut off the wings he so desperately wanted to spread.'

His father, Bomi, on the other hand, was much more relaxed.

'As long as Freddie carried on going to school, everything else was fine by him. After all, they had only just arrived in a foreign country with a completely different culture, customs and traditions. It would all take a bit of getting used to. Bomi was willing to allow Freddie as much time as he needed to adapt to his new environment and get his bearings. His mother, Jer, however, seemed to want her son to reinvent himself overnight. Bomi may have sensed that Freddie was an emerging artist, with talent and potential set to burst. As for Freddie, he truly believed he had a future in music and promised himself he was going to make it his career. He was so determined, nothing could stop him. The home situation grew tense. The more Jer complained, the later Freddie came home, until in the end he was not coming home at all.'

Shortly after commencing his course at Ealing Art College, Freddie found a studio apartment to rent. He longed to live in the heart of the city and soak up everything it had to offer. He had several girlfriends by then but could hardly take them back to his parents' house to spend the night. Bomi understood his predicament. He gave his son money to cover the rent on the tiny flat, and an allowance to live on until he gained his Graphics diploma. After that, Bomi made clear, he would be on his own.

Freddie would return regularly to the family home, to play the piano and sit down to a nice hot meal.

Nothing came easily. He didn't have much. He was always desperate for money, but at the same time felt confident that what he needed was coming to him. He'd treat himself to a few records, the odd book and some posters of paintings for the walls of his drab little flat – appearances really mattered to him – but made do without almost everything else.

'When he visited his family, he'd arrive with a bunch of records under his arm which he would play on their gramophone, because he didn't have a record player of his own,' says B. 'When they bought him his own one for his birthday, he felt like the richest guy in the world.'

. . .

Over time, despite the long separation they had both suffered during his childhood that had put distance between them, Freddie came to know everything about his father. Much of what his dad shared about his own life astonished him. He found it hard to accept many of the things Bomi had been through, such as India's engagement with the British Empire during the First World War, food shortages, inflation created by the war effort, the rise of the separatists and the horrors committed by the British armed forces in order to stop them, the riots, the violence, the extrajudicial executions. Then there was the Second World War, in which Bomi had also served, and all the upheaval of India's quest for independence. Although Bomi was Parsee, India was his country: the homeland where he, his wife and their ancestors had been born and had lived.

'Yes, Freddie came to know all about his dad's life,' says B. 'He knew the full personal history of Boomanshaw Rustomji, long before he became Bomi Bulsara.'

It was the first time I had heard Freddie's father referred to by this name. Bomi's birth names had never been revealed in any previous book or documentary, nor were they mentioned in the feature film *Bohemian Rhapsody*. Here, for the first time ever, was Bulsara senior's legal identity before he left India for Zanzibar, years before Freddie was born. The only record of it that I could find in England appeared among the pages of the *London Gazette*: the UK's official public record, dating back to 1665. In the edition dated 30 June 1970, six years after the Bulsara family left Zanzibar for the UK, Freddie's father is listed under 'NATURALISATION: List of aliens to whom Certificates of Naturalisation have been granted'. His entry appears there as follows: '*Bulsara, Boomanshaw or Bomanshaw Rustomji (known as Bomi Bulsara); of no nationality; 22 Gladstone Avenue, Feltham, Middlesex. 22nd April 1970*' – being the date when citizenship was granted. The Certificate of Naturalisation, also known as a British Citizen Certificate, is issued to non-UK nationals who become British citizens. It confirms that the individual concerned holds the same rights as British citizens born in the UK, including the right of abode.

Immediately beneath Bomi's entry appears the following for Freddie's mother: '*Bulsara, Jer, Bomi; Of no nationality; 22 Gladstone Avenue, Feltham, Middlesex. 22nd April 1970.*' There are no entries at that point for Freddie or his sister, Kashmira. Freddie was seventeen and his sister twelve when the family landed in England during the spring of 1964. Via two temporary lodgings, they settled in Gladstone Avenue that November. Until 31 December 1969, the age of majority in England was twenty-one. On 1 January 1970, it was reduced to eighteen. Both Freddie and Kashmira were legally minors when their parents commenced the application process for citizenship. Freddie did not need to apply in his own right until he had been resident in the country for five years. By then, he would be twenty-three years old: a little over halfway through his life.[1]

. . .

'Freddie was the very image of his father,' B. informs us. 'His facial features – cheeks, jaw, lips – his hands and his gestures were Bomi's. His character, too. Not only his resistance to being told how to behave, what to do and what not to do, his sense of entitlement and his demanding personality, but also his kindness, his attention to others, and his extreme shyness and reserve. He always described himself as Persian and British – *not* Indian, Zanzibari or African, even less Tanzanian,' she tells me. 'His parents lived in Zanzibar for employment reasons. Only those who are completely ignorant of both Freddie's history and that of Zanzibar can describe him as Zanzibari, African or Tanzanian. Even though his stage name and customary name was "Freddie Mercury", he remained Frederick (Freddie) Bulsara until his death. On his death certificate, both "Frederick Mercury" and "Frederick Bulsara" are listed. This was his choice, his decision.'

He honoured and maintained his origins and heritage, in other words. Those who have claimed that he never wanted to look back do not understand him at all.

Another misconception is that he was at odds with his parents.

'He respected them hugely,' his daughter reports. 'Of course he went through his period of rebellion. This is understandable when you consider that he had spent so much time separated from them, thousands of miles away. So they didn't really know each other at that time. When the family came to leave Zanzibar, they lost their previous, relatively elevated social standing, and landed in a totally alien and unknown environment. My grandfather Bomi was very worried about his son, because Freddie was not only not interested in school, he didn't care to find himself a job. It was only later that Freddie understood that his father's attitude towards him had been out of fear for his future.'

It is worth remembering that Brian May's, Roger Taylor's and John Deacon's parents would all express their displeasure when their sons dropped out of education to pursue a music career. Bomi's concerns were entirely justified. His attitude was not unique. In time, the parents of all four young men became immensely proud of them.

Freddie did retain anger towards his parents for having banished him to a boarding school thousands of miles from home, where he was not cared for properly and where he was abused. But he came to understand that without it, he would not have had his excellent education, nor would he have been able to develop his artistic talent. He would not have been able to attend Ealing College.

'Everything else would have been much more difficult for him, if not impossible,' says his daughter. 'He knew that without that terrible decision taken by his parents, he would probably never have had his wonderful artistic career. He came to know how deeply heartbroken his parents had been when they sent him to India. They suffered severely as a result of being separated from their only son. Bomi was very reserved by nature and not given to expressing his emotions openly. But he carried enormous guilt at having inflicted such suffering on his child and on his wife, Jer, Freddie's mother and my grandmother. That guilt came between Bomi and Freddie. It made discussions between them difficult, and at times unpleasant, for several years. Not that Freddie ever lost respect for his father. When he was in London, he made a habit of seeing them once or twice a week. When he was away, he always phoned them regularly.'

Because Freddie's father was an extremely reserved man who kept himself to himself and did not talk to many people, and because Freddie kept his parents away from the press and every-thing to do with his career and business, there were some people who were intent on giving Bomi a bad name, B. flags up.

'These were the same kind of people who sought to portray Freddie as a man who was happy only in gay circles; who still want us to believe that, even though Freddie respected his parents, the only thing he had in common with them was his original surname. They imply that he was cut off from his mother and father and his wider family. But nothing could be further from the truth. While Bomi did not agree with his son's choice to study Art and Design, he was always there for him, and always tried to help him. When Freddie wanted to change course and abandon Design for Graphics, Bomi supported the decision. And when Freddie decided to move out of the family home and find himself a flat' – he moved into 42B Addison Gardens in Kensington, sharing that minute space with flatmates Paul Humberstone and

Chris Smith – 'his father provided funds to cover his rent and living expenses.'

Why did Bomi do all this?

'Because he recognised himself in his son,' B. explains. 'He knew the boy's struggle. He himself hadn't always followed the path that his parents had wanted him to take. As a young man, Bomi had been caught between religious education and indoctrination far more strict than anything Freddie had received. He had longed for much more freedom and fewer rules. As a result, he was more lenient with his own son. He never pressurised Freddie into finding a wife and settling down. He trusted his children to make the right decisions for themselves when the time came and accepted that they must always lead their own lives. He was realistic enough to appreciate that their life and times were vastly different from what his own had been. That was his way of loving his children and being a good father.'

Bomi had taken his time before seeking his own bride and settling down.

'Prior to that,' says B., 'he had left India to travel the world for many years. He had gone his own way and experienced his own adventures, resisting marriage until he turned thirty-six. Which at that time and in their culture was relatively late for marriage.'

Things proved more difficult with Freddie's mother: 'She would have preferred her only son and her pride and joy to follow a more traditional route,' says B. 'She would have liked him to have a more secure career, and wanted him to marry, settle down and have children as soon as possible. She herself had married as a young adult. The age gap between her and Bomi was unusually large for that time. Her daughter, Kashmira, would follow in her footsteps and would marry young too.'

As for Freddie's disastrous education, Bomi was burdened by guilt until the day he died over the suffering he had inflicted on his wife and son.

'He deeply regretted having sent Freddie thousands of miles from home to boarding school in India,' B. notes. 'He tormented himself for years with the thought that he'd made the wrong decisions, and that it would have been better had the whole family returned to India together. He also regretted that they hadn't gone to England in August 1947, after India gained her independence from Britain and when Freddie was only a year old.'

In which case, without the separation anxiety that plagued him and the loneliness and confusion that tormented him and against which he railed, would Freddie have had the need, the drive, the urgency to become an artist and reach for the stars? We cannot know. What we do know, from his own diaries, is that he *understood* why his father had made what he considered to be decisions in Freddie's best interests. Even though it had involved ripping a small, cherished child from his doting mother's arms, banishing him far across the sea for many years and causing them both such insurmountable grief that neither would ever recover, and both would forever bear the scars. Freddie came to accept that Bomi had done what he thought was the right thing at the time, given the very few options available to them. But what Bomi came to recognise as the mistake of his life would haunt him for the remainder of his days.

Freddie could have exploded with rage, walked out and have become permanently estranged from his mum and dad. It was not in his nature to do so. Even though he harboured the hurt, he never let it come between them. His family remained important to him throughout his life. He honoured them, stayed close to them and helped them as much as he could.

'Beneath it all,' explains his daughter, 'particularly because his father suffered from poor health, all Freddie wanted to do was love and protect them.'

CHAPTER 6

DISLOCATION

One of Freddie's good friends at Ealing College, Tim Staffell, played in a band called Smile. They supported Pink Floyd at Imperial College London, where Brian May was a student, and also opened for Family, Yes and T. Rex. Freddie became a fixture at their gigs. In early 1969, Tim introduced him to drummer Roger Taylor and guitarist Brian May during one of their rehearsals. Freddie was so taken with them that he started turning up at their rehearsals whenever he could. With similar musical tastes, Roger and Freddie soon fell in together and became inseparable. Their loyal friendship would last for the rest of Freddie's life.

'They had both gone through bad times at around the same time,' comments B., referring to the sexual abuse Freddie had suffered at school and the painful divorce of Roger's parents. 'Those terrible experiences during their childhood are very important,' says B., 'but there were other factors that caused them to bond, both of which involved close friends. When Freddie left Zanzibar, he did not know and would never in his lifetime find out what had become of the young friends he regarded as brothers.' As for Roger, he had been involved in a horrific road accident in Cornwall in February 1967 when his earlier band, the Reaction, were on their way to a gig. Seventeen-year-old Roger, who had only just passed his driving test, had taken over at the wheel. As their clapped-out old van proceeded along the A30 over Goss Moor close to Truro, heavy fog descended and the van hit a parked lorry. Their vehicle somersaulted, hurling Roger through the windscreen. He escaped serious injury, but most of the other passengers were badly hurt. Roger's best friend Peter Gill-Carey had been destined for a career as a doctor, but was unable to complete his medical degree. Roger was charged by the police but, after seven years' legal proceedings, was cleared. The psychological damage and survivor's guilt would torment him for far longer. Freddie knew exactly how he felt.

'Their pure friendship sustained them,' B. says. 'Freddie and Roger never had a cross word. Freddie loved Smile's sound and could see their potential. He had lots of ideas about their lighting, costumes, visuals and so on. About how they should interact, and how best to build a relationship with their audience.'

In June that year, at the age of twenty-three and having been 'ordinarily resident in the UK and Colonies' for the previous five years, Freddie applied to be registered as a full citizen of the United Kingdom and Colonies under the British Nationality Act 1948. He gave his name as 'Frederick/Farrokh Bulsara' and his current address as '22 Gladstone Ave, Feltham Middx'. He also stated the family's two previous addresses: 19 Hamilton Close, Feltham, a small brick-built, three-bedroom terraced house in a close, at which the Bulsaras had lodged for four months from 4 May 1964 until 31 August 1964; and 122 Hamilton Road, Feltham, a larger three-bedroom end-of-terrace where they had stayed for two months during September and October 1964 before relocating to their unprepossessing permanent home.

• • •

When he finished at Ealing College and his father withdrew his financial support, Freddie's economic status became more precarious than ever. But the summer delivered welcome developments. He and Roger opened a stall in Kensington Market. Freddie met a shop assistant called Mary Austin and fell in love with her. And he joined Ibex, his first proper group. Just as he had with Smile, Freddie fizzed with enthusiasm and ideas as to how to progress the band. But this time he was actually *in* the band, and he could not have been more thrilled. He focused on developing them according to his own vision while working on his stage persona and improving his embryonic stagecraft.

The market stall would never make them a fortune, but Freddie and Roger had fun selling everything they laid their hands on: old clothes, shoes, art, antiques, even Freddie's paintings and drawings. Freddie adored the market's atmosphere. The pair made many friends there. But they were still so penniless and starving that basic bacon and eggs represented a royal banquet. The two moved in together, with other friends.

'Freddie loved those times of great camaraderie and mutual support,' B. shares. 'They played music and wrote songs together as often as they could. It all started there. Freddie said that he and Roger were partners in crime and brothers in arms. They bonded through shared hardship and a burning desire to make it against the odds.'

Brian May didn't seem to share their burning ambition at that stage, Freddie observed, concluding that it must have been because he had enjoyed a happy and stable childhood.

'Freddie thought that the desperate need to *be* someone wasn't there in Brian,' B. explains. 'When John Deacon later came on board,' she adds, 'he brought his own dysfunctional childhood into the mix, having lost his father when he was a child. Freddie felt that this background and psychology explained the bonds between himself and Roger, and himself and John. He never felt able to build the same depth of connection with Brian. It goes some way towards explaining the attitudes of John, Roger and Brian since Freddie's death.'

Freddie lived the bohemian life until spring 1970, when he moved in with his girlfriend, Mary. The couple had first set eyes on each other the previous summer, when Freddie was approaching his twenty-fourth birthday. Mary, born 6 March 1951, was only eighteen.

'He went to the Biba store where she worked, and she visited his stall in Kensington Market where he worked,' reports B. 'They looked at each other and knew in an instant that there was something very special between them. But nothing happened for several months. It wasn't until the end of the year, when Freddie asked her out yet again, that shy Mary finally summoned the courage to accept. They lived together from then on and stayed together until he died. Brian May would later recall that he had introduced them, having previously dated Mary himself,' says B. 'Freddie never mentioned Brian in this context, so perhaps Brian didn't introduce them. They were a group of young people who went to the pub, to gigs and spent time together. Brian is said to have had a crush on Mary, and they are said to have gone on a single date. But the crush was unrequited. Then Freddie and Mary started to get to know each other.'

Freddie admired Mary enormously for the fact that she lived independently at such a young age. He would soon discover that both her parents had been deaf, and that their largely silent house-hold accounted for her quietness and lack of flamboyance. She had also tragically lost her mother when she was about fifteen.

'He was impressed by her tremendous courage, her practi-cality and her cleverness,' B. observes. 'He loved her style, her quick wit and her sense of humour. She made him laugh. He said he knew from the first moment that he would spend the rest of his life with her. He just knew, deep in his heart, that she was the One. He couldn't explain it – who can? He simply felt, he said, as though they'd known each other all their lives. He believed they were destined to be together, and that they would grow old together. As Freddie saw it, they were the same. Two peas in a pod. They spoke the same language, shared the same values, and saw and understood the world in the same way. He insisted that "falling" in love with her was completely the wrong word, because what he experienced was an uplifting, not a fall. They put their love for each other above all else. They completed each other.'

In the little £10-per-week bedsit at 2 Victoria Road on the corner of Kensington Gardens, sharing both kitchen and bath-room with other tenants, Mary and Freddie would talk for hours late into the night. When they turned in, they would lay entwined, sharing stories from their childhood. On days when Mary didn't have to get up to go to work, they would stay in bed all day, just talking, listening to music, making love and enjoying lazing about together. Freddie shared his most painful secrets with Mary and was amazed that she was able to heal some of his wounds. Their relationship became for each of them their safe haven. Until then, Freddie had been burdened by his parents' rejection. He blamed them for having ruined his life by sending him away to school. He still resented some of his fellow pupils at St Peter's for having humiliated and betrayed him. He was also angry with those who had treated him badly when he first arrived in England. But Mary made the misery melt away. She recognised his fears and insecurities, even before he shared a single confidence. She reassured him that she would never reject or betray him. She promised to support him in all he did, and to remain his unconditional love for the rest of time.

'He knew instinctively that theirs was the rarest kind of relationship,' B. reveals. 'This pure, selfless love was something Freddie had never known before. She held his hand. She cared for him, was mindful of his feelings and made him feel special and secure. Not since he'd been abandoned to boarding school had he felt that he was the centre of anyone's world. He cherished her deeply for it. To him, she was the perfect woman, and the mother of his future children. He made no secret of the fact that he adored kids. He loved playing with them, learning from them, and was never, ever afraid of them – unlike his friend Kenny Everett further down the line, who was terrified of children to the point of finding them repellent!'

Freddie had always looked forward to becoming a dad. He regarded fatherhood as the most important and fulfilling thing he would ever do. But all in good time. There were magnificent things to achieve first. Life in a rock band would mean long periods on the road away from home, which he knew was no life for a child.

'He also knew,' says B., 'that touring would be just a temporary phase in his life. After that, he and Mary would settle down, create a home and start their family. He relished the idea of pulling his weight and being a hands-on dad. Long before the West woke up to male–female equality, the expectation that domestic and childcare duties must be shared by both husband and wife was deeply rooted in Parsee culture.'

He would join another band in 1970: an outfit called Sour Milk Sea. But he quit after only a few weeks, having realised that they were cramping his style. His withdrawal happened to coincide with Tim Staffell's departure from Smile to join a band called Humpy Bong. Following a discussion about Smile's future, it was agreed that Freddie could join their line-up as singer and frontman.

'Queen was emerging,' says B., 'with Freddie as its driving force. He had his own vision for the band and knew what they should be about. So he threw himself at the task, dedicating all his time and energy to writing music, developing his songwriting, exploring and experimenting with ideas, and rehearsing as often as they could get together. Much of the pittance he was scraping by on was also invested in the band.'

Weeks later, still going by the name Smile, they performed their first gig: on Saturday, 27 June 1970, at Truro City Hall. The booking had been arranged by Roger's mother, who still lived in Cornwall, as a fundraising event for the Red Cross. When the band arrived at the venue, Freddie contradicted the advertisements for their appearance by announcing that they would henceforth be known as Queen.

• • •

When Freddie and Mary relocated to their first official flat together, a £19-per-week improvement at 100 Holland Road, Kensington, their home had to double as the band's headquarters. The warm, cosy living room became their meeting room, as well as a photographic studio. Their debut shoot took place there. Some of the early images captured by photographer Doug Puddifoot made it onto the back cover of their first album. Mary was always welcoming and attentive, and never minded the intrusion, which was in a good cause.

'She also helped Freddie to create his stage image,' says B. 'She never doubted that he would make it, nor did she allow him to doubt himself. Her support was the one thing he could always rely on, and he did depend on it. She also provided him with his first costumes. She sourced wonderful clothes for all the band at Biba, and also did their make-up. They would sometimes talk through the night about the kind of looks Freddie had in mind. The next day, she would bring home all these incredible garments. Not only was she Freddie's first designer, she was also Queen's. She had tremendous personal style and flair. She knew exactly what suited her, the colours that enhanced her pale skin and blonde hair, and she would never have allowed anyone else to take her shopping! The only person she permitted to tell her what to wear was Freddie. He would occasionally ask her to wear a dress as a change from her usual jeans/jumper, shirt/trousers attire. She would wear her lovely dresses to please him, and he was ecstatic whenever she did. She knew how to please her man, surprising him with new clothes and switching up her look. Her ability to do this enchanted him.'

* * *

Bassist John Deacon joined the band in 1971. After months spent writing and rehearsing, Queen put their stage act together that summer. Luck delivered them to the doorstep of London's De Lane Lea Studios, where they recorded their first professional demo tape. Freddie was over the moon. He knew exactly what an important step this was. They availed themselves of the full range of the studios' facilities. Soon afterwards, discussions commenced with Barry and Norman Sheffield, the sibling founders and owners of Soho's Trident Studios, with a view to them signing the band to a management deal.

'Trident, at that time, was an excellent opportunity as far as Freddie was concerned,' reports B. 'They were a step ahead of every other studio. Queen were promised the opportunity to experiment, improvise and develop their own unique sound during studio downtime, for example in the middle of the night. They accepted the opportunity and took full advantage of it. It was, Freddie observed, the perfect environment for their diverse and very demanding personalities.'

But the road was long. They were nowhere near to signing their contract, let alone to securing a record deal. Their first album release still seemed a distant dream.

'As we know, they got there,' says B. 'When their debut album *Queen* was eventually recorded and released, by EMI Records on 13 July 1973, Freddie couldn't wait to take the first copy round to his parents. No sooner was that first LP out than the band were back in the studio to begin work on the follow-up, *Queen II*. Freddie also started working on his "first" opera about the fantasy land of Rhye. It was the comings and goings of the call girls, the prostitutes, who plied their trade in the St Anne's Court alleyway where Trident Studios stood, that partly inspired him to write "Killer Queen". This was one of the few songs, Freddie said, for which he wrote the lyrics before the music.'

The situation between the band and the brothers grew complicated. Freddie was angry with them because he didn't feel they respected Queen as artists. He was reminded of how he had been made to feel like an outsider by complete strangers during his first two years in England. Was it all worth it, he began to wonder: they weren't even making enough money to live like decent human beings.

'Freddie was torn,' B. tells us. 'He believed in Queen. While he was unable to bring himself to make musical concessions, he was certainly prepared to back down on every business level in order to make things work. He knew he must be patient, even though patience was not his strength. They reached the point of no return when Barry and Norman famously refused John Deacon the advance he had requested in order to buy a house – which he needed, because he and his wife, Veronica, were expecting their first child. That was the straw that broke the camel's back. Freddie was enraged. He decided that Queen's relationship with Norman and Barry Sheffield was done.'

By the beginning of 1975, drowning in a contractual mess from which they could see no escape, Queen were on the verge of calling it a day. But they were so deeply in debt that they couldn't simply quit and walk away. They had no choice but to honour their commitments while working out a way to disentangle themselves. They would eventually achieve their independence from Trident with the help of new manager John Reid: the feisty

Scot well known in the music business for his relationship, both business and personal, with Elton John.

'The only time Freddie was really publicly vindictive towards anyone was against the Sheffields with his song "Death on Two Legs",' B. reminds us. 'But he didn't write the song from a personal viewpoint, nor just over money. He admitted that discussions with the brothers could have gone on and on until they reached an agreement. But to him, the point of no return had been reached when they refused John the advance. Because he was so sensitive and so family-oriented himself, he found that deeply heartless. From that moment on, there was no way that he could continue to work with them. Later on, Norman Sheffield recognised that they should have talked more, and that he should have been more attentive to their feelings. We can only wonder what would have happened had they granted John his request. Queen might have remained under contract with them until they took their independence. They might not have signed with John Reid, so Paul Prenter would not have been around, and wouldn't have got the chance to drag Freddie into troubled waters. Freddie might have met the right man – and with his male partner on one arm and Mary on the other, he would have been a very happy man.'

• • •

Freddie proposed to Mary in 1973, on Christmas Day in the evening. He presented his jade scarab engagement ring concealed – typical Freddie – in small boxes within giant boxes that Mary had to tear her way through until she got to the tiniest one.

'This is the date that he wrote in his notebooks,' B. informs us. 'If you examine photos taken at the launch of their *Queen II* and *Sheer Heart Attack* albums, or pictures from the parties in 1974, you can see Mary wearing the engagement ring. In a BBC documentary, Brian May states that Freddie had said he was "as gay as a daffodil" in a 1978 *NME* interview; also, "That is not a man denying his sexuality." The problem with Brian's comments is that the interview in question actually took place in early 1974, before *Queen II* was released. And it changed everything. Freddie had just proposed to Mary. His comment to the *NME* was made in flash Mercury mode: as his stage persona, and not as Freddie Bulsara. He said it in a cheeky and provocative way, very close to the release of *Queen II*, during a period when the four members of Queen were all wearing women's blouses. They all have access to Queen's complete archives.'

Although his recollection of dates was surely a genuine error on Brian's part, it is understandable that misleading comments inflame B.

· · ·

Inconclusive have been the debates, down the years, regarding who featured where in the pecking order of Freddie's lovers. In what order did they land in his life, and when? Who took precedence? Who usurped whom? Who lived with him harmoniously under his roof, who was banished elsewhere, and who became his worst nightmare? Who shared his bed? Which of them, if any, did he love? And who was it that infected him with HIV? The film *Bohemian Rhapsody* fudges these issues, boiling him down to a compact, convenient Freddie who was passionately, purely in love with Mary while tormented by the homosexual urges that he was helpless to resist. Thus, as the time-honoured story goes, was the Freddie–Mary romantic relationship destroyed – though their close friendship and co-dependence endured to the bitter end. Mary is as good as sanctified on celluloid as the tragic heroine broken by the dawning realisation that there can be no hope for her and her one true love. She tries her best to move on with her life. Freddie is depicted as the cling-on, the possessive ex who just can't let go. He buys his apparent former girlfriend a flat within a minute's walk of his own, so close that he can see through her windows, and she through his. One excruciating scene shows him flashing a bedside lamp on and off while he and Mary converse on the phone. The on-off, on-off signal is symbolic of their everlasting love. The theme throughout the film is that she tries to tear herself away to get on with her own life while Freddie strains with all his might to hang on to her. She represents what for him is an impossible ideal. The implication is that he can never achieve it because of his need for sex with other men. It is by no means an accurate representation.

As previously observed, Mary's worst nightmare was that Freddie would leave her for another woman once Queen were on their way to fortune and fame. His storied confession to her, that he believed himself to be bisexual, and her legendary response – that no, he was really gay – has the merest sliver of the truth. The film condenses Freddie's complicated and multi-layered love life to a single, seamless transition – from Mary to Jim Hutton – and neglects to feature significant others who played pivotal roles in Freddie's life. In so doing, it promulgates the perception that

Freddie was the ultimate tragic figure, a gay man held to ransom by unquellable longings for men, while remaining deeply in love with the same woman for almost all of his adult life.

The reductive treatment is to some extent fathomable. Partly because it was Freddie's own business, and of no one else's concern. Partly because it involved the private lives of individuals not in the public eye who had a right to privacy. But also because, at that point in the evolution of societal attitudes towards sexuality, the requirement of the general public to accept an openly bisexual rock frontman could have been deemed an ask too far.

Queen had a burgeoning reputation to protect, and a musical legacy to preserve. When they came to prominence during the early 1970s, homosexuality had been partially decriminalised in the UK only a few years earlier. Nor did the Sexual Offences Act passed in July 1967 and applicable in England and Wales eliminate prejudice and suspicion overnight. Persecution of gay people prevailed. The band and their management may have feared, quite reasonably, that their popularity could have been compromised and may even have nosedived had their fans got wind of the truth. Few were aware at that time that Freddie's sexuality and domestic arrangements were infinitely more complicated than most could have imagined. Times were changing, but not to the advantage of all. While tolerance of homosexuals was on the rise, bisexuality was still viewed as problematic. More than half a century later biphobia, on certain levels, remains as issue.

But why? Theories abound. One school of thought maintains that many regard homosexuality as 'an aberration of nature' that is not the fault of the 'afflicted' individual. It is argued that a gay person cannot be held responsible for 'the way he is'. Bisexuality, on the other hand, is often sneered at as a stance of greed and/ or choice. Some assume bisexual people to be more promiscuous than homosexuals, because they seem reluctant to 'choose a side'. Bisexual people are often mistrusted because others assume them to be on some kind of journey towards self-acceptance that they are in fact gay. But bisexual humans have existed throughout recorded history. They are no more 'a freak of nature' than hetero- sexuals or homosexuals. They can't be: bisexuality is not confined to human beings but exists throughout the animal kingdom, with more than a thousand species, including bonobos, walruses, giraffes, fruit flies, bottlenose dolphins, bearded dragons, Chilean flamingos and greylag geese, exhibiting same-sex behaviour, which includes co-parenting as well as sexual contact. According to Greenpeace, evidence of LGBTQ+ behaviour among animals 'has existed for hundreds of years but has often been ignored or hidden from the public'. Early scientists described their find- ings as 'unnatural', 'monstrous' and 'hideous'. Queer behaviour between animals has also been dismissed as 'playing' or 'fighting'. In 1912, a member of Captain Robert Falcon Scott's expedi- tion to the Antarctic documented homosexuality among Adélie penguins. But that section of his paper was deleted, only to be rediscovered a hundred years down the line.

In many territories, homosexual behaviours remain illegal. In others, rights for LGBTQ+ people are disregarded or reduced. Some sixty-four countries maintain laws that criminalise homo- sexuality. Almost half of these countries are in the continent of Africa. While some nations, among them Singapore, Barbados and Botswana, have lately moved towards decriminalising same- sex unions and improving rights for LGBTQ+ people, others, including Nigeria and Uganda, have tightened their existing laws. In many places, breaking such laws can be punishable by long prison sentences or even the death penalty.

. . .

'Freddie regarded himself not as gay but as bisexual,' B. states for the record. 'He said so in his own words and confirmed it in his own handwriting. But to him, love, tenderness, affection and emotion were much more important than lust. As he said, "You cannot compare sex to love, because there you are talking about the greatest thing on earth." He had sex and lust with men, and love with Mary. He was physically drawn to men and needed to be dominated sexually, and he was emotionally drawn to women. He needed the unshakeable love he shared with his woman more than anything else in his life. Always polite, respectful and the perfect gentleman, he hated gay men who behaved outrageously out of context. He screamed and exploded with anger and rage at Jim Hutton on more than a few occasions when Jim behaved inappropriately towards women, or uttered disrespectful words. Freddie was proper. He wanted everything "in its place", in accordance with the ancient principle that has long governed Indian society.'

Bisexuality by definition is not binary. This can confuse people who prefer life to be that way. Bisexuals are even accused of stealing limelight for which they have never had to fight. But isn't it mostly about the fact that some people simply love to judge, criticise and persecute? For a private individual to be on the receiving end of all that is harrowing enough. Multiply it by tens of thousands for a celebrity in the global public eye and you see the problem. The plight of bisexuals is arguably 'worse' because they face harassment and abuse from homosexuals, lesbians and transgender folk for not being 'gay enough', as well as the discrimination of the unenlightened straight community. Accused of 'wanting it all', they cannot win.

'If we *have* to label Freddie,' says B., 'then we must use the term "polygamous bisexual male". Was he ahead of his time? He knew that people found it hard to understand his position. He would find it incomprehensible that, more than thirty years after his death, it is still not understood today. The bisexual man is seen in our society as a gay man who refuses to admit it and who wants to keep up appearances. What is strange is that the same society does not project this prejudice onto bisexual women. The repression under which gay men lived has a lot to answer for. The apparently outrageous notion that a person could be both gay and straight has led to the denial of the true identity of bisexual people.'

Freddie's earlier girlfriend Rosemary Pearson rejected him because of his bisexuality. Mary chose to accept him just as he was. Her ability to embrace everything about him sealed their love for life.

'Freddie's duality, incidentally, was revealed for the first time in the Queen crest that he designed for the band's first album in 1973,' says B., 'with two fairies representing himself.'

I was not alone in assuming that Freddie did not share his 'homosexuality' with the world because he did not want to offend his parents or the family's Parsee community. Many of us jumped to such conclusions. We were wrong.

'He never hid his bisexuality, nor the fact that he had sex with men,' says B. 'Had he wanted to hide this aspect of himself for fear of upsetting his parents, he would not have made the public statements about himself that he did.'

Statements such as:

'I've had a lot of lovers. Both male and female. I've tried relationships on either side.'

'I couldn't fall in love with a man the way I could with a girl.'

'I have maybe a wider sexual taste than most people, but that's as far as I'm going to go.'

'I sleep with men, women, cats, you name it. I'll go to bed with anything!'

'I prefer my sex without any involvement, and there were times when I was extremely promiscuous. I used to be just an old slag who got up every morning, scratched his head and wondered who he wanted to fuck today. I just lived for sex.'

And, 'I go out looking for someone who will love me, even if it's just for a one-night stand. My one-night stands are just me playing my part.'

'It is true that in Parsee tradition, homosexuality is not permitted,' agrees B. 'Neither are bisexual relationships. But what were his parents supposed to do about it? Freddie was a grown man. They were fully aware of what was going on, of course: they were not exactly cut off from the world. They were cultured people. They read newspapers and watched television.'

The Bulsaras were not ashamed of their son, nor did they eject him from their lives.

'His mum couldn't have been more proud of him,' says B. 'She cut out and kept all the good articles about him. They were both fully aware of Freddie's statements about his sexuality. As we know, he followed the teachings of Zarathustra. A fundamental rule of these teachings is that sin is not something bad that you do to yourself. It is about bad deeds that you commit against other living beings. According to Zarathustra, sex is not a sin if it's consensual. Well, Freddie's sexual encounters with other men were always consensual. Once he decided how he was going to live his life, but was desperate not to disrespect Mary, they had long and deep heart-to-hearts. They agreed that they didn't want to lose each other. So they redefined, by mutual consent, their partnership and their sex life together.'

She reminds us that sex with men and sex with women are not sins according to the Gathas.

'The Gathas never talk about bisexuality or homosexuality. Don't forget that Ahura Mazda is both male and female: Ahura is masculine, Mazda is feminine. Freddie was au fait with this strict equality of men and women in the same entity. He satisfied his feminine side by having sex with men, and his masculine side with Mary. His ideal lifestyle would have been to be able to live openly in a committed threesome. Unfortunately, during the 1980s – and even today – the victim would have been Mary. She would have been the one people pointed their fingers at. She would have been the one who was ridiculed and humiliated. People would have poured scorn on her and would have pitied her position as the "deceived wife". Freddie couldn't bear the idea of her suffering. Because he did not want to cause her shame or embarrassment, he decided to compartmentalise his life.'

You see Freddie's dilemma. Because he kept his personal life to himself as much as he was able – until former close associates began selling him down the river and drawing attention to his so-called 'shocking and sensational' lifestyle – he attracted intense speculation from both fans and the mainstream media as to what his private life was really about. Press exposés and kiss-and-tell revelations fuelled that fire. A number of people have made a living, since his death, going over and over old ground and coming up with ever more tantalising revelations. There was so much more and so much less to it, comments his daughter, having spent years absorbing and evaluating Freddie's lengthy handwritten account. His fascination with omnisexuality, multi-sexuality and pansexuality, each of these distinct from the others, was inspired by his research into ancient cultures. The sexual customs, traditions, habits and behaviours of earlier civilisations thrilled him and ignited his imagination – particularly those of pre-colonial India.

'The India of the Maharajas, we know, was a constant source of inspiration to Freddie,' B. reminds us. 'Its way of life, its luxury, its sophistication and refinement fascinated him. In that beautiful, ancient land, a libertine atmosphere prevailed. Multiple marriage had long been the custom. For men to have several wives was entirely normal. The nautch girls [professional Hindu dancers who performed at religious ceremonies and in the courts during the time of the Mughal Empire between the sixteenth and eighteenth centuries] were hired to amuse, satisfy and bestow all manner of sexual favours. They were also responsible for initiating young men in the art of sex. The old Indian concept of love separated the woman one marries from the lover with whom one has fun and enjoys sexual relations. "Everybody wants a loving relationship [which he had with Mary] and at the same time to go out and have fun," Freddie told David Wigg during an interview for the *Daily Express*, published in July 1986. "We want it both ways."'

She makes clear her father's understanding and enthusiasm for this ancient concept, which he embraced in his own life, while acknowledging that many in the modern world, especially in the West, cannot find such behaviour acceptable.

• • •

The silly money began pouring in about a year after 'Bohemian Rhapsody' was released and became a sensation. Fame and fortune are well known for their ability to swerve the behaviour of good men and true. So it was with Freddie, further compli-cating matters with David Minns: a music industry professional with whom he had been crossing paths for some time. They met in June 1975. According to Minns's recollections, he was on his way home to his flat on Putney's Werter Road, and dropped in to see his friend Cherry Brown at Rod's, a gay club that would later become the hang-out Country Cousins. It was another friend, Malcolm Grey, who introduced David to Freddie. 'Minnsie' worked in the business in a variety of roles, from costume and wardrobe management to Paul and Linda McCartney's manage-ment company to managing the career of singer-songwriter Eddie Howell. The pair sidestepped the work arena to develop a burgeoning friendship, which led to Freddie introducing his new best friend to Mary, and to David visiting the couple at home in Holland Park. But on the side, David and Freddie became an item, even though Freddie was still living with Mary. As a term of endearment, Freddie bestowed on Minns the feminine nickname 'Dyllis'. During the autumn of 1975, David asked Freddie if he would care to produce a song for Eddie Howell. Freddie agreed to, and worked on the track 'Man From Manhattan' at the beginning of 1976 before Queen were due to depart on their *A Night at the Opera* tour of America.

'Freddie and David Minns had a relationship with a kind of affection,' confirms B., 'although it was chaotic, with a lot of arguments, rows, fights, infidelities, jealousy, abuse and even violence on both sides. They brought out the worst in each other.

'After that studio session with Howell, even though he had met Mary and was well aware of their relationship, Minns took Freddie back to his flat and made a pass at him,' B. says. 'The surge of sheer pleasure that Freddie experienced, his first sexual encounter with another man for fifteen years since the attacks he had been subjected to in Panchgani, confused him terribly. The problem was that he enjoyed it. A lot. He and Minns became passionate lovers.'

At first, Freddie regarded his encounters with Minns as no different from his numerous on-the-road liaisons with female groupies: a common indulgence among touring musicians. Out there between nowhere and someplace, there always seemed to be women for sex. But that was lust, not love. Freddie prided himself on knowing the difference. Years later when he decided to take men for sex, the presence of other women in his bed became superfluous.

'Mary was his one true love,' B. emphasises, 'and the only woman he would now sleep with. The sole exception would be [German actress] Barbara Valentin.' More of whom later. 'And the only man he would sleep with for love as well as sex would be his future boyfriend Joe Fannelli.'

Freddie juggled Mary and David, and grew more and more confused. He was especially troubled by his growing feelings towards Minns.

'He started to think,' says B., 'about a lasting relationship with Minns alongside his relationship with Mary.' He had no desire to end things with her. Quite the opposite. He remained certain that they were partners for life, and didn't see why he couldn't have both. Minns, on the other hand, would not accept this duality. In his anger and frustration, he subjected Freddie to more and more violent physical punishment. Freddie let him have it in return.

'While away on tour, he re-evaluated his relationship with David,' says B., explaining how it dawned on Freddie that Minns's influence was predominantly negative, and that he was in fact trying to control him. 'So Freddie made up his mind to move on from him. When Freddie returned from the Australian leg of the *A Night at the Opera* tour during late April 1976, the first thing Minns did was to demand that Freddie tell Mary about their relationship. It was in this context – his growing feelings towards Minns, his love for Mary and the pressure that Minns was exerting on him – that in early May 1976, Freddie had that time with my mother, and I was conceived.

'It was during the American leg of the *News of the World* tour, at the end of 1977, that Freddie realised the negative impact of David Minns on his life, and saw how Minns was trying to control him. At that time, they were twenty-two months into their relationship. A few days later, Freddie met Joe Fannelli from Franklin, Massachusetts, and broke up with Minns.'

David would not accept that the affair was over. He used all manner of threats and even faked a suicide attempt to try to get Freddie back. The ending of their relationship was violent.

'Freddie felt no guilt over Mary, he recorded in his diary, because David and Mary both gave him something essential, something he could not live without. But his exploration of his sexuality with Minns did lead Freddie to have the very difficult but necessary conversation with Mary. They subsequently redefined their domestic life and partnership, and were able to stay together, building an immense bond based on mutual love and respect.'

It was then, Freddie explains, that he realised he needed both: his 'til-death-us-do-part relationship with Mary, and regular sex with a man. But he loved and adored Mary. How could he expect her to put up with such an arrangement? He was desperate to do the right thing by her, but at the same time did not want to relinquish his new-found homosexual sex life.

'While he was writing songs for the *News of the World* album, he was in a complex emotional state and therefore particularly vulnerable,' reveals B. 'He now knew for certain that he was bisexual, but how would that work out? He was so troubled that he experienced songwriter's block, which was rare for him. Consequently, he was able to contribute only three songs to that album, which was released in October 1977. The songs were "We Are the Champions", "Get Down, Make Love" and "My Melancholy Blues". Of the eight remaining tracks, Brian wrote four, while Roger and John stumped up two each. Freddie was embarrassed. He had never before written so little for a Queen album.'

It is true to say that Freddie struggled with his sexuality and his love life, B. tells us, but not in the way that most people might think.

'The struggle wasn't caused by his need for sex with other men coupled with the fear of losing Mary. Nothing was ever going to come between those two. Not even the fact that he had fathered a child by another woman – which, by then, he had.'

Why didn't that come between Freddie and Mary?

'Because it didn't,' says B.

Why not?

'Because nothing ever could.'

Not even that?

'Not even that.'

Perhaps no one else could understand that nothing could shake their unbreakable bond. But *they* could. So no one else's opinion really mattered.

Nevertheless, Freddie certainly experienced insecurity.

'Opening up to Mary about his need to pursue a bisexual life-style was a major step that could have had serious consequences,' explains B. 'It might have threatened to change their deepest feelings for one another, which he was afraid to risk. Then he remembered how, between late 1975 and mid-1977, during the period when I was born, their bond had grown even stronger. If that were even possible. In the end, he concluded that Mary would be able to accept the situation as long as he was always honest with her. He was proved right. The point is that he never struggled to suppress his needs. His "struggle" related to the fear of admitting his bisexuality, because it could have had a negative effect on his and Mary's feelings for each other.'

Freddie bit the bullet and initiated the conversation with Mary just before Queen's departure on the *News of the World* tour – which would commence in Portland, Maine in November 1977 and conclude in London the following May. As he prepared himself for their heart-to-heart, he was beside himself with nerves. But Mary took it well. There were no histrionics. Calmly and lovingly, she let him know that she accepted it and encouraged him to feel comfortable with his sexuality.

'Crucially, she didn't reject him,' says B. 'She showed him that if he was brave enough, he could live the sexuality he truly felt. Though he was worried about social norms and how things would look, Mary simply spoke about feelings. After he said to Mary that he thought he was bisexual, and not gay or purely heterosexual, it is always stated that Mary replied that she thought he was gay. But the discussion didn't end there, as Freddie makes clear in his notebooks. After that, they had a long talk during which Freddie explained to Mary his true feelings, and why he was bisexual and not gay. This part of the conversation is never included.' While she has all due respect for bisexual people today, B. points out that their experience is very different from what Freddie lived through in the 1970s. There are numerous identities and nuances today, but Freddie regarded himself as, and identified as, a bisexual man.

'Freddie and Mary both knew it wasn't going to be easy,' says B. 'They would have to learn not to be jealous, and to give each other space. Their new lifestyle wouldn't fall into place overnight, either. They would no longer have penetrative sex together, but would remain faithful to each other emotionally for as long as they lived.'

Freddie would still have married Mary. He fully intended to.

'He had postponed their wedding when it ought to have happened for lack of money, and because of business complications,' B. reminds us. 'He at last got around to wanting to rearrange it during the 1980s, but by then the situation had changed. The disease had arrived.'

Not wanting to deprive his partner of the opportunity to become a mother, he encouraged Mary to think about finding someone else to father her children. But none of that changed the way they felt about each other.

'Mary was always his wife and he her husband,' says B. 'He always behaved as though he were her husband' – gay sex aside – 'kept his promises and stuck to his commitments. They never parted. So by the time he left for the *News of the World* tour, they had agreed a way forward together and his mind was soothed.'

• • •

Mary continued to work for Freddie, managing his various companies. The sequence of those companies is complicated.

'Freddie had created Marlhouse Productions Limited in July 1975, when the band began to take back their independence from Trident,' says B. 'At the end of 1976, Marlhouse Productions became Mercury Songs Limited, which became Goose Productions at the end of 1978. Meanwhile, at the end of 1977, Freddie had created Pond Productions. At the end of 1978, Pond Productions became Mercury Songs Limited.'

• • •

'The devil' looked in during 1977, in the form of Paul Prenter, a radio DJ from Belfast, Northern Ireland, who lived an openly gay lifestyle, met Freddie in a bar, perceived what he was going through, spied an opportunity and moved in swiftly for the kill.

'Employed by Queen's then manager John Reid, he started out working with the whole band, but soon took over Freddie's personal management,' recalls B. 'That situation would continue until 1985.'

Prenter introduced Freddie to yet another lifestyle that was new to him: 'Freddie was fascinated by that freedom,' says B. 'It was a lifestyle he'd had no idea of before. At that time, Freddie rarely indulged in gay sex. He was incredibly shy, he never took the initiative with other men, he always needed a matchmaker – and, later on, a beater.'

Why? Because the thought that he could be seriously hurt during an encounter, but would be helpless to do anything about it, was to Freddie the most irresistible turn-on.

'The first time Prenter took Freddie to one of the more notorious New York gay clubs, Freddie was initially shocked to witness so much violence,' reveals B. 'He did not long to join in, he was content just to be a voyeur. He wanted to see not only how far people would go, but also how much pain they could endure. You only have to listen to "Get Down, Make Love" on the *News of the World* album, which was inspired by the nights he spent in clubs with Paul Prenter during the period when he was interested only in voyeurism. He enjoyed it. It excited him. It also inspired him. The song "Body Language" on *Hot Space* was about what he lived during his wild period, when it was no longer merely about words and titillation.'

Prenter now had Freddie hooked. It was thanks to him that Freddie changed his look, adopting the distinctive 'gay clone' look.

Contrary to gossip and rumour, Prenter and Freddie were not sexual partners. Although Freddie was not out – and would never in his lifetime out himself as gay, simply because he wasn't – he and Prenter frequented gay bars together. The relationship was to sour in autumn 1984. The other members of the band were disgruntled by the influence over Freddie and even their music that Prenter appeared to wield. The consensus has long been that Freddie was putty in his hands, and that Prenter was the architect of Freddie's downfall.

'He appealed to Freddie's outrageous tendencies by showing him the most sordid places,' B. explains. 'It was he who got Freddie hooked on the sleaziest practices. Sex can be a dangerous drug, and Freddie became helplessly addicted to it. He was easily led, time after time, deeper and deeper, into a self-destructive world of promiscuity and depravity, rent boys, random sexual encounters and forbidden drugs.'

This was such a turn-around for him. Until then, Freddie had always been incredibly shy, sensitive and romantic.

'But suddenly,' says B., 'he could not get enough of this debauched new world. He wrote in his notebooks that he was never shocked in the worst of those sordid clubs. The reason was that he looked, but didn't touch. It was more voyeurism on his part, an indulgence that he enjoyed … rather too much on many an occasion. It inspired and excited him. He watched, became aroused, then he would look around, pick up men to take home for the night, and spend the night having sex with them. Over time, his tastes in men changed. It was soon the

case that men with dark hair and moustaches became his preference for one-night stands. His favourite kind of sexual encounter
was hard sex, no strings, in which he was the passive partner.
He indulged in countless flings, sometimes with many men in a
single night. But he drew the line at violent, abusive and sordid
practices, even though violence and abuse had tended to hall-
mark his relationships with other males.'

Not so with Joe Fannelli: a twenty-seven-year-old American
chef whom Freddie was believed to have picked up while Queen
were on the 1978 US *Jazz* tour. 'We all – myself, Queen Productions, those who worked for Freddie – have always misspelled his
name,' says B. 'He was in fact born Joseph FANNELLI.

'Freddie's relationship with Joe was totally different from his
relationships with David Minns or any other man,' says B. 'With
Joe, Freddie found real affection and tenderness. To be accurate
about when their love affair began, they met *not* during the 1978
Jazz tour, but in late 1977' – in other words, during Queen's
twenty-six-show jaunt around the US as part of their *News of the
World* tour 'Back and forth between the US and the UK Joe
flew for the next two years,' says B. Their affair contrasted starkly
with the one that had preceded it. Freddie was happy. The relationship they had together was peaceful. With love, affection
and tenderness as its hallmarks, it had plenty in common with
what Freddie shared with Mary. 'Reassured by Mary regarding her commitment to their relationship and living in a second
loving relationship with Joe,' says B., 'Freddie was both upbeat
and serene when he turned to writing songs for Queen's seventh
studio album, *Jazz*. This time, he was more prolific, contribut-
ing five numbers – "Mustapha", "Jealousy", "Bicycle Race", "Let

Me Entertain You" and "Don't Stop Me Now" – to Brian's four and two each by Roger and John.'

. . .

Almost anyone would have struggled to juggle so complicated a lifestyle. But Freddie did not see it as a problem. By his own reckoning, he had it made. He shared the cosy Phillimore Gardens love nest with Mary, and his 'shag pad' Stafford Terrace with his male lovers and one-night stands. During the daytime, Mary would also work there. At night, more often than not, she and Freddie continued to sleep together in the 'marital bed'.

'Whether or not he had a current boyfriend,' says B., 'he regularly spent the night with Mary. And whenever Mary joined him on tour, they kept to an arrangement that worked for all. Freddie always stayed in a two-bedroom suite: one bedroom to share with Mary, the other for fun with his rent boys.

'Yes, odd though it may seem, Mary knew exactly what was going on, because she was only on the other side of the wall. There were no secrets between them. She had come to accept the arrangement because the alternative was unthinkable. They didn't want to lose each other.'

Late at night, after a gig, Freddie would go clubbing with his entourage, pick up whoever took his fancy – sometimes more than one – bring them back to his hotel, have his fun, then send them on their way and spend the night with Mary. How in heaven's name was she able to put up with that?

'It worked for them,' shrugs B. 'Freddie would kick the boys out when he'd finished with them, shower meticulously, and join

Mary in bed. Both of them were able to compartmentalise. It was more complicated at times when Mary had a boyfriend but still wanted to spend the night with Freddie. Not many partners will turn a blind eye to that. But Freddie and Mary were in their own little bubble. Their love was their haven. Strange though it may seem, it was above mere bodies and sex. It was about the joining of two souls, and about endless love. They lived a version of this arrangement for thirteen years.'

His one-night stands and rent boys never betrayed Freddie, B. asserts, because 'they knew why they were there. They knew exactly what to expect. But he was always betrayed by his male lovers, with one exception: Joe. Sometimes, one of his one-night stands would become his boyfriend for a few days or months, or even a "steady relationship", as with Jim Hutton. But in the end, it was always the same thing: they hurt, abused and betrayed him. Those one-night stands and rent boys aside, Freddie never played with his lovers. He always fell in love too quickly, but he really wanted his relationships to work. As I have said, he wanted both the unconditional, everlasting and mutual love that he shared with Mary and a beautiful simultaneous relationship with a man. Trust was the most important element in his relationships. He really wanted things to work, and was thoughtful, loving and caring. Once betrayed, once hurt, however, he was the extreme opposite. This was a recurring theme, but never with Joe.'

Joe, whom Freddie nicknamed 'Liza' in keeping with his habit of bestowing women's names on his men,[1] eventually grew tired of the secrecy and the subterfuge.

'He wanted a relationship that was out in the open,' says B. 'But because of Freddie's love for and commitment to Mary, and because of societal prejudice with regard to bisexuality at that time, Freddie could not give him that.

'Joe was very much like Freddie's quiet side,' she adds. 'He was private, discreet, quiet and shy. He was also a fit, strong man who led a healthy lifestyle. They shared the same sense of humour, and liked funny games. Joe was interested in and curious about everything, including things that did not interest Freddie. Which was often helpful to him. He was passionate about what he did, and very meticulous. And he could always calm Freddie's fears, his tantrums and his panic attacks. It didn't bother him to stay in the shadows away from the limelight and out of sight. On the contrary, it suited him. It was all the agitation around Freddie that made him uncomfortable, because he didn't want to be exposed. When Paul Prenter began taking Freddie to more and more sordid places, Freddie was increasingly intrigued and fascinated by uglier and uglier practices. But not Joe. Not at all. He just didn't have a wild party-animal side.

'When Joe told Freddie he was leaving him to go home to Massachusetts, there was a scene, of course,' B. says. 'But the break-up was just like their relationship. No fights, no violence. Freddie understood Joe's feelings, and Joe understood Freddie's. The affection and tenderness they had shared did not end. Love turned into a deep and strong friendship, despite Freddie being devastated by the split. His heart was broken. It was after their break-up', explains B., 'that Freddie turned wild.'

Although it has been written and said that Joe came back into Freddie's life full-time in 1983, the pictures tell the story.

'You can easily find photos on the web of Freddie and Joe together between 1980 and 1982,' says B. 'Joe was with Freddie during Queen's *The Game* tour. There is a picture of them together that was taken in Brussels in 1980. He was also with Freddie in Japan in 1981. At the Japanese premiere of *Flash Gordon* in Tokyo, Joe was pictured sitting to the left of Peter Freestone. Although it has been reported that Freddie had to suffer the indignity of sitting all the way through a film without fidgeting, he didn't attend the screening of the movie on 10 February 1981. He stayed back at the hotel with Peter Morgan, to the chagrin of both the promoters and the fans, using the excuse that he needed to take care of his voice and throat, which had been compromised by pressurised cabin air during the long flight to Tokyo.' After the screening, the other members of the band were invited up on stage for interviews and a photo opportunity in front of their hysterical audience, with female teen-idol singers Hiroko Yakushimaru and Hiromi Ōta and singer, actress and DJ Yuki Okazaki. Freddie took no part in any of this. Japanese press reports from the time make clear that he was not there.

There are also photos of Freddie and Joe together in Argentina in 1981, in Venezuela that same year, and during the 1982 Munich recording sessions. 'For all that time and all the way to the end,' says B., 'Joe was Freddie's main personal assistant. He lived at Stafford Terrace even after he and Freddie broke up, before he moved to Garden Lodge. And during the final three and a half years of Freddie's life, it was Joe who was with Freddie in Montreux.'

Having made his way back to England, but before he returned to Freddie's household, Joe sought employment as a chef in a string of London restaurants. Freddie would help him with visas, work permits and references wherever necessary. Residual fondness between them kept the doors open. They would later resume their friendship, and it flourished. The realisation that Freddie could trust him implicitly was what prompted him to invite Joe to live at Garden Lodge, where he worked for him as his chef and main personal assistant for the remainder of Freddie's days. Yes, that was Joe, not Peter. Like Freddie, Joe eventually contracted HIV, which led to full-blown AIDS. He would die not long after Freddie, of a brain seizure.

'Joe's responsibilities increased after Paul Prenter was sacked,' explains B. 'That happened after Queen's visit to Brazil in January 1985.' This was during their *The Works* tour, when the band took part in the first Rock in Rio festival at the City of Rock on 11 January that year. The festival also featured AC/DC, George Benson, Rod Stewart and others. 'That was when Freddie put an end once and for all to his professional relationship with Prenter,' says B. 'It was Joe who was now charged with keeping unde-sirables and unwanted attention away. He always knew where Freddie was, and with whom. He prevented any unpleasantness. He facilitated Freddie's secret moments without disturbance and was always able to circumvent and avoid conversation with Freddie's current lover.'

Freddie trusted Joe with his life, he revealed. He relied on his discretion and reserved personality. Joe did not blab. He saw all but said nothing.

'It's the reason why Freddie never believed that it was Joe who gossiped about Freddie's condition,' says B. 'I don't believe it either. Because only Joe, Mary and Terry Giddings the chauffeur knew Freddie's medical schedule inside out. Crucially, some of the information published in the press was detailed enough to strongly suggest that it had been shared by someone at Garden Lodge, but there were enough inaccuracies to demonstrate that they had been given by someone who didn't know much.

'Joe was,' adds B., 'a really nice guy. Patient and calm. Not a hypocrite. Not calculating. He didn't have ideas above his station. He never wanted to be what he was not. He was frank, clear and direct, even with Freddie. Perhaps especially with Freddie, who could tell him about absolutely anything. Whatever it was, Joe remained loyal to Freddie. Joe did have his own life outside Freddie's circle. He wasn't confined to living "the normal life of Freddie", whatever that was. He was a very soothing and pacifying person to have around, which Freddie appreciated. He never pushed himself to the front, he stayed in his corner and was happy that way. He both did the job he was paid to do and was there for Freddie as a friend. Freddie knew that he could rely on him and could not have asked for better.

'Joe died too soon, in June 1993. He was only thirty-nine: way too young. But had he lived, I believe he would have had exactly the same attitude that Mary has had all these years. You know, he was one of the few who knew about me. Freddie trusted him even with that. And he used to make me the most delicious crêpes bretonnes whenever I had to wait around for Freddie.'

• • •

The Münchner Winnie Kirchberger notwithstanding – for Freddie and he had not yet met – David Minns and Joe Fannelli were the only two men for whom Freddie felt genuine affection, B. confirms.

'He had hoped that he could continue to share love and tenderness with each of them. But both relationships let him down badly. Freddie realised that he couldn't fall in love with a man the way he was in love with Mary. Nor could any man ever love him the way Mary loved him. At first, this awareness caused him deep disappointment and hurt. Once he had evaluated his dilemma and came to understand its implications, Freddie was able to have what seemed for a long time like the best of both worlds: a fine, beautiful woman with whom to share an exclusive, loving, romantic relationship, and as much hard sex as he could handle with as many men as he liked.'

· · ·

Throughout 1978 and 1979, Freddie lived abroad, in tax exile: 'But not exclusively in New York,' B. reminds us. 'He spent much of his time in Munich between mid-1979 and late 1985. His sojourns in Manhattan during that period were the most sordid of his life. Whenever Mary was not with him, it was easy to go out and pick up a man for the night. There was no better place for such activity. He could be anonymous there. Gradually, the one-night-stand thing became his routine. After Joe left him, sleeping with men became an addiction. To begin with, it was just for fun. All Freddie wanted was sex without involvement. But addiction took hold and led him towards the dark side. He started craving rougher and more dangerous sex. Caught in the whirlwind, his desire and need increased. He was all too aware that he was out of control, but he couldn't escape. He needed more and more alcohol, cocaine and poppers (amyl nitrate, a muscle relaxant) to kill the pain. It didn't help that people continued to tell him how great he was, or that more and more people wanted to hang with him because of his fame and money. Freddie saw them all having fun and convinced himself that he was having fun too. Part of him was. He threw extravagant parties and spent exorbitant sums, never pausing to count the cost. He partied without any thought for the consequences. His nights became a merry-go-round of entertaining and socialising, of wildness and insanity. Some of it was shockingly depraved. But by day, he was his old, real self again. He described himself as Dr Jekyll and Mr Hyde, or Gizmo and Mogwai.[2] After Joe, many dozens of men dipped their biscuit in his cup of coffee, to use Freddie's quaint expression. But no love was ever lost. It was all merely sex, a mechanical act. He couldn't have what he wanted, so he pretended to be happy that way.'

• • •

Freddie met DHL courier Tony Bastin from Brighton towards the end of 1979. Although he was yet again smitten, he had a feeling that he couldn't trust this one.

'During *The Game* tour,' B. says, 'Bastin was unfaithful to Freddie one time too many. Freddie learned of this in August 1980, after Bastin had left. That night, Freddie drowned his sorrows and anger in alcohol, then got in touch with Tony and begged him to return to the US. As it turned out, Freddie had only summoned him to humiliate then sack him. Due to technical problems, Queen's show the following night was a disaster. Freddie's emotional state did not help. Tempers blew, and Freddie flew into a mad rage, rejecting everyone. On that occasion, only tour manager Gerry Stickells was able to calm him down.

'Freddie fled to New York for a few days to drink himself stupid and get over it. While there, he met and became enamoured of one of the group of gay men who called themselves the New York Daughters. At that point, he set himself a rule that unfortunately he was to break time and time again: that he must no longer allow himself to fall in love too quickly. His one-night stands spiralled out of control, as did his life-threatening lifestyle. Boosted by coke and pills to shed his inhibitions, he also became dependent on Paul Prenter – whose self-styled purpose was just to keep telling Freddie he was untouchable. Taking no precautions, Freddie frequented the dingiest back rooms and darkest corners of New York's under-belly. Picking up boys indiscriminately, he took them back to his hotel room and had his way. But Freddie was the perfect target. In the end, wasn't it they who were picking him?'

• • •

One of Freddie's daughter's most prized possessions is a photo-graph, taken in 1981, of her four-year-old self with her father and David Bowie, captured at Le Picotin: the charming chalet home of Montreux Festival founder Claude Nobs in the village of Caux, a thousand metres above Lake Geneva (Lac Léman in French) and the resort of Montreux.

'Along with Phillimore Gardens, Caux was one of Freddie's cherished refuges,' explains B. 'Walks to the Col de Jaman moun-tain pass and to Rochers de Naye, a truly beautiful alpine trail with breathtaking views over Lac Léman, were his favourites.

Freddie loved to walk, and it's so peaceful up there. He was also fond of strolling in the mountains above Munich. But it would take a day to get there and back, and he rarely had the time to spare. If some "difficult" discussion was needed, for Freddie there was no better place for it than on a mountain walk. We used to talk a lot on such walks. There was no possible escape. I also believe it made discussions easier, because part of our brains and attention were focused on the walking. I soon learned the ploy myself, and would take him up there whenever I needed to ask him an awkward question. Later on, the promenade along the lake and the lawns that slope down to it became the preferred circuits. They were much easier for him once he became ill and could no longer manage anything strenuous. Consequently, I find it impossible to revisit those locations today. They are loaded with memories of his final months and weeks. I find I cannot go near the lawns or the lake. But up there in the mountains, where the landscape and the views take your breath away – whatever the weather – I feel close to my father in a very serene way. The strange feeling I get up there is hard to describe. It is heartbreaking, yes, but without the anger and regret, and without the lack and the loss. Up there, I am relieved of any sense of injustice. It's all much easier to deal with. Those journeys into the mountains feel like pilgrimages in a way. Up there, away from it all, I am fine.

'My father used to show and teach me about the immensely big and the infinitely small,' she says. 'About the whole painting, and about the smallest detail in one corner. About the majestic height of an entire tree, and the tiniest detail of one of its leaves. He would point out small, bright spots in the sky, and remind me that each spot was far greater than us, our little planet Earth. And he would marvel at a snowy landscape while talking about the minute perfection of the crystals in a single snowflake. When you look at all this beauty, he would say, you cannot accept that it happened by accident. Sometimes even now, up there on the mountain, I will ask him whenever I need help. Maybe the simple process of "asking" him is what gives me strength, solutions and my answer.'

As for Claude Nobs, he emerges as one of Freddie's greatest allies, as well as a man of exceptional kindness and infinite honesty.

'He was a wonderful friend to my father and me,' B. says. 'He understood the ways in which Freddie compartmentalised his life and many aspects of it, because he had worked with multiple artists over many years who did the same kind of thing. I have also come to believe that discretion is a characteristic feature of people from this region of Switzerland. Whenever Freddie asked him for something, Claude never queried it. He didn't ask the ins and outs or the whys and hows. He simply accepted, and he provided wherever he could. He was a great help to Freddie in Montreux, especially during his final years. With Claude, there was often no need for third-party involvement, which Freddie really appreciated, given the circumstances. Claude knew Freddie inside out. He knew a great many private things about him but never shared what he knew during his lifetime. Claude died in January 2013, following a ski accident from which he did not recover. Today, his former partner Thierry Amsallem shares stories, some of which he cannot have experienced first-hand because he was not yet part of Claude's life when they happened.'

For example?

'One of the numerous evenings that took place at Le Picotin (the chalet Le Grillon had not yet been built during Freddie's lifetime. Freddie knew only Claude's original home Le Picotin, and Claude's extensive collections were a good deal more modest in those days) and the fireworks display that Claude put on for Freddie and David Bowie when they went to his home for dinner in July 1981, during the recording of "Under Pressure",' she says. 'That famous firework evening, incidentally, took place while Bowie was still living in a chalet in nearby Blonay. David left that house in 1982 when he purchased the Château de Signal in the hills of Lausanne.

'It's scarily fascinating to me how some Freddie-related people can seem inclined to support each other's versions of things they could not have experienced because they were not present. Thierry was Claude's partner and so owed no particular loyalty to Freddie.[3] Claude was Freddie's loyal friend, and he did not speak about Freddie. When I say that we owe them a lot – Claude and Vicky Vocat – we really do.'[4]

Still, Freddie refused to give up hope – of finding himself a compatible male partner prepared to love him and share him with Mary. Time and time again, he convinced himself he had found the One. One minute it was body builder and gay porn star Peter Morgan, whom he saw from autumn 1980 until March 1981. The next, it was Bill Reid from New Jersey. But Bill treated him badly. Freddie became depressed. His frail mental state caused him to lose his way in early 1983, while writing songs for his solo album, *Mr Bad Guy*.

He is candid in his journals about each of these partnerships, describing them as 'violent' and 'destructive'.

'His problem was still that he fell in love too quickly,' B. reiterates. 'Either that, or he *thought* he was in love. You know that rush, the excitement at the beginning of something new with someone. But as quickly as he fell for a guy, he would all too soon find himself desperately disappointed when his lover started treating him badly. It took a long time for him to grow out of his need for this kind of relationship.'

Not knowing how else to deal with the pain of loss, Freddie again resorted to full-on party-animal mode, living blindly for sex night after night.

'It was his fix,' says B. 'Sex for the sake of sex. Paul Prenter kept him well supplied. Even when Freddie didn't feel like it, Prenter would always insist on finding him someone, and Freddie felt obliged to go through the motions. Prenter was remorseless. He took advantage for his own personal gain, knowing that Freddie could never sleep alone. Freddie carried on kidding himself that he was having the time of his life. But the fun never lasted. Whenever he wanted to make himself feel better, he'd take a large drink and a line of coke. The highs were too high, the lows too low. He would wake the next day, remember what had happened the night before, and feel horrified and disgusted by his behaviour. He felt more lost and alone at that point in his life than he had ever felt before.'

Given the horrors of his school days and the genocide, that was saying something.

Also in 1983, Queen spent a few weeks in Los Angeles for the first sessions and recordings for their *The Works* album.

'That was when yet another new man came into Freddie's life: Vince "the barman" Gioielli,' says B. 'They enjoyed a tender and non-violent relationship, and Freddie really believed he was in love. Not since Joe had he experienced such harmony with another man. He was so happy, he hoped and prayed that *this* was the One.

'Maybe he was in love,' reasons B. 'But that relationship lasted only a few weeks. When the work was done and Freddie invited Vince to accompany him to Europe, Vince declined. Like Joe, he ended it with Freddie because he wasn't prepared to give up his own life to follow his boyfriend around the world. This aroused unprecedented feelings in Freddie. Although he understood and respected Vince's position, the snub broke Freddie's heart.

'He couldn't even turn to Mary for the moral support he needed, as she was now enjoying a romantic relationship with musician Jo Burt,' says B.[5] 'Freddie was bereft. He skulked back to New York with his tail between his legs for one last hit, knowing that when he left America this time, he would never return.'

. . .

Post-Vince, Freddie fell into a deep depression. Sucked into yet another vortex of self-destruction, he lost himself completely for a while.

'The Wild Years turned slowly but surely into the Dark Years,' says B. forlornly. 'He projected an air of happiness, but it was alcohol-induced and false. Determined to make the best of things, he knuckled down and wrote another bunch of good songs. Everyone was happy. But his spiral of decline got worse. The Monster, as he described it, took him deeper than he had ever wanted to go, and it was consuming him. Work took a back seat as he focused on his nocturnal activities. But even on his nights out, he couldn't pace himself. He went to the total extreme in about ten minutes. He couldn't wait. Freddie was living a lie, pretending to be the happy gay macho man, and everyone around him thought he was having the time of his life. Part of him was happy. He got wilder and wilder by the night, fuelling his compulsive need for sex. He was completely indiscriminate. Literally any man would do. But at the end of every night, he went home suffering. He wanted to believe that he was doing all this for love, but he knew in his heart he was only pretending. The Monster had taken up residence and demanded to be fed. Constantly. Which meant that Freddie could never be sober or alone.'

• • •

In 1987, Paul Prenter sold a kiss-and-tell about Freddie to a national newspaper. In the ultimate betrayal by a friend, he shared private photographs and sordid details about Freddie's lifestyle, and claimed that he had slept with hundreds of men. He also revealed that two of Freddie's former lovers, Tony Bastin and airline steward John Murphy, had died of AIDS. Prenter is believed to have collected in the region of £32,000 for his revelations. He lugged his ill-gotten gains back to Belfast, squandered the lot, then went back to Freddie to ask for more. He didn't get past the doormat. He would die of AIDS in August 1991, three months ahead of his former boss and friend.

• • •

'Because their romantic relationship continued for the rest of his life, Freddie was always very wary of bringing Mary into disrepute,' says B. 'He writes about how fearful he was of causing her embarrassment, and how sickening he found the thought of heaping shame on her. But although he did all he could to keep his private life private, information began to leak. There are eyes and ears everywhere; always someone willing to sell a titbit to a newspaper. He began to come under increasing scrutiny from some of the tabloid press. His hard exploration of his sexuality led to a further full and frank discussion with Mary. She was very understanding. By closing the door on their lovemaking and moving forwards in another kind of relationship, Freddie and Mary were able to remain faithful to each other.'

Mary actually saw it like that? *Really?* Even though Freddie was indulging in countless encounters with strange men night after night?

'Only they could understand what they meant to each other,' B. repeats. 'Freddie and Mary both knew that she was never going to be able to give Freddie the hard sex he needed, never mind the idea of bringing other partners into their relationship. Mary simply wasn't made that way. Barbara Valentin [the Munich-based German actress who would soon become Freddie's lover] was much more willing to indulge in that kind of activity. He never reproached Mary because she couldn't do that kind of thing for him.'

So together, B. says, 'they went on in their domestic life and partnership, and built an immense lifelong bond. Only those who were truly part of their inner circle – and this did not include certain assistants – knew precisely what their arrangement was, or what exactly was going on. To the outside world, they had ended their romance and were now no more than good friends. Mary carried on working closely with Freddie, and they remained devoted to each other. They would have been the first to admit that their unusual partnership overshadowed their relationships with others. As Freddie told journalist Nina Myskow for the *Sun* newspaper in November 1979 – later picked up by the Dutch-language Belgian magazine *Joepie* – "Other people who come into our lives just have to accept it."'

Freddie's daughter believes it is vital to set the record straight and to correct previous misstatements about Freddie's relationship with Mary Austin. She does not believe that this information is harmful to Mary, given everything that has previously been written and said about her and her relationship with Freddie. What B. has to say here about Mary is not only no more intrusive than all that has gone before, but it is also entirely to her credit. B. loves, admires and supports Mary. She finds the prevailing belief that Mary was merely a footnote in Freddie's life, and that they spent no more than a few years in a compromised relationship before he moved on to a predominantly homosexual lifestyle, frustrating and insulting. She wonders why certain individuals, especially those who command respect from Queen fans, feel the need to perpetuate this myth. She believes strongly that Mary should be acknowledged and respected for having stood by the love of her life, just as he stood by her, and for having brought Freddie more happiness and security than anyone else, ever.

Business as usual, then. Freddie and Mary continued to live together, and to enjoy their private home life away from the fray.

• • •

Even though Mary hadn't been able to accompany Freddie across the Atlantic for Queen's American tours in 1974 and 1975 due to lack of money, she did take holidays with him. She also joined the band's other wives and girlfriends on a trip to Hawaii for a break ahead of their first tour of Japan in April 1975 – where Queen performed eight dates, commencing and finishing in Tokyo.

Freddie and Mary separated, after seven and a half years together, during the autumn of 1977. But that wasn't really the case. They remained together for life.

'They continued to live together at 12 Stafford Terrace, Kensington until late 1978,' B. points out. 'Joe Fannelli lived there with them too.'

Imagine all that. Having accepted a proposal of marriage along with a ring – as Mary had, over Christmas 1973 when she was twenty-two, Freddie was twenty-seven and they had been together for three years – she was forced to relinquish her dreams for their future together. She had to forget all thoughts of a blissful wedding and happy-ever-after marriage, and settle for being Freddie's secret life partner, wing woman and 'official girlfriend'. In other words, a cover for his apparently self-centred bisexual lifestyle. I analysed this dilemma at length in *Love of My Life*. I posed the obvious questions: why didn't she jump ship and walk away, resume her independent life, be her own woman, marry some other guy and have the children and domestic life she had always craved? Why settle for the humiliation of relegation from first violin to second fiddle because 'everyone knew what he was up to'? The answer can only be because she and Freddie believed they were soulmates, pre-destined. Because she loved and adored every cell and sinew of him as much as he loved her. And because neither could see the point of life without the other.

'A signature on a piece of paper is terribly Western and civil,' remarks B. 'The truth is, Freddie *did* get married to Mary, in pure Parsee tradition. According to those customs, his gift of a ring to her made their marriage contract "pukka" – in other words, complete. It was real, authentic and genuine, not pretend, and it could not be dissolved. The reason that Freddie proposed to Mary on Christmas night was that, in the Parsee tradition, the nuptial ceremony commences soon after sunset. The ring he gave her was of jade: a valued stone in Parsee culture, and as prized as diamonds, emeralds or pearls. Freddie chose the scarab design, a symbol of the sun and of eternal fire, which is the most important element of the Zoroastrian faith. This was his simple but massively meaningful gift to her. A few years later, after Queen had made it and Freddie was very wealthy, he also gave her a beautiful solitaire diamond engagement ring that she never removed from her finger.'

* * *

Freddie purchased Flat 2, 14 Phillimore Gardens, within spitting distance of 12 Stafford Terrace, during early 1978, affirms B.

'That residence, as I have said, became Freddie's and Mary's love nest. He bought it via his company Mercury Songs Limited, which later became Goose Productions Limited.' The secluded home was theirs and theirs alone. 'It became their sanctuary, their haven and their safe harbour,' she explains. 'Freddie and Mary decorated it meticulously and with good taste. They shopped together for pieces of furniture, artworks and decorative objects, which Freddie, with his flair, artistic sense and attention to detail, took time to arrange to their best possible advantage.'

Freddie and Mary lived there privately and intimately, away from prying eyes. Although it appeared to the outside world that they had ended their relationship, we now know that they never did so. This new property afforded them the privacy and seclusion to continue that relationship without damage to Mary's reputation because Freddie was, with Mary's blessing, indulging openly in multiple gay affairs and one-night stands.

'Theirs was a life of love, affection and sensuality,' says B. 'Freddie always found shelter, comfort and cosiness there. He never felt insecure when he was at home with her. He could reveal his vulnerability to Mary without fear of threat. After every break-up, or when he left New York or Munich on a whim, or whenever he just needed to remove himself from "being Freddie Mercury" and the whole gay scene, it was to Flat 2, 14 Phillimore Gardens that he would return. Right until the end. Other than only a couple of times, Freddie and Mary were never apart for more than a week.'

He continued to take his one-night stands back to Stafford Terrace.

'But to the end of his days,' B. adds, 'Freddie never stopped behaving like Mary's husband. He loved her, looked after her and of course showered her with gifts. He especially enjoyed buying her wonderful feminine clothes, expensive lingerie and exquisite pieces of jewellery.'

. . .

Mary knew everything. The more Freddie sank into self-destruction and excess, the more he wanted her by his side. He felt safe and secure only when his longtime love, his 'common-law wife', his 'Old Faithful' as he called her, was right there within touching distance. Mothering him. Picking up the pieces. Reassuring him that everything would be all right. He started asking her, ever more frequently, to join him in New York, Los Angeles, Munich, Montreux, and always on the road when Queen were touring. During their separations they would phone each other every day and talk for hours. Freddie would also write her endless notes and cards, scribbling away in the privacy of his room. He would present her with these in person as soon as they next got together. This continuous correspondence, dating from Queen's earliest gigs to their final recording sessions in Montreux, ran to hundreds if not thousands of hand-written notes. Their content reveals the inner Freddie Bulsara and the depth of his feelings for Mary. He would begin each one with 'Honey', 'Sweetie', or 'My Love' before pouring out his love across the page. Every last billet-doux was saved. Not a single note was ever discarded. The couple kept them together at Phillimore Gardens, concealing them in the large, beautiful, lacquered boxes of which Freddie had always been so fond.

. . .

I remember seeing Mary backstage at the gigs I covered on *The Works* tour of 1984–1985, and on the *Magic* tour in 1986. Whenever Freddie appeared, there she was too. They looked happy and contented together. 'Like a proper couple,' people would remark, though we all knew otherwise. At least, we thought we knew. Mary, we all agreed, was Freddie's walker, his beard. Most journalists on the scene at the time must have been aware that 'Freddie was gay'. Fellow reporters and I certainly were. It was accepted, not that anyone cared. We didn't write about it. It was his business. We could not have known that Freddie's relationship with Mary was much more complicated than it appeared, and that it was as strong and as close as it had ever been. Freddie had not broken off their engagement and abandoned Mary to live a reckless gay lifestyle. On the contrary, in some ways. If only we had known.

I have in the past, along with others, been critical and judgemental of Mary Austin. Now that I am aware of what Freddie had to say about their situation and their relationship, I regret some of the assumptions I made. Freddie's and Mary's alliance was never a lie. His treatment of his true love did not humiliate her. While most wives and partners would never dream of accepting such an arrangement, for Mary and Freddie it was the obvious solution. No one else's opinion mattered. Would the world have understood? Highly unlikely. Society hadn't yet evolved to the point that it could. Had the truth of the matter leaked, it might have dented the band's reputation and affected both their popularity and their record sales. So they kept it to themselves. They were consenting adults. It was nobody's business but theirs. Although unmarried in the legal sense, they were committed, devoted, and together because they wanted and needed to be. For them, there was no alternative. Having created their own quiet chaos, they would deal with it privately in their own way.

There were failings on both sides. Perhaps, had Mary been more assertive, she would have refused to put up with it, insisted that they seek counselling, and backed Freddie into a corner to make a choice. We could look at it another way. Didn't she know something that most of us miss: that to enforce convention on an unconventional individual would be to kill their spirit and destroy the essence of what made them unique? Freddie's love for Mary and hers for him was just the way it was. Complicated and confounded by the extreme elements of fame and celebrity, by prying eyes and by professional and personal obligations, it weathered all storms to remain steadfast and true. They came to realise that they did not need permission or approval, and that they were not obliged to live as others did. Their lives were up to them. Each was answerable to no one except the other.

Was it fair? Nothing is. Many have denounced Mary down the years, writing her off as a gold-digger. She has been accused of sticking around for the fancy lifestyle, luxury travel and bottomless pit. But think about that. She would never have been homeless or penniless, whatever the outcome. Freddie, an honourable partner and a man of his word, would have been more than happy to provide her with her own home and even an allowance had they gone their separate ways. She had a purpose – running his companies – and she was valued both profession-ally and personally. She could have surrendered her position, accepted a fat pay-off that would have set her up for life, and departed to start again elsewhere. It was much more difficult for her to stay. She knew that she would be reviled, pitied, pilloried and dismissed within Freddie's inner circle, as well as by the general public and fans. She stayed because she loved Freddie and simply could not give him up. She chose to weather those challenges because he was hers.

'Freddie said that he opened up to Mary more than to anybody else,' B. says. 'And so did she. They saw through each other to the real person. She was his rock, his support, his "repos du guerrier".[6] They went through just about everything together until the end.'

. . .

Mary has never been in the habit of giving interviews. She would have reasoned that she was neither a performer nor a celebrity. Freddie trusted David Wigg, in those days a high-profile journalist on the *Daily Express* who later operated as a freelance, often on behalf of the *Daily Mail*. He and I remain friends. Mary would talk to him occasionally during Freddie's lifetime, and granted him a couple of exclusives after Freddie's death. Inaccuracies occasionally crept in between the filing of copy and the pieces appearing in the newspapers. Copy passes through many stages before it reaches the printed page, while headlines can in certain circumstances suggest other than what had been intended when the interview was agreed. Freddie knew enough about such procedures not to blame the scribe, for whom he had the utmost respect, and whose loyalty and admiration for his famous friend has never waned.

. . .

Freddie and Mary's mutual understanding was what saved their relationship. He knew that his hard libido would wear out eventually. He recognised that few people have the same sex drive at sixty years of age as they had at thirty, and that sexual desire for one's lover at the beginning of a relationship will naturally have dwindled by the time a couple has been together for fifteen years or more. He explained that the sex he had with men was merely a physical pursuit.

'He loved Mary, and his love was based on emotion and tenderness,' B. tells us. 'It was to him a pure love, and not about sex. In a similar way, he thought rock 'n' roll was for young people and knew that one day soon he would stop touring. Mary and Freddie never gave any thought to having children at twenty-five or thirty years of age. When the time came to settle down – which for him meant at forty or forty-five, when he would have been too old to tour the world in a rock band – he would then have had time to be present for his wife and children. Mary would by then be thirty-five or forty, so it would not have been too late for her to start a family. How many women these days have children after the age of thirty-five?

'Freddie wanted to get his penchant for a decadent lifestyle out of his system before having children. He was very cut and dried about that. It was one of the things about Barbara Valentin that he disapproved of vehemently – her careless mothering. He would reproach her for the choices she made, and for her unmaternal attitude. Barbara's son, Lars, would have been a young adult at that time, while her daughter, Minki, was still a teenager.'

Freddie described with longing how desperate he was to have a family and to live a family life.

'His writings show,' says B., 'that he wanted to be there for them more than anything. Physically, mentally and emotionally, he would have to be there. He didn't want to have to leave them at home while he went off on tour. That feeling of having been rejected by his parents had never left him. He realised, he said, that the only way he was ever going to console and heal his inner eight-year-old was to have children of his own. He wrote about all this with a great deal of passion.'

Freddie spoke of his intention to have only two children.

'He didn't want more,' B. reveals, 'because as he said, he had only two arms. He needed to be able to hold his children at the same time. He had it all planned, all mapped out. After reading his impassioned outpourings, it didn't surprise me at all to learn that he had thrown himself into fatherhood as soon as I came along – spending all the time that he could with me and making sure that I was never less than secure and well cared-for.'

June 2025

Freddie Mercury was and is my father. We had a very close and loving relationship from the moment I was born and throughout the final fifteen years of his life.

He adored me and was devoted to me. The circumstances of my birth may seem, by most people's standards, unusual and even outrageous. That should come as no surprise. It never detracted from his commitment to love and look after me. He cherished me like a treasured possession. I was, naturally, devastated by his death.

Shortly before he died, he gave me a collection of private notebooks that he had been writing since 1976, before I came into the world. They revealed, in at times, excruciating detail, the story of Freddie's whole life. They were written in his own handwriting, in ballpoint pen, in his own words.

He entrusted to me, his only child and his next of kin, the written record of his private thoughts, memories and feelings about everything he had experienced.

His gift to me was our secret. Although those who lived with him and shared his life knew of the existence of the notebooks, none of them knew, after his death, what had become of them. His family, fellow band members, closest friends, associates and management have had no idea until now that he gave them to me as a present.

Mary Austin - the wonderful woman who was to all intents and purposes his wife, until death parted them - knew absolutely everything about him, including all his undisclosed secrets.

The others - his real, true friends whom he could count on fewer than the fingers of one hand; the band; the great army of so-called friends, employees and hired help, those with whom he had working relationships (journalists, designers, film makers, roadies, fan club staff); the even greater army of so-called personal this or that (personal assistant, personal film maker, personal designer, personal photographer...); wider acquaintances and everyone else - knew only what Freddie wanted them to know. Which wasn't much.

Freddie was an intensely private man. He gave so few interviews that he was famous for it. Because of this it has been easy, since his death, for many people to exploit and betray him. To twist his words, to rewrite his story, to speculate and make up this theory or that about his life, in order to equate him to the image of the Freddie Mercury that they seek to portray. Their versions of Freddie are far removed from the man he really was. They have done this for their own profit and ego. Freddie would have been deeply wounded by it all.

After more than three decades of lies, speculation and distortion, it is time to let Freddie speak.

I had read everything that Lesley-Ann Jones had ever written about my father when I wrote to

her towards the end of 2021, with the intention of
offering her the responsibility of sharing his true
story. I had been meaning to contact her for years,
having read so much of her work: not only about
Freddie, but also about other artists. I was struck by
her obvious pursuit of the truth, and by how closely
she came to capturing "the real Freddie". Her book "Love
of my life: The Lives and Loves of Freddie Mercury",
published in 2021, portrayed him more accurately
than anything I had ever read. So much of what
has been written and committed to film about him
by so-called friends, former loves, employees and
colleagues has been at best a gross distortion of the
truth, at worst an exercise in exploitation.
Those who have been aware of my existence kept
his greatest secret out of loyalty to Freddie. That
I choose to reveal myself in my own mid-life is my
decision and mine alone. I have not, at any point,
been coerced into doing this.

Lesley-Ann and I talked intensely for many
months from late 2021. We continue to communicate to
this day. Our long discussions have been very moving, at
times unbearable and heartbreaking. I revealed to her
who my father was. I told her the truth about his childhood,
his life, and everything that built the infant, the boy,
the teenager, the young man, the grown man, the Dad
he was to me, the stage persona and the Mercury mask
that he created. I explained to her how he
compartmentalised his life, and of course talked at
length about our precious time together.

Lesley-Ann flew to Montreux in May 2023. I do not live there, but the city was chosen because of Freddie's attachment to the place. She made the journey to meet me and my family there, to see Freddie's seventeen notebooks, cards, private notes, letters, bank statements and other relevant documents, to view photos and private videos and to listen to audio. She tried for a long time to persuade me to publish some of my photographs. It is by no means her fault that I decided not to agree to this. Although I understand very well the importance of illustrating a book, I had to decline to publish the records of our time together. They are from a father to his daughter and only child. They are records of my Dad and grandfather of my children. We cherish them, they are private, and we want them to remain private.

None of these personal items will ever be exhibited to the public. Nor will they ever come up for auction. It is, however, my legal right to share everything I learnt from my father's notebooks. It is also my right to destroy the notebooks, should I see fit to do so. Freddie's fans, the lovers of his music and the millions who honour his memory must respect this. I hope and pray that they will. If they cannot, that will prove that I was right to keep our mementoes to myself.

The life I live with my husband and our family in another country is intensely private. We want things to stay that way. We cherish our peaceful and anonymous life, and we want nothing to disturb it.

Nobody needs to know who I am. I will have nothing more to say beyond what I have revealed in this book. There will be no further interviews other than those I have given to Lesley-Ann.
I owe it to my father to cherish privacy as one of the most precious privileges in life. As he himself said, it was the thing he regretted giving away so readily. The one thing he wished that he could get back.

Here, then, for the first and only time, is Freddie Mercury's true story. I have chosen to entrust it to my dear friend Lesley-Ann Jones. Every syllable that you read here was revealed to me by Freddie himself.

B

CHAPTER 7

PERNICIOSUS

A few months after they moved into Phillimore Gardens, Freddie asked Mary to start searching for the family home of their dreams.

'He wanted a house large enough for them and their children,' says B., 'and to be able to see them grow up, but not so large that the family would grow distant from one another within the home and lose touch with each other. Mary, as we know, found Garden Lodge in Kensington. It was the perfect house. But Freddie being Freddie, perfection would have to be improved. They planned the renovations and redecoration together. This was the reason why Mary changed hardly anything about the house after Freddie died. She was more than happy with it just the way it was. One specific change that she made after he left us was that she had a garden "à la française", in the French style, constructed there. Freddie had wanted one so much and had even designed and drawn up the plans.'

Mary's gesture of honouring a promise and a commitment was a reflection of the way Freddie had always done things.

They acquired their future family residence, seven-bedroom Garden Lodge on Logan Place, Kensington, in early 1980. Freddie paid the £500,000 asking price in cash. The neo-Georgian brick house had first been advertised in *Country Life* in 1978. Offers in excess of £300,000 had been invited. Mary and Freddie went to see it together, and he decided to buy it on the spot. The property required extensive renovation and updating to turn it into the home of their dreams. That work would take several years. He would move in permanently during the late summer of 1986, and would live there until his death in November 1991.

Zanzibar and India being Freddie's lost paradises, one of the first things he did for the house was to commission a huge, spectacular mural of the Panchgani region of India, plus several paintings of his vision of Zanzibar as he imagined it must once have been like.

'India and Zanzibar remained special to him throughout his life,' says his daughter. 'To all those who said that he turned his back on both, left his past behind and reinvented himself when his family moved to England, these paintings were proof that it was not true. There are other things that demonstrate this too. For example, for what he believed would be his final birthday, Freddie ordered himself a birthday cake in the shape of the Taj Mahal. Not Big Ben, Buckingham Palace, the Eiffel Tower or Versailles. Not the Brooklyn Bridge, the Statue of Liberty, Marienplatz (in Munich) nor Theresienwiese (the location of Munich's annual Oktoberfest). Every one of those places was special to him, but he wanted the Taj Mahal, because it is a symbol of India. For one of Mary's birthdays, he ordered her a cake in the shape of a tiger. The royal Bengal tiger is India's national animal, as well as one of its most sacred creatures. And it was Freddie who suggested to Roger Taylor the name Tiger for his unborn child. Roger named his son Rufus Tiger. Three years later, he called his second child Tigerlily.'

• • •

Between the summers of 1985 and 1986, whenever Freddie was in London, he would occasionally spend a few days and nights at Garden Lodge.

'Otherwise,' says B., 'he lived at Stafford Terrace or at Phillimore Gardens. He began spending more and more time at Garden Lodge from spring 1986, and started moving his things there from Stafford Terrace so that he could enjoy his wonderful garden that summer. He took up permanent residence there only in August 1986, at the conclusion of Queen's *Magic* tour. Meanwhile, over the next several months, he continued to take men from his close circle of regular partners back to Stafford Terrace.'

After his death, Mary found it impossible to let the Phillimore Gardens flat go.

'It was their haven,' B. reminds us. 'The place that had sheltered their love for thirteen years, from mid-1978 until mid-1991. She took partial residence of Garden Lodge during early 1992 and ran Freddie's companies from there. She lived between Phillimore Gardens and Garden Lodge from February until October 1992 before moving into Garden Lodge permanently at the end of that year. She had always run Freddie's businesses, houses and everything else from their home: first from the Holland Park flat, then from the Stafford Terrace flat. From 1978 it was from Phillimore Gardens, then finally from Garden Lodge.'

● ● ●

Mary auctioned the contents of Garden Lodge and most of Freddie's possessions – in 1,406 lots – through Sotheby's in September 2023. Following more than 41,800 bids, the sale fetched £39.9 million in less than a week. Almost all the lots sold for prices in excess of their high estimates. Some – including Freddie's Wurlitzer 850 jukebox that went for £406,000, his military-style jacket for £457,000 and his 'Six Cats' waistcoat for £139,000 – were purchased anonymously by his sister Kashmira, who spent £3 million buying back possessions she felt should remain in the Bulsara family. The move hinted at a long-running feud between her and Mary Austin. Of the proceeds remaining after fees had been deducted, Mary donated a percentage to the Mercury Phoenix Trust and another to the Elton John AIDS Foundation. A few months later, in February 2024, forty-four years after Freddie had acquired it and where he had died in November 1991, Garden Lodge was listed for private sale, inviting offers in excess of £30 million.

'This house has been the most glorious memory box,' commented Mary, quoted in *Country Life* magazine, 'because it has such love and warmth in every room. It has been a joy to live in, and I have many wonderful memories here. Now that it is empty, I'm transported back to the first time we viewed it. Ever since Freddie and I stepped through the fabled green door, it has been a place of peace, a true artist's house, and now is the time to entrust that sense of peace to the next person.'

Her dignified message echoed loudly between the lines. This courageous final act of surrender of the love of her life, his earthly possessions and the precious home they had created together was made not to set herself free of Freddie. On the contrary, as she must have known all along, it would return him to her.

• • •

Until Freddie's death, neither he nor Mary engaged in any significant or long-term relationship with anyone else.

'Mary was never involved with another man for more than a few months, except when she was seeing musician Jo Burt,' B. confirms. 'She was later with decorator Piers Cameron, yes, but for a totally different reason.'

There is some confusion in the reporting, here. Some dates have either been misremembered, or have been written up erroneously. 'In your last book,' says B., 'you quote Jo Burt as having said that Freddie flew them to New York for his fortieth birthday [the legendary party that had been planned to span a weekend, but which dragged out over three debauched and drunken weeks]. You also quote Jo as saying, "For five years we were in each other's pockets." It wasn't for Freddie's fortieth birthday party but for his thirty-fifth, in 1981, just before *The Game* tour *Gluttons for Punishment*. Unless Jo is talking about Mary's birthday party in Munich in 1984 … but that one didn't last for three weeks.' There is no suggestion that Jo Burt has been untruthful, only that elements of three separate birthday parties seem to have been recalled as one and the same. 'Also, the relationship between Mary and Jo Burt didn't last for five years, but for four years. It began in mid-1981 and ended mid-1985. But Jo never lived with Mary, not at Phillimore Gardens or anywhere else. They never actually resided under the same roof. Jo did visit Phillimore Gardens regularly but never lived there with her. That residence remained Freddie's and Mary's private love nest. Later on, Piers Cameron did park his suitcases there for a while, but that was a different situation, which we will come to.'

Jo, who was born in 1956 and was five years Mary's junior, was and remains a bass player. A member of Tom Robinson's new-wave band Sector 27, founded in 1979, he went on to perform along-side drummer Jason Bonham in rock band Virginia Woolf during the late 1980s. He also played bass with Black Sabbath on their 1987 tour, and contributed fretless bass to Freddie's only solo studio album, *Mr Bad Guy*, released in 1985.

It was Freddie, B. reveals, who engineered the separation between Mary and Jo: 'Because he was jealous! He was terrified of losing his Mary. He invited Jo to play on his album, which he saw as a means via which he could control the situation. But a row that broke out between Freddie and Jo one day led to the cooling of the relationship between Mary and Jo. In the end, it killed it completely.'

• • •

Having spent the summer of 1979 in Munich, working at the then-famous, now-defunct Musicland Studios with producer Reinhold Mack, all four members of Queen developed an addiction to that city and its smorgasbord of off-grid delights. For Freddie, the Bavarian capital's exuberant gay scene was its main attraction. Queen's music and their approach to recording began to veer in different directions as a result of influences to which they were exposed there. All were keen to maintain the Munich connection. Queen were by then in the habit of record-ing abroad anyway, for tax reasons. In July 1979, they acquired their own recording facility: Mountain Studios in Montreux, Switzerland, where seven Queen albums would be crafted. When they returned to Munich in 1981, they were still officially tax exiles. They planned to begin work on another album there.

Between 1980 and 1985, Freddie admits, he was monstrously promiscuous. Between 'steady' relationships, whenever such a liaison began to crumble, and during long absences while away on tour, he shared himself around with abandon.

'He had different levels of relationship with men,' B. explains. 'In his journals, he refers to countless one-night stands. An eye-watering number, actually. There is not much more that I can say about that.'

Then in 1983 and for the next two and a half years, Freddie became immersed in a 'strange relationship' with a rugged German restaurateur by the name of Winfried Kirchberger. Freddie renamed him 'Winnie', of course, maintaining the women's-names trend. Their affair was complicated by Freddie's involvement with the flamboyant German actress Barbara Valentin. That set-up would soon become further entangled by a new liaison back in London, with Irish barber Jim Hutton. The moment he took up with Winnie, Freddie quickly vacated the band's digs at the depressing Arabella-Haus apartment hotel above Musicland Studios to share the home of his new boyfriend.

'His relationship with Winnie was odd,' B. relates. 'It was strong to begin with and had real potential: because Winnie loved Freddie for himself, not for who he was. He wasn't showbiz-y, he wasn't impressed, he didn't care about any of that and he was very down to earth. He was also a busy man. He had his own business to run, with its many obligations. When they first met, Freddie was calm, in a good state of mind, and was working on his solo album. But a few months later, when Queen's *The Works* tour kicked off, the usual problems began to rear their heads again.'

The tour commenced in Brussels, moved on to Dublin, spent three nights in Birmingham and proceeded to four consecutive shows at Wembley Arena. The second of these, on 5 September 1984, coincided with Freddie's thirty-eighth birthday. Out of the blue, Winnie presented him with a ring. Freddie was delighted by the gift and wore it in public for the first time at his birthday party at Xenon nightclub in London's Piccadilly, straight after the Wembley show. The band then rolled on through West Germany, Italy, France, the Netherlands, Belgium and Austria before departing for their controversial Sun City visit, following which they voyaged on to Brazil. Next on the schedule were New Zealand, Australia and Japan. Queen were consuming the world, and should have felt on top of it. But all Freddie could care about was his love life. The trouble was that old habits die hard. The minute he got back on the road, he resumed his promiscuous lifestyle and indulged in so many one-night stands, it was as if he was trying to break a record.

'When he discovered that Freddie was being unfaithful to him,' says B., 'Winnie hit back blow for blow. Not with the obvious, by taking other lovers himself. It was much worse than that. To begin with, he treated Freddie with indifference. He then began rejecting him, as well as his many gifts – including a brand-new Mercedes, which was delivered outrageously wrapped complete with a huge ribbon bow, because Freddie never did anything by halves.

'It's an oft-related tale, but nobody ever tells it to the end,' sighs B. 'Winnie never accepted the car as a gift. Freddie was forced to compromise. They came to an arrangement. Winnie would drive the car when he and Freddie were going out somewhere together, or when Winnie had to drive Freddie somewhere. Otherwise, Winnie never agreed to keep it for his own personal use. What Winnie valued more than a Mercedes was Freddie turning up towards closing time at his restaurant and helping him around the place with dishes and sweeping and generally clearing up before they went out on the town. That's the kind of guy that Winnie Kirchberger was.'

When Winnie started treating him coldly, Freddie was at a loss.

'He was bewildered,' says B. 'He couldn't cope with being treated that way. What had he done to deserve it! We must remember that all this was taking place during an intensely chaotic time, thanks to the explosion of the AIDS crisis. The gay community was terrified, everyone was paranoid and most of them were looking over their shoulder.'

Who's doing what with whom and who's going to give it to me was the prevailing fear.

Freddie moved out of Winnie's home into drab furnished rooms at the Stollbergplaza apartment hotel, where he happened to meet Barbara Valentin: a locally well-known actress who resided opposite. They fell in together, became lovers, and at that point Freddie entered his most hedonistic period yet. His obsessions with both Winnie and Barbara took his eye off the ball, and ultimately damaged his creativity.

'Many individuals have denied that Freddie ever had a sexual relationship with Barbara,' B. reminds us. 'But how would they know? Only four people ever knew what really happened,' she points out. 'They were Freddie himself, Barbara, Winnie and another member of their close circle of regular partners in that three-/four-in-a-bed set-up. Forget whatever else you may have heard. No one else was ever in the bedroom with them. Freddie never discussed his relationships with women with his roadies or his employees. He did publicly acknowledge the importance of Barbara in his life by thanking her, in the *Mr Bad Guy* sleeve notes, "for misconduct". What does anyone *think* he was talking about? Of course he had sex with Barbara, he says so himself! The thing is, he was never Freddie Bulsara with Barbara. He was only ever Freddie Mercury, the outrageous Mercury, with her.'

Peter Freestone in particular has long been resolutely of the impression, and has discussed it at length with me on several occasions over the years, that Freddie's and Barbara's relationship was most likely platonic. In the 2004 Channel 5 television documentary *Freddie's Loves*, later quoted in the *Daily Express* in October 2020, he commented, 'I can't tell you yes or no if sex happened. If it had, Freddie could not have been quiet about it.'

'But it was certainly not with Peter Freestone that Freddie ever discussed this,' remarks B. 'Freddie wouldn't discuss his relationships with women with any of the men in his "gay" circle. It seems to me that many individuals would like to reduce Barbara to nothing more than Freddie's and Winnie's interpreter.

'Why would anyone deny something today that was obviously so important to Freddie during his lifetime?' she asks. 'No one can deny her significance in Freddie's life throughout the two years that their relationship lasted.'

Only now, decades after the fact, does the complex reason behind Freddie's involvement with Barbara begin to emerge. Unexpectedly, it came about as a direct result of Mary's relationship with Jo Burt. Even though Mary had put up with so much from Freddie, he, it appears, was not prepared to do likewise.

'As I have mentioned, Freddie was jealous of Jo Burt because his relationship with Mary looked set to last,' comments B. 'Mary, on the other hand, did not feel jealous of Freddie's other lovers. Knowing that she would always have her place at his side, and that only she could give him what no man could ever give him, Mary was relaxed about Freddie's male relationships. Freddie, however, found it difficult to see Mary apparently happy with another man. Even though they had redefined their physical relationship – for what was intended to be just a phase, but then HIV came along and ruined everything – their love for one another never wavered. Freddie feared, however, that this time, with Jo, could prove to be the turning point. The idea that another man could give Mary what Freddie gave her really scared him. It wasn't that their bond had stopped growing, more that Freddie was a highly sensitive man. He was not very confident about personal issues, so this was an unsettling time for him. He couldn't see that Mary was not as happy with Jo as Freddie thought she was. To him, Mary was in a stable relationship while he was shouldering heartbreak after heartbreak, abusive relationship after abusive relationship with his string of male lovers, with no prospect of stability in sight. This is probably the reason why he developed his relationship with Barbara Valentin: to redress the balance. Unfortunately, Barbara misread what Freddie needed.'

Desperate to have Freddie for herself, Barbara plunged him deeper and deeper into troubled waters, pandering to his basest instincts, believing that to be the way to keep him. She told me this. But it backfired on her, serving only to exacerbate Freddie's deepest insecurities.

'His consumption of drugs and alcohol increased, taking him to the most hedonistic, life-threatening period of his life from late 1984 to early 1985,' explains B. 'Barbara gave him something that he must have needed to survive that period, but she was never able to give him what Mary had always given him. It's no surprise that the Monster cracked when Mary broke up with Jo Burt. Freddie no longer felt afraid that he might lose her. It must have been very difficult for Barbara to deal with that.'

●   ●   ●

By Freddie's own admission, his life at that time was a mess:

'He produced a lot of unworthy songs during that period,' says B. 'There was a great deal of tension within the band. He really struggled with the songs for *Mr Bad Guy*. During the recording of that album, just after the festival in Montreux, so during late May 1984, he took a bad tumble in a Munich bar one night. It was only a fall, not a fight [as has long been reported]. He was enjoying a happy evening out, the drink was flowing, and the friends started riding on each other's shoulders. Up, down, up, down they went, until Freddie lost his footing, fell, and tore a knee ligament. His leg was in plaster until the shoot for the "It's a Hard Life" video on 22 June 1984.'

Freddie's alcohol and drug consumption during that period reached Himalayan peaks. He fell apart during the *The Works* tour while in South Africa and during the first half of 1985. He describes in his diaries how he lost respect for himself, to the point where he felt 'filthy' inside.

His state of mind was further troubled by the baffling controversy that raged over Queen's acceptance of an invitation to perform at the Sun City pleasure resort in South Africa's Bophuthatswana – a rich white enclave in the middle of a poverty-stricken black land – during the struggle against Apartheid and a United Nations boycott, thus earning themselves a Musician's Union ban. He had always believed that music is for everybody: for the people, not for governing bodies. He cherished its universal and apolitical language.

'He said that if you refuse to perform in certain countries, you must also refuse to sell records there,' says B. 'But what about history? Surely every territory had dark episodes in its past. If you took into account every war and injustice, every repugnant and murderous regime, the only place you could play without offending anyone was Antarctica. Freddie refused to allow any of it to interfere with his music.'

When Queen were accused of thumbing their noses at worldwide efforts to end Apartheid – not that they were the only artists ever to have played there – Freddie inadvertently put his foot in it. He retorted arrogantly that there was a lot of money to be made there and implied that was the reason why they had agreed to do it. He said the following during a press conference in Munich in March 1984, excerpts of which were published in German magazine *Musikexpress* and *Sounds* that June and which were requoted widely down the years, including in the *Big Issue in the North* in October 2006 to commemorate what would have been Freddie's sixtieth birthday:

'We're thinking about going to South Africa and it's going to be very political and everything, but I don't give a shit. As far as I'm concerned, I'm just playing music to people. We were one of the first groups to go to South America. It was an amazing experience. Two weeks after we'd finished Britain was at war with Argentina. But that shouldn't matter as far as musicians are concerned. Music is for everybody. I want to go to Russia. We wanted to go there three or four years ago but they looked at our album covers and decided we would corrupt their youth. These are the things that I want to get to – the other corners of the world – before I give it all up. Music is for everybody. I absolutely don't want politics to interfere with my career. Politics enters into my thinking, yes, but I discard it because we are musicians. I don't like to be political …'

His comments were of course made tongue in cheek. South Africa was a financial abyss. But Queen were not making a political statement. Their performances there were in the name of entertainment only. In that case, scoffed their critics, they would presumably have danced to the tune of the Nazis had they been offered a fat enough purse.

'People forgot that Freddie had technically been born African, even though he was Parsee and Indian by heritage and culture,' says B. 'Because he presented as Persian, and that was how people regarded him, the circumstances of his birth in Zanzibar were overlooked. Freddie had lived there for nine and a half years, not including his years at boarding school in India, before his family fled to England during the genocide. At that point, at the age of nearly thirty-eight, he had lived in Africa for about a quarter of his life.'

• • •

Back in London, Freddie threw himself into his new relationship with Jim Hutton. The pair had first crossed paths two years earlier at the Copacabana, a Kensington gay bar that stood just a short walk from Freddie's home. Jim was involved with another man at the time, so nothing came of the encounter. By 1985, the situation had changed. One night in March, Jim joined Freddie and his friends during a night out, and the gang ended up back at Freddie's flat. Freddie couldn't get over the likeness between Jim and Winnie, which was striking. Now he knew exactly what to do to gain Winnie's commitment. He would use Jim, Freddie resolved, to make Winnie jealous. So he began a sexual relationship with Jim, then gifted Winnie a very expensive and beautiful ring.

'This is another story that people often rewrite and re-tell only partially,' says B. 'Freddie and Winnie got into a fight that night, it is true. Freddie asked Winnie again to come and live with him in London. Again, Winnie refused. He was dismissive of Freddie's gift, which he regarded as an attempt to "buy" him. They had a huge row, but they didn't break up that night. The split was to happen six months later, in spring 1986. It's wrong to say that Winnie threw the ring, and that it was lost. Winnie had big fingers. As it was too small for his ring finger, he went to put it on his little finger but somehow managed to drop it. It fell to the ground. That's all. One of them picked it up, Winnie put it on his pinkie, and there it stayed until the following spring when they went their separate ways.

'Of course, all this provoked Jim's jealousy,' recounts B., 'But Freddie did it to provoke *Winnie's* jealousy, so that Winnie would be persuaded to follow him to London. And when things fizzled out between them – which was a shame, as Winnie was a good guy – that was when Freddie began his full-blown affair with Jim. Who, in turn, gave Freddie a birthday ring, for his fortieth in September 1986. But when Jim turned thirty-eight the following January, Freddie did not reciprocate. He did give him a piece of jewellery: the gold Cartier bracelet that was Freddie's favourite gift to his men friends; he gave away dozens of them. But he did not give Jim a ring, which to Freddie was too symbolic. We must remember that Mary had been wearing his engagement ring all this time. Jim was devastated. He refused Freddie's gift, accepted a cheque, and went off to select and purchase his own ring with it.'

That relationship, such as it was, did continue, but only on Freddie's terms. Jim moved into Garden Lodge and remained part of the household in an evolving capacity until Freddie died. Freddie makes clear in his diaries that Jim was never more than what amounted to a personal rent boy: a convenient partner for sex once Freddie was no longer able to go out cruising to pick up other men.

'Their relationship was hallmarked by a lot of big, violent rows, infidelity and abuse,' says B. 'Eventually, in 1989, Freddie put a stop to it. Jim, however, was not going to go quietly. He really didn't want to leave Garden Lodge. Freddie was too afraid to kick him out, because he was terrified that Hutton would go to the press, just as Paul Prenter had done. So he decided to let him stay on, allowing him to tend the garden and take care of bits and pieces around the house.'

. . .

Freddie's bond with Barbara Valentin, B. explains, 'was built on Barbara's unrestrained willingness to share her bed with Freddie and his male one-night stands, as a parody of love, acceptance and happiness. Between Freddie and Mary, we know, it was love. With other men, and also with Barbara, it was simply lust. While Mary was his true love – in effect, we know, she was Freddie Bulsara's wife – Barbara represented sexual exploration. As such, she was Freddie Mercury's mistress. You see the difference. As Barbara herself said, with her he "could have sex with someone else present between them, because that was the way Freddie liked it". She gave him whatever he wanted, and became his partner in debauchery, depravity and decadence.' No wonder Queen neglected to depict her in their film. To do so would have exposed a less savoury side of Freddie that they must have been keen to keep hidden, for fear that it could tarnish their legend and perhaps even turn fans off them.

Freddie mentioned Barbara only once during an interview, B. reminds us: with journalist Sharon Feinstein for the *News of the World*'s *Sunday* magazine supplement on 14 April 1985.

'What he said was, "Barbara and I have formed a bond which is stronger than anything I've had with a lover for the last six years. I can really talk to her and be myself in a way that's very rare." Note, he said "*formed*" a bond, not "*built*" a bond, which was the way he would talk about what he had with Mary. "The last six years" means "since 1979". To him, his bond with Mary is unreachable. Also, his bond with Joe Fannelli was always greater than anything he had with Barbara.'

To be fair, Freddie did love Barbara in his way, B. agrees:

'She did accompany him to Rio on tour with Queen in 1985. Then again, so did many others. And while they were there,

Freddie shared his master bedroom with Mary, not with her. When the band travelled on to Japan and Australia that same year, it was Mary who accompanied Freddie. Not Barbara.'

Imagine how confused and unsettled Winnie, Barbara and Jim were made to feel by Freddie's skittishness. How unnerved they must have been whenever he gushed about his feelings for Mary in interviews. Embroiled in simultaneous sexual and emotional relationships with him, each of them dropped every-thing for him and came running whenever he called. It must have felt, to them, like out of sight, out of mind, and can't have done much for their self-esteem. But Freddie appeared not to give a fig about any of them when he wasn't actually with them. Although Barbara had been with Freddie at the Munich press conference for *The Works*, it was Mary who was in the Munich control room during the playback of *Mr Bad Guy*. Was he toying with all their emotions, then, or simply so self-centred that he was careless of them?

'Like all the others before them, Barbara, Winnie, Jim, Peter Freestone and the rest could never fathom the domestic arrange-ment between Freddie and Mary,' says B. 'Nor could they work out why they could never replace her.'

Perhaps he could have taken the time and trouble to explain it to them? Maybe their own arrogance had deluded some of them into believing that they would make a more suitable part-ner for Freddie than Mary did. Perhaps their pride wouldn't allow them to back down, forcing them to stop at nothing until they 'got' him for themselves. It does seem curious that Barbara 'accepted having sex with Freddie with someone else present between them, but that she could never accept Mary', B. opines.

Freddie did purchase a Munich flat with Barbara. I visited her there in 1996. She showed me his things, none of which had she been able to discard or give away. Silver-framed photographs of him, and of them together, graced every surface. It was clear from our conversation how much she adored him.

'If Barbara was so important to Freddie,' asks B., 'why did he never clarify her share of ownership legally, on paper, so that she would not have had to fight his management in order to keep her home after he died? Why didn't he simply bequeath his share of the flat to Barbara in his will? He could have prevented so easily her subsequent suffering, stress and indignity. He could have done that for her, but he didn't. All I can tell you, because of legal restrictions, is that he had his reasons.'

Marriage to Barbara, we know from Freddie's journals, was never discussed.

'For a video or even just for fun, Freddie could have taken part in an outrageous fake wedding,' says B. 'But never anything more than that. To say otherwise would be to betray Freddie's feelings. He did love Barbara in his own way for a while, it is true. He says so himself. But it was Mary, always Mary, who was as good as his wife. It was out of the question that Barbara should ever compete with her. He may have arrived at his 1984 birthday party with Barbara and Winnie, but it was around Mary that he put his arms. When Mary was travelling to Munich almost every week during the period when Freddie lived there, he would usually go to the hotel and stay with her, and they would sometimes stay at his flat. Whenever Mary was around, he was never to be found at Barbara's or Winnie's places.'

His relationship with Barbara, according to Freddie, lasted for just two years: from early 1984 until late 1985. After that, says B., 'he cut ties with her. They later became friends again, from mid-1988 until late 1990. Beyond that point, Freddie had no further contact with her. She did go to stay at Garden Lodge during the summer of 1988. But that was just a friendly visit, nothing more.

'Nowhere in his notebooks did he talk about Barbara between late 1985 and mid-1988,' she stresses. 'It was not that he had come to hate her. In any case, hatred was impossible for him. He would loathe certain behaviours in someone, but not the individual. Not even those who betrayed him. He could behave indifferently towards them, but he was incapable of hatred. The difference with Barbara was that, from late 1985 onwards, he no longer wanted to see her alone. She talked about being in Ibiza with him, but she had been going there for years before him. When they ran into each other there in 1987, it was not at Freddie's instigation. When she would visit him for a couple of hours whenever she happened to be in London between late 1985 and mid-1988, Freddie never initiated it. He did write in his notebooks in mid-1988 that he was happy to see her. But how come there is nothing about her between the end of 1985 and mid-1988 if, as she suggested, they continued to meet on a regular basis? When he put an end to his wild lifestyle, he also ceased contact with Barbara. They did come to forge a friendship later, but he ended it during the last year of his life. Having said that, I have never doubted the relationship they once shared.'

She did harbour some resentment towards Barbara, B. confesses: 'Because, had she adopted the same attitude as Mary, and had she tried to keep Freddie's feet on the ground rather than taking him deeper, he might have avoided or at least limited his HIV over-exposure and hyper-infection, so his immune system might have resisted the virus for significantly longer. Instead, she was his willing and enthusiastic partner in depravity and decadence. I don't doubt that she really loved him, nor that he loved her in his way. But that was not what Barbara wanted. She probably never understood, still less accepted, the life Freddie and Mary shared together. But it is absolutely true that Barbara was much more to Freddie than a mere interpreter between him and Winnie. No one should ever dismiss her as that. She and Freddie shared so much more. I think she did try to take advantage of him. She may have sold some stories to the press: about Freddie Mercury, not Freddie Bulsara. She was well aware that she had screwed up her relationships with her own children. We know Freddie was reproachful about her maternal attitude and choices. I believe this is the reason why she never revealed what she knew about me. In this, she is more loyal to Freddie than her detractors would have us believe.'

Barbara discovered that Freddie was a father quite by accident: 'I was with him in Munich for a brief stay, following which I had to return to school,' remembers B. 'My nanny, Maria, was taking me. Maybe less than ten minutes after I'd left the house, I realised that I'd left a school book behind at his place. We turned around to go back and get it. We couldn't let him know that we were on the way back as there were no mobile phones in those days. But Barbara had arrived, meanwhile, earlier than Freddie was expecting her. When Joe opened the door, I went running in, saying that I had forgotten my book. There was nothing Joe could do to prevent it: Barbara and I came face to face.

I remember saying, very solemnly, "Bonjour, Madame." Barbara and Joe looked at each other. Neither of them uttered a word. Freddie, who was in the next room when I got back, suddenly came out. All three of them glanced at each other. Still nobody said anything, it was as if someone had put the movie on Pause. My nanny, who had brought up the rear, simply explained that we'd had to return to retrieve the book. Barbara guessed immediately who I was: I couldn't be Joe Fannelli's child, nor the nanny's.'

Some people find it impossible, she despairs, to accept that Freddie loved women but had hard sex with men.

'Not that he made life easy for himself. He always felt torn in two. But the most important thing to say here is that both Mary and Barbara accepted that they had to share Freddie with men. Each of them understood that what male lovers were able to give him was something they would never be able to provide. Sadly for both of them, the gay men in his life were never able to accept the women in return. David Minns, Paul Prenter, the New York Daughters, Jim Hutton and all the other ex-lovers, even Peter Freestone, could never understand or accept that what Mary and Barbara gave Freddie, no man could give him in their place. Their rejection of the women he loved hurt Freddie deeply.'

But in the end, what any of them thought didn't matter at all. He would never have given up Mary for Winnie, Barbara, Jim, or anybody else.

'Many people do seem to have wanted to erase Mary and Barbara from Freddie's life. They assign them menial roles: "the beard", "the cover", "the interpreter". For what reason? Freddie never hid the fact that he had sex with men,' B. reminds us. 'So he was partial to one-night stands. Those encounters were never about love, only sex. Nor did he ever hide his love for Mary. He managed to maintain both until 1989. Only love lasted until the bitter end. The rest was offloaded. To be clear, those who seek to label Freddie as "gay" or "straight" are denying half his true feelings, emotions and needs. How he would have hated this. Above all, and it's important that I say it, he would have loathed more than everything else having been cast as a global gay icon.'

. . .

Freddie's bond with Mary continued to grow meanwhile, 'and it was for them alone', B. affirms. 'Freddie never lived the life he shared with Mary with any other lover. Not with Barbara, not with Jim, and certainly not with any of his "friends" or other male partners. You can dismiss everything you have ever read in which others discuss their relationship. As if they could possibly know! They knew nothing. They were not involved. Mary was the only one in his heart. There wasn't room there for any other lover.'

. . .

Freddie's friend Elton John collected works by the artist Henry Scott Tuke, a late-nineteenth-century/early-twentieth-century Cornish artist who painted boats and naked boys. Freddie acquired a Scott Tuke for Elton, and had it delivered to him by a mutual friend after he died.

'But Freddie himself didn't collect paintings of boys and young men,' B. informs us. 'The only paintings of men in his possession were of himself, with his cats. The subjects of paintings, sculptures and other *objets* that he owned were always women, never men – except for his collection of drawings representing mythological gods. Men are represented rarely in the works of art that he acquired. He had no taste for that kind of art. And in his own art, he invariably drew or painted women. With the exception, that is, of Jimi Hendrix.'

Another telling revelation is that Freddie never needed drugs or alcohol to aid him in his personal relationship with Mary, whereas he needed to consume both in vast quantities in order to be able to indulge in sex with men.

'So is Freddie a homosexual man who also made love with women, or is he a straight man who also had sex with men?' asks B. 'Does it really matter? Might we not ask of ourselves instead, which is more important: love, loyalty, trust, emotion and tenderness, or hard sex and lust? Isn't a relationship that brims with sensuality and affection but no longer penetrative sex still a fulfilled and happy relationship? Aren't the majority of straight, middle-aged marriages just like this? By the same token, can a sexual relationship that includes penetrative sex but that lacks love, emotion and tenderness be a truly fulfilled relationship? I must say, yet again, that Freddie always regarded himself as bisexual. Love, tenderness, affection and emotion were much more important to him than lust.'

There were others of Freddie's acquaintance who found themselves in similar predicaments. Yves Mourousi, for example, a French journalist and news anchor with a reputation for a raunchy nightlife. Freddie often accompanied him to Le Marais, Pigalle and similar places when in Paris. Mourousi lived a gay lifestyle until 1985, when he fell in love with and married a woman. A few days before their wedding, he was humiliated publicly by two of his closest friends, who staged a mockery of a wedding. It was unacceptable at that time that a gay man should suddenly become straight. Society was outraged. The Mourousis were subsequently blessed with a daughter. But then, tragically, his wife contracted meningitis and died in 1992. Yves himself died six years later, at the age of only fifty-five. Their little girl was orphaned. Then there was Patrick Dupond, a danseur étoile (principal ballet dancer) whom Freddie had seen on stage in Paris. Dupond succeeded Rudolf Nureyev as dance director at the Paris Opera Ballet. Openly gay, he committed to a relationship with sacred oriental dancer Leïla Da Rocha in 2004. In 2017, he declared that his previous homosexual lifestyle had been both a mistake and a parody of love. Although he took care to explain that he was speaking only for himself, he was castigated and ridiculed. Again, it was deemed unacceptable that a gay man could become straight. Dupond died in 2021. While we are on the subject, dare I mention David Bowie? Not sure if he was a boy or a girl, he enjoyed many affairs with men but married two women, Angela Barnett and Iman Mohamed Abdulmajid, and fathered a son and a daughter.

'Why does gay communitarianism treat such individuals as gay men who betrayed the cause?' wonders Freddie's daughter. 'They had loved or slept with men for a while, and they had loved or slept with women for a while, during the course of their life. So were they gay, straight or bisexual? And did it matter? As far as Freddie was concerned, and regardless of what anybody else has to say about it, Freddie was bisexual and Mary was the love of his life. It is a sad fact that so much of what various people have had to say on this subject has kindled huge and unacceptable animosity towards Mary. They seem never to have taken Mary's or Freddie's feelings into consideration.'

Why, in the many books, blogs, interviews, documentaries and videos, B. also asks, do they persist in erasing Mary from Freddie's history? Why is it deemed necessary to portray her in a subservient role?

'In much of the output,' she says, 'Mary seems practically non-existent, despite the fact that she was Freddie's permanent partner for the last twenty-two years of his life. In other words, for as good as *half* of his life. Could it be that some people deeply resent her? Did Peter, Jim and others feel animosity towards her because, whenever they wanted to take a day off or go on holiday, it was to *Mary*, not Freddie, that they had to go to ask permission?'

She has pondered the question over and over, B. says, and she arrives at this:

'Freddie's love for Mary and Barbara doesn't fit with the gay image that others have sought to imprint on Freddie. So the only solution is to erase them completely.'

But nothing could break the bond between Freddie and Mary, nor between Freddie and Joe. 'Joe, we know, had always had a special place among Freddie's former lovers,' reaffirms B. 'He was a genuine partner who loved Freddie and accepted Mary's position. Joe and Freddie went on to build a strong relationship. Joe had broken Freddie's heart when he left him, but he never walked out of Freddie's life for good. Apart from a brief absence, Joe stayed with Freddie. He satisfied Freddie's demands and expectations, accepted his terms and decisions, and was content to live to his timetable.

'Peter states that he had heard about Joe Fannelli in 1979 during the *Crazy* tour and met him for the first time in 1983 for Freddie's birthday – which marked the rapprochement between Freddie and Joe. He said that the next time he saw Joe was in 1985. He must have forgotten that Joe was at Freddie's side in Japan, Argentina and Brazil in 1981, and also on several occasions during 1982. Peter later said that he was always there with Freddie, quite often in the same room, at worst in the next room. But that wasn't Peter. It was *Joe* who was the only one, other than Mary, who could calm Freddie during his panic attacks when they struck, allay his fears, and reassure him.

'Freddie had several such attacks, some more violent than others. He recounted a number of them in his notebooks, and sometimes the reasons why they had happened. During the period when his attacks were at their most intense, Joe Fannelli was with him as Freddie's main personal assistant. Joe knew exactly how to react and what to do during these episodes.'

Peter lost Freddie's trust in 1984, B. reminds us. Peter himself has acknowledged and discussed this.

'It was Joe and Terry Giddings, his driver, who accompanied and attended Freddie from then on. Peter did return to his post in a partial capacity while Freddie was working with Montserrat Caballé, because he had worked in the opera world and knew the ropes well. When the renovation work at the Mews was complete, he relocated from Garden Lodge to live there instead. When the time came, only Joe and Jim were made aware of Freddie's condition. Joe continued to live at Garden Lodge. It was he who took charge of screening all calls to the house.'

Freddie's diaries make clear that he never talked to his employees or casual friends about his childhood, background, religion or inner feelings; his relationships with women, his love life, his domestic partnership with Mary; his inner thoughts and desires, or his opinions about international news or politics.

'He confined conversation on such matters to his real, closest friends,' says B. 'Those whose loyalty speaks for itself, more than thirty years later. Those who have never talked or written about him, and who have never betrayed his trust.'

. . .

Freddie continued to collect men as though his life depended on it.

'He acted with increasing disrespect for himself and stopped being honest with himself,' B. tells us. 'He pushed the boundaries, beyond the limits. He was the puppet master, choosing the miserable, the uneducated and the penniless over men who were his social equals. He needed to be dominated in his sexual life. He allowed himself to be abused by his sexual partners, and he deliberately stirred up their jealousy. All that sex devoid of love and emotion, playing one lover off against another, took its toll in the end. Freddie collapsed mentally, and his empty existence was filled with evil. The victim of his own contradictions, he continued to convince himself that he was having a good time. He wound up entangled and trapped in a very dark place, in which most of his acquaintances were betraying him.'

As Freddie said, he had only himself to blame. It was he who had created the Monster that he could no longer control.

'And when he woke up in the mornings,' recounts B., 'he wished to God that he was no longer Freddie Mercury. Because that Freddie, the outrageous Freddie, was burning away his life. He had gained the upper hand over Freddie Bulsara, the quiet, gentle man who adored and felt totally secure in his domestic life with his Mary; the lover of art, classical music, opera and ballet; the talented musician, composer and songwriter. My father wrote that at last he began to grow conscious of the Monster's hold on his life, of his own downfall, and of his deep and desperate misery. He said that from the writing of the *Mr Bad Guy* album and his songs for Queen's *The Works* album onwards, his music and lyrics began to become deeper.'

The Works, released on 27 February 1984, features Freddie's deeply introspective songs 'It's a Hard Life', 'Man on the Prowl', 'Keep Passing the Open Windows' and 'Is This the World We Created', written with Brian May. His composition 'Love Kills', written with Giorgio Moroder, was recorded for *The Works* but failed to make the final cut. It was reworked as a Freddie solo and later appeared on the *Metropolis* soundtrack. Released as a single, it was included on Queen's 2014 album *Queen Forever*. 'Man Made Paradise' was also re-recorded as a Mercury solo track, and released in 1985 on *Mr Bad Guy*. 'There Must be More to Life Than This' was recorded originally by Queen for *Hot Space* in 1981. They were going to conclude *The Works* with it, but then Freddie and Brian May came up with 'Is This the World We Created', which elbowed it out. Freddie re-recorded it with Michael Jackson in 1983. Freddie later recorded it again for his solo album *Mr Bad Guy*. The re-worked Queen version with the Freddie and Jacko duet appeared on *Queen Forever*.

Slowly but surely, B. reflects, 'Freddie Bulsara began to regain the upper hand over Freddie Mercury.'

His tragedy was that the reversal came too late.

• • •

Privacy was everything to Freddie – as proven by the fact that he was able to father a child, play an active part in her upbringing, travel with her – although rarely on the same plane – and develop an intense, mutually fulfilling relationship with her while pretending to be a footloose and fancy-free millionaire rock star who belonged to no one and had zero responsibilities except to himself. For almost fifteen years, throughout Queen's global reign, the world's media never knew that his daughter existed. So close to his chest did he keep her that not even members of his own household knew anything about her. Only those who needed to know, those whom he trusted with his own life, ever knew the first thing. Had someone told them, the chances are that they would never have believed it. It all seems extraordinary and far-fetched now. But reader, it happened.

'Freddie kept his private life especially private,' B. reflects. 'Because of that, the more he played the Monster or the Great Pretender, the more the press were drawn to his "monstrous" stage persona. They confused it with the real him. The two became indivisible. They seemed driven to try to expose him as a homosexual, despite the fact that homosexuality was no longer illegal in Britain, so why the big deal? What was so shocking and shameful about it anyway? The harder they tried, the more he withdrew to protect his personal life. This was not primarily for his own sake, but for the sake of those whose privacy he was striving to protect – especially mine. That's why the Monster and the Great Pretender became so invaluable to him. Those constructs helped him to divert press attention away from the real Freddie. In his notebooks, where he is completely alone with himself, he lays himself bare. He recorded on those pages his own naked truth. The journals were his outlet. They enabled him to sidestep sensitive and highly personal issues in prying interviews.'

Getting stuff out of his crammed head and onto the page was Freddie's essential therapy.

'When he talked in interviews about his real self and his privacy, did you really think that he was talking about his gay side? I sincerely hope not!' she says. 'Because several journalists and one or two broadcasters did know that side of him. They knew about his nightlife and his male partners. Some of those journalists indulged in the very same nightlife! They frequented the same gay bars and clubs. Whenever they saw Freddie out and about with Mary on his arm, many assumed her to be no more than his beard companion. They treated her as such and were dismissive of her. But as I have said, over and over, that was never the case. If only they had listened and looked for the clues. Freddie spoke often in interviews about his feelings towards Mary. He also talked about his male partners, and even about his sex life.'

Freddie made public statements such as the following:

'I've had a lot of lovers, of course. Both male and female. I've tried relationships on either side.' [August 1984 interview with David Wigg, published in the *Daily Express* that September, and part of a 1987 interview with the same writer].

'I couldn't fall in love with a man the way I could with a girl.' [April 1985 interview with Sharon Feinstein for the *News of the World*].

'I have maybe a wider sexual taste than most people, but that's as far as I'm going to go.' 'Everybody wants a loving relationship, and at the same time go out and have fun. We want it both ways. I live life to the full. My sex drive is enormous. I sleep with men, women, cats, you name it. I'll go to bed with anything! My bed is so huge, it can comfortably sleep six. I prefer my sex without any involvement, and there were times when I was extremely promiscuous. I used to be just an old slag who got up every morning, scratched his head, and wondered who he wanted to fuck today. I just lived for sex.' [Excerpts published in *Freddie Mercury: A Life in His Own Words*, the compilation of quotations by Greg Brooks and Simon Lupton, 2006].

'People always ask me about sexuality and all those things, right from the early days, but I couldn't fall in love with a man the same way as I am with Mary. All my lovers ask me why they couldn't replace Mary, but it's simply impossible.' [Sharon Feinstein, *News of the World Sunday* magazine supplement, April 1985].

About Mary, Freddie said this to Nina Myskow for the Sun newspaper in November 1979: 'I know a lot of people find it hard to understand our relationship. Other people who come into our lives just have to accept it. That's something nobody can take away from us. It's unreachable.' To David Wigg in August 1984, he said: Mary is my common-law wife. To me, it's a marriage. What is marriage anyway, something that you sign? As far as we were concerned, we were married, and we carry on now like we are. Marriage is a term of other people. It's where the heart is that matters. We're happy with each other, and it doesn't matter what other people think. We believe in each other, and that's enough for me. Nobody should tell us what to do. As far as I'm concerned, we are married. It's a God-given situation.' [Brooks and Lupton, 2006].

He also said this, as reported by Nina Myskow in the *Sun* in November 1979, and by Rick Sky in the *Daily Star* the same month the following year:

'I am as fond of her now as I have ever been. I'll love her until I draw my last breath. We'll probably grow old together.'

CHAPTER 8

DILEMMA

It has been written and said that Freddie often suffered 'seizures'. This was not true. Many men with full-blown AIDS died of seizures in those days: it was one of the primary causes of death among them, after pneumonia. 'But Freddie experienced panic attacks, not seizures,' explains B. 'His panic attacks, exacerbated by alcohol and cocaine, had plagued him for years.

'He first experienced them when he was a teenager. He learned to control them quite easily most of the time. But whenever he was having difficulties dealing with certain situations, and when at the same time his emotional state was running high, causing him to overindulge in alcohol and cocaine, he was not able to control them. He was especially prone to panic attacks between late 1984 and the first half of 1985. Joe Fannelli was one of the only two people – the other was Mary – who were able to calm him down.

'This was a major turning point in his life,' she reflects. 'The Monster continued to crack. His life in Munich with Winnie and Barbara was destroying him. He wanted Winnie to come and live with him in London. But Winnie's business was in Munich, and he couldn't just up and leave. Besides, he didn't feel comfortable in London. By then, despite having so many people in his life, Freddie felt desperately alone. He had everything a man could want, but feared life was slipping through his fingers. He wore his usual brave face, but inside he was screaming. The endless nights spent trawling Munich's clubs, drinking himself legless, taking too many drugs and indulging in too much madness, then plunging into bed with whoever happened to be around to play sordid games with, had long lost their attraction. He had also lost interest in sex. When he realised that he was just going through the motions and that none of it thrilled him anymore, he knew he had to change.'

On the professional front, rumours had begun to circulate that Queen had called it a day.

'It's certainly true', says B., 'that their *The Works* tour was torture for Freddie, and that in some ways it nearly destroyed him. But Freddie was unequivocal: the band was and always had been his main framework. Roger, John, Brian and Freddie were a family. But they were not only a unique partnership, they were four strong individuals with clashing egos who some-times needed to escape. The only time Freddie truly feared that the band might collapse was in 1985. He was terribly anxious about it. He knew how impossible he could be. He would not have blamed any of them for walking out on him. And if John, Roger or Brian decided to quit, Queen would be no more. Freddie firmly believed that they couldn't exist as a band with-out all four original members. He made his feelings known. Had any of the others left, he would never have carried on as Queen without them.'

Had Freddie lived longer, she says, things would have changed as the years went on.

'He would not have undertaken another major tour. Tours going forward would have been limited to just a handful of dates. Queen would most likely have become primarily a studio band. But I can assure you that Freddie would never have left the others. He needed them more than they ever knew.'

. . .

Freddie's only solo album, *Mr Bad Guy*, produced by Reinhold Mack using local session musicians in Munich, was released in 1985. Compared to his success with Queen, it was not a smash hit. It did well enough, however, making it to number six on the British album chart.

'His music and lyrics on this album are deeper,' B. flags up, 'because at the time of writing and recording, he was doing battle with the Monster. His intention had been to call it *Made in Heaven*, the title of one of its tracks. But for commercial reasons, he did not get his way. After his death, Queen decided to call their final album *Made in Heaven*. For that, they reworked the tracks "Made in Heaven" and "I Was Born to Love You" from his solo album. This was odd, as Freddie had insisted he didn't want his solo album to sound like a Queen album. That had been the point of making it. He actually thanks them in the *Mr Bad Guy* sleeve notes for not having interfered with his creative process on this album. But then Brian, Roger and John appropriated the core elements of Freddie's solo album to make a new Queen album. If we take only the first ten songs from *Made in Heaven* – because track eleven, "It's a Beautiful Day", is a repeat of the first track; track number twelve, "Yeah", is not a song; and track thirteen, untitled, is an experiment – we find that Freddie wrote seven of the ten songs. In other words, seventy per cent of that Queen album.'

. . .

Paul Prenter – toxic, ruthless and menacing with his tiger smile – was at this point still in the frame, still orchestrating Freddie's lifestyle and needs. During the latter half of 1984, Freddie's existence had become so sordid that he could hardly bear to look at himself in the mirror. When word reached him, that autumn, that former lover Tony Bastin had been diagnosed with full-blown AIDS, he momentarily became more mercurial than ever. 'I was extremely promiscuous,' he told David Wigg in March 1985, during an interview at a CBS conference in Munich. 'It was excess in every direction.' But he was looking back on a time of his life that had ended. By then, Freddie had changed his lifestyle dramatically. His locking of the stable door, however, proved futile. The nag had bolted. By the following year, both Bastin and another of Freddie's lovers, airline steward John Murphy, were dead. Freddie saw the writing on the wall.

Prenter was ousted from his quasi-managerial role in spring 1985. The pair remained friends for a while after that, until the end of 1986, when Freddie cut him out of his life. It was on 4 May 1987 that the first of Prenter's series of articles under the banner headline 'All the Queen's Men' appeared in the *Sun* newspaper, exposing Freddie's booze-and-drug-fuelled gay lifestyle and revealing, with photographs, the identity of several of his male lovers.

. . .

Jim Hutton's November 1994 memoir *Mercury and Me*, and the many interviews he gave after Freddie's death, exaggerated their relationship beyond satire. Jim acknowledged this in part to me when I spoke to him for my own books about Freddie. He placed the blame squarely on his ghostwriter, the respected journalist Tim Wapshott. There is no suggestion that Wapshott invented anything.

In 1996, nine years after we had last seen each other, Jim welcomed me to the home that Freddie's money had built in Bennekerry, County Carlow, Ireland. He gave me his undivided attention, cooked meals for me and put me up. Hanging out with him was pleasant. He confessed that some of the content of his best-selling memoir had been at best an exaggeration, at worst 'reimagined': in other words, untrue. His excruciating account of the sequence of events on Freddie's final day, for example, which was later echoed in Peter Freestone's 1998 memoir, was a largely fanciful recollection in which creative licence played a robust part.

As he told me, and as I reported in *Love of My Life*, 'I wasn't there. The fact is, I wanted to be there. Maybe I felt I needed to validate myself, my importance in Freddie's life, by being with him at the exact moment he crossed over. Because I wasn't far away. I was in the house, but not in the room. It seemed symbolic and was perhaps another example of me needing him more than him needing me. Maybe I did force my needs onto him. The wedding rings and so on, the calling each other "husband", all the "I love yous". Freddie was the first to say it, if you want to know, and of course I leapt at that and grabbed it, because it was all I wanted. To be his one and only, you know. It took me a long time to work out that whenever Freddie said, "I love you," he wasn't telling you, he was *asking* you. He was needy of love and affection for himself, not expressing to me that I meant the world to him and that he couldn't imagine his life without me.

'I did behave like a spoiled eejit sometimes, I don't mind telling you. Because I think I had worked out deep down that what we were was a bit of an act, as far as Freddie was concerned.'

If Freddie told his lover negative things about his father, B. muses, Jim must have misinterpreted Freddie's meaning.

'Jim's statements on the subject are pure imagination,' she states. 'Freddie probably said to Jim that he had rebelled a lot, and that he had asked himself many questions. But in 1986, when he and Jim were together, Freddie was by then a quiet man. He also had a very good, well-restored and peaceful relationship with his dad. They talked a great deal, about everything.'

Freddie wrote bluntly about Jim in his diaries. Hutton was, said Freddie, no more than a sexual partner, kept on hand as little more than a personal rent boy. Male concubines – *concubinus* – had been legally and socially recognised during the Roman Empire. Well read on the subject, Freddie saw this sexual-convenience arrangement as the perfect solution to his new predicament. Jim was retained to meet the physical needs of his master at a time when Freddie could no longer gad about. Hooking up with multiple partners was no longer possible because AIDS had become a death sentence. The regrettable aspect of this scenario is that Jim's status was never spelled out to him. Freddie had Jim categorised and compartmentalised as to what he was 'for'. He must have known that Jim would find such a set-up unacceptable and that, had he been enlightened, he would probably have made himself scarce. His presence in

Freddie's household was entirely for Freddie's benefit, not Jim's. Freddie toyed with him, was dismissive of him, and even treated him with contempt. It is yet another unfortunate aspect of stardom, that the star is central to all proceedings and considerations, and that his acolytes must dance to his tune. The central figure is able to justify such a situation with the argument that such people receive a salary, are given a roof over their heads and are privileged to be part of a superstar's all-expenses-paid life.

'But was Jim really honest with Freddie?' B. wonders. 'Jim actually rejected Freddie the first time they met. He didn't know who Freddie was. Hutton said Freddie followed him and tried for several months to find out where he was. But when Jim found out that the man coming on to him was the great Freddie Mercury, it was he who changed his habits and the bars and clubs that he frequented – not Freddie. The next time they met, Jim accepted a drink from Freddie, and later on a date. To begin with, Freddie used Jim to make Winnie Kirchberger jealous. Some of Jim's friends had been close to people Freddie knew before Freddie and Jim met each other.'

Even though they were now officially an item, there were clear signs that Freddie's relationship with Jim was disingenuous. After *Live Aid* in July 1985, for example – Jim's first-ever experience of a rock gig – Freddie went on holiday to Ibiza with Winnie Kirchberger and Barbara Valentin. Jim was not invited.

'And when Freddie gave Winnie the ring,' says B., 'he provoked Jim's jealousy. Because by this time, Jim was living at Garden Lodge alongside Peter Freestone, who was looking after the place and overseeing the last of the renovations and the decorating. Throughout this period, Freddie was living between Phillimore Gardens with Mary, at Stafford Terrace, and in Munich with Winnie and Barbara.'

At the beginning of his involvement with Freddie, Jim behaved nicely. He demonstrated no animosity towards Mary. Freddie and Jim began their sexual relationship in mid-1985, while Freddie was still involved with Winnie. Not until that affair ended in spring 1986 – when, during the final days of rehearsals for Queen's *Magic* tour, Freddie removed Winnie's ring – did the relationship between Jim and Freddie truly begin.

'When Jim wanted to surprise Freddie in Paris during the *Magic* tour, and turned up without letting him know that he was coming,' says B., 'he unwittingly provoked Freddie's enormous rage.'

It wasn't for Jim to call the shots. He wasn't in charge. How dare he! The way Freddie saw it, only *he* was allowed to make such decisions and perform such grand gestures. He was utterly furious with Jim for having taken matters into his own hands. His anger over this would not subside for months.

After the *Magic* tour concluded in August 1986, Freddie moved permanently into Garden Lodge. But he continued to avail himself of his 'shag pad', taking male partners back to Stafford Terrace for the night. He knew, however, that his days of zipless sex were all but over. At that point, Jim came into his own. But he misinterpreted the development. Who could blame him for thinking that Freddie had stopped sleeping around because he had fallen for him? In Jim's mind, he was now Freddie's exclusive choice. Because of that, his attitude towards and treatment of Mary began to change.

'Freddie writes that he was also trying to rekindle a relationship with David Minns at that time,' reveals B.

Given their past history, Minns would surely have been his preference as a regular partner.

'Jim then gave Freddie the fortieth-birthday ring. As we know, Freddie did not return the compliment. Worse, Jim had to fight Freddie to prevent him from taking the ring off,' she says. 'Shortly afterwards, they took their "million-pound" trip of a lifetime to Japan, which Jim later described as their "honeymoon". But to Freddie, it was no such thing. As far as he was concerned, it was no more than a shopping trip and a holiday in a country that he loved.'

It was on 4 January 1987, Jim's thirty-eighth birthday, that Freddie gifted him the infamous solid gold Cartier bracelet and Jim, deeply offended, seized Freddie's cheque and flounced off alone to Cartier to buy himself a ring. This marked the cooling-off and decline of their relationship, which ended altogether in 1989. Although Jim remained at Garden Lodge until Freddie died, it was over between them.

'Back in the early days, Freddie had been glad to see that Jim wanted to keep his financial independence, to the point of paying a token rent at Garden Lodge,' reflects B. '"Finally," Freddie thought, "a man who is not in it only for the gifts." But when Jim refused that lovely bracelet because all he wanted was a ring, Freddie realised that Jim was no better than all the others. He was in love with Freddie's money, fame and stardom, not with the real him. From then on, Freddie refused to let Jim continue to pay rent, not only to maintain control over him but so that he owed him nothing.'

Some months later, Jim quit his regular job as a barber at the Savoy. It was Freddie who decided that the 'arrangement' was

impractical. He convinced Jim that he would be better off working for him as his gardener.

'His job,' says B., 'was to rake and collect dead leaves, mow
the lawn and pull up the weeds. He worked six days a week from
9 a.m. until 6 p.m. Freddie would lose his temper if the work
was not done properly and the garden wasn't immaculately maintained. He hated it when it appeared that his employees were
being paid to do nothing. He always found some other work for
Jim to do whenever the garden needed less attention.'

At that time, Freddie records, Jim was pleasant and civil
in Mary's company. Freddie was content. This was the reason
behind his statement to David Wigg in Ibiza during the summer
of 1987: 'I'm very happy with my relationship at the moment,
and I honestly couldn't ask for better. There is this kind of solace
that I've got now. I don't have to try so hard. I don't have to
prove myself now. I've got a very understanding relationship.
I've finally found that niche that I was looking for all my life.'

'Freddie wasn't just talking about his relationship with Jim,'
B. points out. 'At long last, he had the best of both worlds: on
the one hand the unconditional, everlasting and mutual love that
he shared with Mary, and on the other a man to service his sex
drive who accepted his love for and domestic partnership with
a woman; a man for his physical needs who knew he was only
there for sex, and who was agreeable to the idea of avoiding the
limelight and keeping his distance from the cameras.'

A simple 'friends with benefits' arrangement, then. But
things are rarely that simple. One partner or the other will soon
throw their toys out of the pram and start demanding more in
the way of commitment.

'The relationship soon disintegrated into the usual endless round of arguments, rows, fights, infidelities, jealousy, violence and abuse,' reveals B. 'In 1989, Freddie ended it and asked Jim to leave. But Jim knew all about Freddie's health condition. What was to stop him going to the papers? So he changed his mind. Otherwise, he thought, Jim would be the next to betray him. Sadly, he was not wrong! Jim moved into a small bedroom at Garden Lodge, not the larger guest suite that he claimed to have taken. And there, until the end, he remained.'

• • •

It had long been Freddie's habit, at formal dinner parties, to have Mary Austin seated beside him on his left-hand side, and his current male partner on his right:

'But from 1989 and the end of the relationship between Freddie and Jim,' says B., 'you will notice in photographs that Mary was always on his right, while Jim sat further away. For Freddie's forty-fourth birthday in 1990, Jim found himself lost between Queen manager Jim Beach, aka 'Miami', and Gordon Atkinson, Freddie's loyal doctor since the mid-1970s. Those two sat deep in conversation and Jim Hutton was left out on a limb.'

Freddie wrote unequivocally that his relationship with Jim was simply a masquerade that he had conjured himself.

'Once hurt, as he was by Jim in January 1987,' B. reveals, 'Freddie was never again tender with him, just as he had never again been tender with any of his previous male lovers after they had hurt and betrayed him. The exception is Joe, because Joe never hurt Freddie by being unfaithful, disingenuous or greedy.

'Maybe Jim did love Freddie and wanted to be important to him, as he said and wrote in his book. But the truth was that Jim was no more than a puppet in Freddie's hands.'

Over time, she says, 'it occurred to Jim what was really going on at Garden Lodge. The realisation upset him dreadfully. He couldn't accept that Freddie loved only Mary. He then made a fatal mistake, by nurturing resentment and animosity towards her. This pained and angered Freddie. Jim would have been better off accepting that Freddie didn't love him the way he wanted him to and never would. He should have just enjoyed the status quo for its own sake.'

Was it Freddie who infected Jim with HIV? Freddie didn't think so, but he didn't draw any conclusion on this. Several of Jim's ex-lovers had either died of AIDS, developed full-blown AIDS or had tested HIV positive ahead of Freddie's own diagnosis.

'We never spoke about this,' says B. 'And by the time he was made aware that Jim was HIV positive, my father had already given me the notebooks. After Freddie's death, some people accused him of having spread HIV and called him a criminal. Some are still saying this even today. Of course he took risks. Of course he was extremely promiscuous. But that was all at a time when the world knew nothing about any new disease. When details emerged, conflicting theories raged. In the autumn of 1984, when Freddie learned that Tony Bastin had developed full-blown AIDS, he started to change his behaviour. By the time he started seeing Jim – after the first Rock in Rio festival in Brazil in January 1985, which was one wild time too many – he had ceased being promiscuous. He then limited himself to safe sex with the same partners in Munich and London. Once Freddie knew he was HIV positive, he and Jim stopped having penetrative sex altogether. But Jim carried on having numerous sexual relationships on the side. Considering that, in 1987, there was a new type of treatment and therefore new hope, it's strange that Jim didn't do a test that year. Or perhaps he did, and the test was negative. He did later take one, as he'd had numerous one-night stands after he ceased intercourse with Freddie. The test was positive. Jim survived Freddie by eighteen years, and never developed full-blown AIDS. So it's highly likely that Jim became infected during one of his post-Freddie one-night stands.'

· · ·

After the Monster cracked, the *Live Aid* extravaganza changed things.

'It at least gave Queen another chance not to disband. But things between them remained uneasy. Most of the time, they worked in pairs in two different studios: usually Freddie and John in Munich, while Brian and Roger worked in Montreux. Because of personal issues, the *Magic* tour was not the long, quiet river that some people seem to think it was. At the end of that tour, the decision was made to take some time out. Freddie seized the opportunity to work on his second solo album.'

CHAPTER 9

FOOD OF LOVE

One of the first songs Freddie wrote soon after arriving in England in 1964 was 'Green'. Its lyrics reflected his new-found freedom. He would adapt and complete this song with his early group Ibex, who later evolved into Wreckage. A home recording of a 1969 rehearsal of it in his flat can be found on YouTube. The recording was also included on the *Freddie Mercury Collection* box set released in 2000. 'The idea that "there's nothing you can do to stop me", "don't stop me now"/ "no one's gonna stop me now, it's hopeless to even try" is already there on "Green",' B. points out. 'It will be there ten years later in "Don't Stop Me Now" on Queen's 1978 album *Jazz* [released as a single in January 1979] and yet again in "It's a Beautiful Day"' – which was written by Freddie in 1980 and released in 1995 after his death, on the album *Made in Heaven*.

According to Brian May, 'There was a feeling that ["Don't Stop Me Now"] lyrically represented something that was happening to Freddie which we kind of thought was threatening. We were worried about Freddie at this point.'

'I didn't really take to it in the beginning,' Brian further reflected to *Guitar Player* magazine and the *Daily Express* in April 2021. 'I didn't feel totally comfortable with what Freddie was singing at the time. I found it a little bit too flippant in view of the dangers of AIDS and stuff.'

'Did Brian know about AIDS as early as 1978, long before HIV had been identified by scientists?' asks Freddie's daughter.

Apart from that, she struggles to make sense of these misgivings: 'It's like those who say that Freddie knew he was going to die because he alluded to not wanting to die and wishing he'd never been born on "Bohemian Rhapsody",' she reasons. 'Freddie wrote "Don't Stop Me Now" during the first half of 1978. He was enjoying a peaceful and loving relationship with his American boyfriend Joe Fannelli at the time. After two tumultuous years [1976–1977] with David Minns, he had kicked the latter out of his life. During the autumn of 1977, when of course he was already a father, he opened up to his fiancée Mary Austin about the lifestyle he'd been experimenting with in New York. He and Mary subsequently redefined their relationship. He met Joe at the end of 1977, and Joe followed him to Europe. Even though Freddie was into the New York gay scene and its nightlife, he was so far removed from his future unrestrained lifestyle with multiple partners and copious drug use that he wasn't yet risking his life. That dangerous phase began in 1980, not 1978. He threw himself into it after his break-up with Joe, and it peaked between 1983 and 1985. So just as "Green" had been, "Don't Stop Me Now" was an ode to freedom, and to the relief he experienced having rid himself of David Minns. He would go on, we know, to discover new horizons in his personal and sexual life. But this was far removed from the reckless lifestyle he would live between 1980 and 1985.'

· · ·

In London, since his arrival in 1964, Freddie had enjoyed a life of freedom not even he could have imagined.

'He suddenly had the Swinging Sixties right on his doorstep, not just at his fingertips in magazines,' says B. 'He was thrilled by the wide variety of people and artists, the many fashions and refreshing attitudes. There were new-found pleasures for the taking, such as live music, bars and girls. Freddie adored women. He enjoyed their company, their presence, their bodies, their perfume, the beguiling ways in which they blended strength with femininity. He loved and wanted females in his life, to touch, to flirt with and to feel comfortable around. The way women made him feel would never leave him.'

Teenage Freddie had started going out to clubs with his friends and immersing himself in live music for the first time ever.

'His creativity overflowed as he stood there watching others perform,' she says. 'He often felt driven, he said, to rush home and write down all the music he had in his head. He would get in late at night and sit and play everything he had listened to earlier. He would then spend the whole night writing and working on his own songs. He would set it all out on paper as a sort of puzzle. It was amazing how organised his disorganisation was, he said; or maybe his organisation was disorganised. Years later, if he couldn't remember a song he'd written the next morning when he woke up, he wrote it off, dismissing it because it couldn't have been good enough ... he wouldn't have forgotten it otherwise. "Bohemian Rhapsody", one of those that he did not dismiss, was another of the first songs he wrote shortly after arriving in England.'

Widely regarded as Britain's 'second national anthem', the song that quickly became Queen's signature arguably knocks

'McArthur Park', 'American Pie' and 'I Am the Walrus' out of the park in terms of likely everlasting obscurity. Its radio-unfriendly length of almost six minutes, impenetrable lyrics, clashing genres and absence of a recurring chorus should have doomed it from the moment of its 1975 release. Against all odds, it transcended time and taste to top the UK charts for nine weeks, conquered rankings around the world, and returned to the British top slot for a further five weeks after Freddie's death in 1991. At the time of writing, it stands as the UK's third-bestselling single of all time behind 'Candle in the Wind'/'Something About the Way You Look Tonight', Elton John's 1997 reworking of his 1974 tribute to screen goddess Marilyn Monroe in homage to the late Diana, Princess of Wales; and 'Do They Know It's Christmas?', the 1984 Band Aid charity fundraiser record that awoke the world to the famine in Ethiopia and led to global jukebox event *Live Aid* the following year.

But what is it about? Fifty years after it first appeared, theories still rage. Freddie resisted his interrogators and never surrendered an explanation, not even to his own bandmates. All he would say about it was that its meaning pertained to relationships. The other members of Queen have long resisted attempts to interpret it, but tend to agree that the lyrics feature disguised references to Freddie's own troubled personal life. 'Freddie was a very complex person: flippant and funny on the surface, but he concealed insecurities and problems in squaring up his life with his childhood,' said Brian May to *Record Collector* magazine in July 1993. 'He never explained the lyrics, but I think he put a lot of himself into that song.' Brian has also said that the members of Queen agreed that the essence of a song's lyrics were a matter for the writer alone. They were happy for Freddie to conceal and protect its meaning. Freddie himself was always vague about it. 'It's one of those songs which has such a fantasy feel about it,' he said. 'I think people should just listen to it, think about it, and then make up their own minds as to what it says to them ... "Bohemian Rhapsody" didn't just come out of thin air. I did a bit of research, although it was tongue-in-cheek and mock opera. Why not?'

Fellow lyricist Sir Tim Rice, a close friend and collaborator of Freddie's – they co-wrote songs for *Barcelona*, Freddie's album with Montserrat Caballé – concurred with his pal that the song is 'about relationships'. He was convinced, Tim told me, that its undercurrent is a confession of homosexuality. 'It's fairly obvious to me that this was Freddie's coming-out song,' he said. 'I've spoken to Roger Taylor about it. There is a very clear message in it. This is Freddie admitting that he is gay. In the line "Mama, I just killed a man," he's killed the old Freddie, his former image. With, "Put a gun against his head, pulled my trigger, now he's dead," *he's* dead: the straight person he was originally. He's destroyed the man he was trying to be, and now this is him, trying to live with the new Freddie. "I see a little silhouetto of a man": that's *him*, still being haunted by what he's done and what he is.'

Every time he heard the song, Tim continued, he thought of him trying to shake off one Freddie in order to embrace another. 'Do I think he managed it? I think he was in the process of managing it, rather well. Freddie was an exceptional lyricist, and "Bohemian Rhapsody" is one of the great pieces of music of the twentieth century.'

Freddie's erstwhile lover Jim told me after Freddie's death that my own theories had been correct. 'Freddie was never going to admit it publicly,' Hutton reasoned, 'because he had to carry on the charade about being straight, for his family. But we discussed it many times. It was Freddie's confessional. It was about how different his life could have been. How much happier he would have felt, had he been able to be himself. The world heard a masterpiece of imagination. It was so intricate, and had so many layers, but its message was simple. "Bohemian Rhapsody" was Freddie as he truly was.'

Freddie's own explanation, however, as revealed in an early volume of his diaries, confounds all other theories and explanations. As he described it, Queen's magnum opus had nothing to do with any kind of coming-out, least of all sexual. Nor did it pertain to the apparent end of his relationship with Mary Austin.

'Freddie and Mary "broke up" during late 1977,' his daughter reminds us, as confirmed by Freddie in his journals. 'Not in 1976, still less in 1975, as is so often quoted. They continued to live together until towards the end of 1978. To be clear, Freddie and Mary pretended to the outside world that they had ended their relationship, so that she would not be embarrassed or ridiculed publicly by Freddie's gay promiscuity. In fact, they had not ended it. They never did, but remained committed and devoted to one another until the end of Freddie's life. "Bohemian Rhapsody" was recorded during the summer of 1975. But Freddie had written it a long time before he got together with the musicians with whom he would form Queen.'

The first elements of the song, she reveals, were written ten years ahead of its recording: 'As I said, it was one of the first songs Freddie wrote when he landed in England. Because he did not have a piano, he wrote it all in his head.'

He completed the song on the Yamaha baby grand that would sell at the 2023 auction at Sotheby's London for £1.7 million, during the mass sale of his possessions by Mary Austin, who had inherited them. The song's handwritten lyrics fetched a further £1.38 million. Jim Hutton would later claim that Freddie had gifted the lyrics to him, and that he was prevented from retrieving them from Garden Lodge. Freddie's daughter disputes this, on the grounds that it would have been contrary to what Freddie believed a gift should be.

'To Freddie, a gift was something that must be thought about and personalised. You must add value by spending time on it with the recipient in mind, or by spending money to acquire it. The lyrics had been written years earlier, and not with Jim in mind. To Freddie, that would not have been a valuable gift to give to Jim. I'm not even sure that Freddie so much as showed Jim the lyrics. This may seem strange to just about everyone on Earth, but to Freddie, writing songs was simply his job, his bread and butter. Once it was done, it was done. A car, a flat, diamonds, gold bars, jewellery, precious fabrics, beautiful works of art: these were the things Freddie gave as gifts. Not sheets of paper on which he had scribbled some songs. No, never. And if by some fluke he *had* gifted those sheets, he would have personalised them in some way: for example, with "To Jim" and his own initials, plus something along the lines of "Lots of love" – to ensure that the person receiving the gift would know that it was for him personally.'

Freddie developed the structure of 'Bohemian Rhapsody' while he was a student at Ealing College: 'He explained that he linked three songs together to create it,' B. says. 'The song is about a young man who had been forced to leave Zanzibar, and who arrived in England with a different skin, accent and look from most of the people he saw around him. His early days in a foreign land were not easy. He was teased, ridiculed and humiliated, and suffered racial attacks. In order to get the better of his tormentors, he toughened up and began to play "the Persian Popinjay". He put on his costume and strutted his stuff in defiance. Slowly but surely, Freddie Bulsara retreated into his shell. Freddie Mercury emerged. That, according to what he wrote about it himself, is the thrust, the true meaning of "Bohemian Rhapsody". "Bohemian" because at that time he was living a bohemian and itinerant life-style. And "Rhapsody" because, in Greek antiquity, a rhapsody was a series of poems featuring a range of highly contrasting moods, and was something that Freddie was fascinated by.'

Ancient Greek rhapsodies or oral epic poems were sung by professional *rhapsōidos* or rhapsodists. *Rhapsōidein* means 'to sew songs together'. These 'stitchers' would interlace standard, memorised passages with their own improvisations, depending on the location of the performance and the type of audience the minstrel was charged with entertaining. This moving from place to place and the customisation of performances with stories, myths and jokes suggest that the art form was a very early type of pantomime – which itself can be traced back to ancient Rome. Rhapsodes are known to have competed for prizes at religious festivals. These travelling minstrels would later be deployed primarily to recite the *Iliad* and *Odyssey* of Homer in their received versions. The six-minute 'patchwork quilt' that is Freddie's 'Bohemian Rhapsody', with its distinct sections –

intro, piano ballad and solo vocal, guitar solo with an improvised flavour, operatic section, hard-rock interlude and balladic outro that reprises the opener – and total lack of chorus, is nothing if not a reflection of the ancient Greek *rhapsōidia*. It is wonderful to know the song's origins at long last, as well as to hear that Freddie's magnum opus was partly inspired by both the artistry and art forms of the Ancients. How intriguing that its rich history was never explained. Then again, who could blame him for having buried the torment and feelings of inadequacy that had led to its composition? For leaving behind the hurt hidden within it, and choosing to rise above?

'Love of My Life', also from 1975's *A Night at the Opera*, says B., began as a distinctly different song. When Freddie first worked on it, he explains in his diaries, he split it into two songs. One retained the melody, while the other consisted more or less of only the lyrics. That melody plus some of the lyrics eventually morphed into 'Love of My Life'. The remainder later became 'You Take My Breath Away' on *A Day at the Races*. He used a Japanese pentatonic scale to write the melody. Years later, that phenomenon would repeat itself with the embryo of a Roger-penned song, 'A Kind of Vision', which a few weeks later divided into 'It's a Kind of Magic' and 'One Vision'.

Contrary to popular opinion, 'Love of My Life' and 'You Take My Breath Away' were not written for Freddie's lover David Minns: 'During the period when Freddie wrote the embryo of the two songs,' affirms B., 'he and David Minns didn't even know each other. Both songs were actually written for Mary, but not in the way people tend to understand them. In both songs, Freddie is expressing how distraught he would feel if ever Mary were to leave him one day. The melody having been written before the lyrics, the tenses and verb conjugations are adapted to the rhythm, melody and phrasing of the song. Songwriters are familiar with this process. Melody and phrasing determine the sound of words. Incidentally, the only song Freddie ever wrote for David Minns was "Don't Try Suicide" on their eighth studio album *The Game*, released in 1980, and the one that features "Crazy Little Thing Called Love" and "Another One Bites the Dust".'

. . .

'I could give you a complete song-by-song study of Freddie's works, but it would take me years to get through them all,' says B. 'As you might imagine, he had so much to say on every single song that he ever wrote. But as an overview, I can tell you that Freddie loved gospel and most religious songs. From a very young age he was fascinated by the polyphonic overtone singing prayers of Zoroastrian celebrations. These influenced him on "Jesus" (*Queen*), "The Golden Boy" (*Barcelona*), and "All God's People" – written in 1987 but recorded much later for *Innuendo*. He admired Aretha Franklin hugely. *Amazing Grace*, her 1972 live album, was, he said, probably his favourite album of all time. "Somebody to Love" was massively influenced by gospel and Aretha.

'Many of his songs are inspired by Zoroastrian and Parsee songs in terms of melodic content, rhythm, phrasing and harmony,' she reveals. 'He said that a lot of his melodies and lyrics had their foundation in the Gathas: the seventeen Avestan hymns said to have been composed by the prophet Zoroaster that are the core of the Yasna, the Zoroastrian liturgy.'

So both Zanzibar and India inspired Freddie's songwriting far more than has ever previously been known.

She singles out 'Love of My Life' from Queen's 1975 album *A Night at the Opera*. Queen spent a month during early summer 1975 rehearsing in a Surrey barn on a farm that would later become Ridge Farm recording studio. They moved on that July, making their way west to a rented house in Kington, Herefordshire, before repairing to Rockfield Studios in Monmouthshire, south-east Wales. It was there, from August into September, that they recorded this track.

'Mustapha', the first track on Queen's 1978 album *Jazz*, was dismissed by Freddie as 'complete gibberish. It isn't any language at all except in a few spots.'

'Yes but …' B. reminds us, 'Freddie spent part of his childhood in Zanzibar, where nearly all the local citizens were Muslim.'

The presence of Islam on the Swahili Coast, which includes parts of Mozambique, Tanzania, Kenya and the Comoro Islands off the south-eastern coast of Africa, can be traced back to 1000 BCE. The oldest archaeological evidence of the religion in the region is the Kizimkazi Mosque in Zanzibar. Its Kufic inscriptions date back to the 1100s. Today, ninety-nine per cent of Zanzibar's population is Muslim.

'Complete gibberish?' muses B. 'Yes, but … he spent eight years in India, a country with more than four hundred native languages and a rich diversity of religious beliefs and practices. The Zoroastrian Gathas are composed in one of the idioms of the Aryan group of Iranian languages. The language of the Gathas, spoken only in a small region of the Persian Empire, slowly faded away with the collapse of the Empire and was forgotten for about two thousand years. During this period, not a phrase of it could be understood. But the Zoroastrian priests learned the Gathas by heart and passed them down as an oral tradition from one generation to the next. Complete gibberish, then? Oh, yes, it was … to *most* people. To Freddie, it made complete sense. The "gibberish" reflects the many sounds of multiple languages in which he was bathed during his childhood in Zanzibar and India.'

The characters Mustapha and Ibrahim who feature prominently in the song and who are referenced repeatedly in the lyrics are none other than Freddie's boyhood best friends. Along with the fourth friend of the group, Ahmed, they were once joined at the hip. The beaches and dusty streets of Zanzibar's Stone Town were their playground. We know that Freddie mourned his enforced separation from the friends he loved, and the abrupt curtailment of his childhood, for the rest of his life.

'Zanzibar symbolised a period of precious innocence to which he longed to return,' B. reminds us. 'It was, Freddie said, such a charmed and beautiful life. Ahmed, Ibrahim, Farrokh and Mustapha had spent all their free time together there. One of the boys had a go-kart, which they played with constantly, taking turns to ride and push. They also rode their bicycles around the streets. If the song "Bicycle Race" was inspired by Le Tour de France – when the stage between Morzine and Lausanne passed by Montreux on 19 July 1978 – and its beautiful hostesses at the start of the race and on the podium, the bells on this track are also a direct nod to his childhood. There had been very few cars in Stone Town in those days. It was the reason why Freddie and his friends were able to ride their bikes so freely through its narrow streets. He remembered that they would ring their bicycle bells all the time, just for the fun of it, in a constant cacophony that was such music to their ears that it sounded like a symphony. The thrill of that noise lingered in his heart. It was to those carefree, magical days that Freddie harked back on "Bicycle Race".'

She calls me out for having stated erroneously that 'Don't Try So Hard', a track on *Innuendo* – Queen's fourteenth studio album and the final one to be released during Freddie's lifetime – was a John Deacon composition.

'The problem with the internet,' she points out, 'is that one person will write something false on a fan website and ten minutes later it has gone around the world. Everybody accepts it as the truth without taking the time and trouble to check the information. They take it on board as "fact" simply because that snippet of misinformation has been repeated and re-posted again and again.

'"Don't Try So Hard", as confirmed during his lifetime by Queen's late engineer and co-producer David Richards, is *Freddie's* song. This changes everything when it comes to understanding what it is about. Freddie wrote it with a particular person in mind. It is for a specific individual who is very dear to his heart. The song is a final message, engraved forever ... I will leave you to guess who it was for.'

He wrote it, she confirms, for none other than his only child.

'By then,' she says, 'he knew that happiness did not derive exclusively from loving and being loved. It is also to be found in life's smallest things, in its tiniest miracles. He had somehow learned to be satisfied with the many little things. Achievement no longer had to be about impressing the world. Just being quiet at home and treasuring one's privacy could also be considered an achievement. "Don't Try So Hard" is Freddie's antithetical response to some of the conditions dictated in Rudyard Kipling's poem "If –".

'A lot of people have said many things about "Under Pressure". I can tell you exactly what Freddie really thought of that song. He described it as the most powerful he had ever written: a pure, heartbreaking love song that he wanted to sing at every single gig, and which they did perform at every gig – except at *Live Aid*. I can also tell you that, despite their momentary discord, my dad was always very fond of David Bowie.'

When Freddie wrote 'Crazy Little Thing Called Love' for Queen's *The Game* album, he completed the whole song in about five minutes.

'Freddie commented that Brian was sometimes filled with doubt when he wrote a song,' reveals B. 'With Freddie, it was the opposite. He was a perfectionist but knew right from the start exactly what he wanted. He always had the whole picture of the song in his head. He could see it. If it didn't come quickly, he would drop the whole thing, because he knew it wasn't good enough. It wouldn't be worth it, not according to his very exacting criteria. From the tiniest idea he could make something really great: sometimes huge pieces such as "The March of the Black Queen", "Bohemian Rhapsody", "Somebody to Love" or "Innuendo", at other times those he called the "crazy little songs", such as "Killer Queen", "In the Lap of the Gods … Revisited", "Delilah" or "Crazy Little Thing …" itself. He thought Brian's problem was that he could have a really good idea but would then go and ruin it, because he rarely had the whole landscape of the song in his head before he started.'

'Somebody to Love' (released in 1976 and on *A Day at the Races*) was written during a very difficult period.

'He met his lover David Minns in early July 1975,' B. reminds us. 'During early 1976, they had sexual intercourse for the first time, and quickly developed a relationship. But there was conflict, because they did not see that relationship in the same way. Minns wanted him to dump Mary, Freddie just wanted to love and be loved, and things got worse when Freddie returned from the road. It was in this context that he spent time with my mother, which led to my conception. He also began writing his notebooks and wrote and recorded "Somebody to Love". The song was in fact a sad echo of Solomon Burke's "Everybody Needs Somebody to Love". It encapsulated Freddie's quest for bisexual love, and the life that he was doomed to search for, as long as he lived.'

When John Deacon started to write 'Another One Bites the Dust', she tells us, 'Freddie said that John wanted to do something totally different from everything Queen had written before. He'd always liked the funk-rock disco sound. Freddie listened to it with enthusiasm, and helped him develop the idea. Roger didn't like it at first, Dad said. Brian was said to have hated it. But Freddie, as usual, decided that he wanted to do it, so they did it and that was that. Huge hit. Their bestselling single.'

Freddie wrote 'It's a Hard Life' from 1984's *The Works* about American lover 'Vince the barman', and not about his German restaurateur boyfriend Winnie Kirchberger, as has been claimed.

'He hadn't yet begun his relationship with Munich-based Winnie,' says B. 'He began writing the song towards the end of summer 1983, while he was still in Los Angeles. He loved the video for "It's a Hard Life" because it was an accurate reflection of part of his life at the time, which was a clash of exuberance and sadness. It was by his own definition both a fanciful and sad life. The theatre, the stage and the performance were the brilliant illusion. But the moment the lights went out, he was totally alone.'

Living life to the full, the search for happiness and the universality of love are recurring themes in both Freddie's life and lyrics.

"Who knows what might happen tomorrow?" was his stance,' she says. 'So he decided to do whatever he wanted whenever he wanted. It was another thing he taught me: to do things for myself and not because they were what other people wanted me to do. The notion of freedom was there in his very first songs.'

• • •

Although it is one of the tracks with which his name is synonymous, Freddie did not write 'The Great Pretender'. That song was written and composed by the Platters' manager and producer Buck Ram. The Platters' recording of it was released in 1955. Freddie's cover of it appeared more than thirty years later, in February 1987. His version topped the US chart and scored a number-five hit in the UK. Its memorable video features Freddie walking himself through a series of his own visual incarnations, with drummer Roger Taylor and his actor friend Peter Straker as his sidekicks and backing singers.

'Many people misunderstand his version of "The Great Pretender",' agrees B. 'Of course, the song is about a man who spends his life acting and pretending. But the question to ask in connection with Freddie is, what was *he* referring to when he sang it? What pretence was *he* talking about?

'The Great Pretender of Freddie's interpretation dated back to his school days in India. He was also partly the sad clown in Ruggero Leoncavallo's opera *Pagliacci*, a life-and-soul-of-the-party character who touched him deeply and with whom he identified; and partly this man who was physically drawn to other men. He was a man who needed to be dominated in his sexual life, who even wanted to be in love with a fellow male, but who always found himself very wounded by them, to the point that he was forced to resort to mechanical sex with them that was devoid of sensuality or love. In other words, just going through the motions. He was pretending to be happy that way, while in reality he was anything but. The Great Pretender figure was a clone of the macho gay: the character he had by that time been portraying on stage for several years. And ultimately, of course, the character subsumed the original Freddie, to the point that it became his image: the identity he reserved for the gay clubs, while spending time in the company of certain friends, and also the image that he presented to the media in interviews and during press conferences. This was Freddie's new disguise, behind which he could hide. It fitted him perfectly. You only have to read some of the remarks he made on the subject:

'"All these sort of visuals and these sort of, these images that I've portrayed over the years, is a kind of pretence, because I mean there was no way that I was real on stage."

'"I wore costumes and I sort of put myself into different atmospheres and different characters."

'"I've been pretending all this time, doing all this stuff."

'"It's a kind of pretence, whereas I mean, underneath it I'm still a musician. And so I thought I'd bring it up in that level, where all these sort of costumes, where a lot of people took it so seriously, well I didn't give a damn. I just thought, my God, and they read far too much into it, I just thought that this is a nice way of sort of covering this whole sort of era of mine. It's just been a bit of fun. Actors *portray* somebody, they don't *become* those people. Then they go back and do something else." [Part of an interview given by Freddie to David Wigg in February 1987, excerpts published in the *Daily Express*].'

The Great Pretender, B. explains, is not the man who was deeply, emotionally in love with Mary Austin; the man who depended on the unshakeable love affair they shared. 'Nor is the Great Pretender the man who showed that beloved woman all his scars, his many failings and his weaknesses,' she says. 'He is not the devoted father who spent his at-home days unshaven and in a tracksuit, playing piano or chess or other board games with his little girl; telling her incredible stories, teaching her to fly her kite, listening for hours to all that she had to say and never, ever being bored by her.'

• • •

'Freddie said that "We Are the Champions" from *News of the World* was the most egotistical and arrogant song he had ever written. It's his way of saying that we are all champions in some form or another. The song is about hope over adversity, and about humankind.'

His songs have always been obscure and difficult to understand, his daughter reflects.

'His lyrics are not exactly crystal clear. Many of them could have several meanings, making it hard for fans to work out what inspired them. His only songs that lack double meaning or innuendo are "The Fairy Feller's Master Stroke" and "A Winter's Tale", both of which are purely descriptive. Freddie's songs have hardly ever been interpreted correctly, mainly because he gave very little explanation, only what he felt like giving. There is always a bit of himself and his own feelings. But in many cases a song would be inspired by several things, with a central theme but breaking down into different forms. He used to say that if he had to rewrite any song he had written years earlier, it would come out completely different from how it had been the first time around. But songs also changed for him between the initial writing and the recording of them. They would develop according to his mood, what was going on in his personal life and so on. He would also say that the tracks on an album are not the end of the process, but the birth of something that grows again and again on stage, that changes over time and according to emotions.'

• • •

In his daily life, B. reveals, Freddie was not at all rock 'n' roll.

'When he sat at the piano and played for fun, he didn't play that kind of music. His songs that I like the most, not in terms of lyrics but because of their musical mood, are "Bring Back that Leroy Brown" [on *Sheer Heart Attack*], "Lazing on a Sunday

Afternoon" [*A Night at the Opera*], "Seaside Rendez-Vous" [*A Night at the Opera*], "The Millionaire Waltz" [*A Day at the Races*], "Good Old-Fashioned Lover Boy" [ditto], "My Melancholy Blues" [*News of the World*], "Crazy Little Thing Called Love" [*The Game*], "Man on the Prowl" [*The Works*] and "Keep Passing the Open Windows" [ditto]. The Freddie on these songs is the one most like the Freddie he was during our time together.'

Father and daughter would sometimes duet together on Queen songs: 'We had our own special version of "Let Me Entertain You" [from *Jazz*],' she reveals. '"In the Lap of the Gods ... Revisited" [*Sheer Heart Attack*] was the first Queen song I ever sang. At that time, I sang only the "whoa whoa lalala ..." It's something that still comes naturally to me today, anytime and anywhere. It's a little passage in my head that follows me around. Whenever I hear it now, I think to myself, people should stop spotting a "coming-out" in so many of Freddie's songs! In a recent documentary on ITV, [latest Queen frontman] Adam Lambert said he thinks that "In the Lap of the Gods ... Revisited" is about Freddie *thinking* about coming out! Well, I can tell you that it isn't, not at all!

'As we know, the relationships between the band members and the Sheffield brothers of Trident were very complicated. The band, especially Freddie, were in open conflict with them. During the *Queen II* tour, Brian had health problems and gigs were cancelled. Trident put pressure on them. They wanted a hit, and asked them to reduce costs and to reimburse their studio expenses. The road was long, and the contract was to their disadvantage. Freddie talks about this in "Flick of the Wrist". Queen's debut album and "Keep Yourself Alive" were not successful. If *Queen II* and "Seven Seas of Rhye" were more successful, they were still not successful enough. They were burdened by their debts to Trident. They came very close to disbanding and resorting to bread-and-butter work, but couldn't, because they had to pay back their debts. Freddie and the band wanted to make great music. The Sheffields spoke primarily about money. "In the Lap of the Gods … Revisited" is all about this situation.'

She confesses that the songs of Freddie's that she enjoys most are not exactly 'songs'.

'It's what he recorded on tape, the *drafts* of songs, that please me most. They are my favourites because they take me back in time to when I'd be in the room with him, playing with something or reading a book while he worked at the piano. Sometimes on these tapes, while Freddie is playing, you hear this little four-year-old girl asking him to come and help her, or to play a few notes for her of this or that: "The Carnival of the Animals", "Peter and the Wolf", "Entrance of the Gladiators", "Sabre Dance", "The William Tell Overture", "Peer Gynt", "In a Persian Market", "The Rite of Spring" … At other times, he and I can be heard singing this or that together. Sometimes it was a game, Freddie singing that I must do this or that – take a nap, dance for him, sing with him, get on with my homework – and me answering him, "No, no, *NO!*" with all the different tones of voice that I could do. Or it would be him singing that I was this or that, and me answering him, "Oh, I *know*, Dad!" On later tapes, you can hear our exchanges and discussions while he was playing some music softly, with me sitting next to him on the piano stool. These tapes are very moving, and incredibly precious to me.'

She shares that she is fond of 'La Japonaise' (from *Barcelona*). Also, that the recorded songs that move her the most are 'Goin' Back' (1973, recorded under the name Larry Lurex; the single was later released as part of the box set *The Solo Collection* in 2000 and appears on the CD *Lover of Life, Singer of Songs* in 2006. A sample of it also features at the end of 'Mother Love' (*Made in Heaven*, 1995)) and 'These Are the Days of Our Lives' (*Innuendo*).

'I really can't listen to "The Show Must Go On" or "Mother Love" – the last song Freddie ever recorded,' she confesses.

When the test result showed him, in spring 1987, that he was HIV positive, she explains, he wrote 'How Can I Go On' as an outlet for the misery it caused him.

'Four years later, Freddie also co-wrote the lyrics for "Mother Love" with Brian, up until the line about his heart being heavy and his hope all gone. The rest of the song was written by Brian alone. You can hear, in the rhythm of the lyrics, that it's not the same writer. It's no wonder that Freddie never wanted to go back into the studio to finish it. Those additional lyrics are heartbreaking. Freddie was managing to deal with his fate, immersing himself in his work in order to feel alive, then this song changed everything. It was as though his death had suddenly been thrown in his face. He recorded the song, along with "The Show Must Go On", because he wanted so badly to sing. His work helped him to deal with the disease and its progression. So it's a tragic irony that "Mother Love" ruined his state of mind. When he closed the door of the studio behind him that day, he knew that he would never be going back.'

Freddie's solo album, *Mr Bad Guy*, and his album with Montserrat Caballé, *Barcelona*, are of course his most autobiographical works.

'Both were written at particularly significant times in his life,' she says. 'The first from the Dark Years until the Monster cracked; and the second when there was no longer doubt that he was HIV positive.'

. . .

A word about Freddie's voice. Because he was so self-conscious about the way that his teeth protruded, Freddie was quizzed all the time as to why he didn't submit to corrective dental work.

'Freddie never wanted to fix his teeth because he knew how vital a role teeth play in resonance, in the projection of the voice, and in harmonies,' reveals his daughter.

'He feared that dental surgery might change the sound of his voice. Even if only a little bit, so barely that the majority of listeners would never even have noticed it, it would have been different for the elevated perception of his ear. He simply couldn't risk it.'

. . .

Freddie was incredibly proud, she tells us, of his many framed gold discs.

'Yet to him,' she says, 'they were only the starting point of a brand-new challenge. That was why he didn't display them anywhere other than in his "office". At Stafford Terrace, they were not in the living room but in the basement: the room that served as his sitting room/office room. At Phillimore Gardens, they were stored in a closet. And at Garden Lodge, they were displayed away from prying eyes, visible only to those invited into his bedroom.'

Whenever Freddie gave what he considered to be a bad show, he said, he was infuriated.

'He knew how hard people worked to pay for their tickets, and he felt they deserved the best of him,' she tells us. 'And he was always conscious of recognising the time when he should call it a day. He did believe that a day would come when he would be too old to be a rock 'n' roll performer. He never wanted to become a ridiculous shadow of his former self.'

For Queen's final couple of albums, Freddie was prolific, writing more than ever before.

'He was more creative than ever, and more of a perfectionist too,' B. says. 'For the *Miracle* album, he co-wrote many songs that made it onto the album and discarded many others. He co-wrote "My Baby Does Me" with John about Mary, the one person in the world whom he was born to love forever. Also with John, he co-wrote the song "The Miracle". This one is so full of hope, it's incredible. At that time, Freddie had been given hope that there would soon be treatment for HIV and AIDS. He really believed that a miracle would happen. As he said, if it's possible to conceive a baby human in a test tube, there was every possibility of a cure for that disease. Having accepted his HIV-positive diagnosis but not yet that he was dying – acceptance of that came much later – he became more and more contemplative in his everyday life.'

There has been much discussion and debate about 'Face It Alone'.

'Many have taken the song to be related to his illness,' she says, 'but it wasn't. Freddie remained positive, even during those final two albums. It wasn't ever intended to be a sad song. But because Freddie didn't think it was good enough, he discarded it early on: thirty years before its eventual release in 2022, when Brian and Roger got it back out and dusted it off. A "gem"? Certainly not as far as Freddie was concerned!'

The *Innuendo* album was apparently more difficult.

'By then, Freddie was very weak,' she says. 'But he wanted to work because it helped him to keep going. And he remained a perfectionist right to the end. Some have described it as his Swan Song. To me, it is the opposite. It demonstrates his desperate desire to live.'

• • •

Musically, each member of the band dealt with the news of Freddie's impending death in a different way.

'As soon as Brian knew, the songs he wrote for Queen became lamentations. "The Show Must Go On" was the only song he wrote for *Innuendo*. "Headlong" and "I Can't Live with You" were not written for this Queen album originally, but for Brian's solo album. Later, he wrote only "Mother Love" with Freddie for the *Made in Heaven* album. "Too Much Love Will Kill You" was written before he knew that Freddie was sick. Roger wrote "These Are the Days of Our Lives" about his kids and about Freddie the man, not the showman. He stayed positive, even though it was the harder thing to do. He did it because it was what his old friend Freddie wanted. As for John,' she says, 'he just couldn't write anything anymore. He had written "My Life Has Been Saved" before he was made aware of Freddie's diagnosis.'

Queen's video for the song "These Are the Days of Our Lives", shot in a London studio in May 1991 only six months ahead of his death, was the last time that Freddie worked on camera. In it, he wears the waistcoat featuring pictures of his beloved cats. His parting shot is a gaze into the lens as he whispers the words 'I still love you.'

'It was with "I'm Going Slightly Mad" that he completed the circle, with the party and the photos used in the booklet of their first album, because he believed that this video was his final video,' says B., 'before he headed for "the other world". During one of Queen's first parties as a band, the four of them had worn the same kind of costumes as those in this video. Some of the photos taken at that time feature in the booklet of the first Queen album. The illustrations for the album and singles were inspired by Grandville's *Un autre monde* 'Another World'. It is absolutely not a coincidence.[1] He never thought he could do the video for "These Are the Days of Our Lives", but he rose to it.'

Freddie's ability to write songs did not desert him after he tested positive for HIV.

'Up to a certain point,' she reminds us, 'he was more prolific than ever. His music was nourished by love, hope, beauty and happiness. But then came the moment when the disease gained the upper hand. During the final months, his creativity left him. It was in fact life itself that had nourished his music, and which had been his inspiration. When there was nothing to his life but endurance and suffering, the music in Freddie disappeared. That was in the summer of 1991. From then on, he could still be happy at times, and even funny, but the music in him was gone. He wrote the final entry in his notebooks that July. Not even that was a coincidence.'

• • •

'I don't remember when my father started making me listen to opera and classical music,' B. muses. 'There wasn't a specific moment, I suppose. It was always there. He used to give me recordings all the time. He taught me how to listen out for many features such as arpeggio, ostinato, decrescendo, cadenza, con delicatezza, con dolcezza, pianissimo, sforzando, glissando, ritenuto, legato and pizzicato. And we wouldn't only listen to grand opera or bel canto, but to more obscure composers such as Birmingham-born Albert Ketèlbey: a brilliant graduate of London's Trinity College of Music who became famous for his light orchestral music for silent films and who, in the late 1920s, was Britain's first millionaire composer; and the Soviet Armenian composer Aram Khachaturian, who like Ketèlbey created wonderful orchestrations and exotic scenes, as well as some very famous ballet music including the "Sabre Dance" for *Gayane*. Freddie loved and appreciated so many composers that I can hardly name them all: Mahler, Stravinsky, Tchaikovsky, Balakirev, Scriabin, Satie, Debussy, Schönberg, Bartók. He adored their complex orchestrations, their blending of diverse influences. Unfortunately, I was also given Mozart and Chopin and made to work on them at the piano over and over until it practically made my ears bleed. I hated it so much. Having been introduced to a vast musical universe by my dad, being made to slave over boring waltzes and études was torture. But my father would not hear my protests. He'd always turn a deaf ear to my moaning and complaining. A compromise was struck, allowing me to play whatever I wanted to once I had completed my compulsory studies. He was as adamant about that as about school homework and other commitments. On the other hand, he could be very liberal and permissive about pursuits I loved but which he didn't care for. For example, he never liked skiing, while I enjoyed it immensely. Heights made him dizzy. However, he did let me go climbing.'

Nowhere on Earth, Freddie knew, could greater resonance be found to rival the kind that quivered among the mountains. Nowhere else, he felt certain, whenever he reached for those lofty reverberations, could he get any closer to God.

CHAPTER 10

DANCE WITH MY FATHER

'Freddie always kept his promises,' agrees his daughter, echoing Freddie's own words.

'If he didn't marry Mary formally in a civil ceremony, it was to spare her the humiliation of appearing to be the scorned and deceived wife whose husband was living a homosexual lifestyle behind her back. Again, Freddie was acutely aware of the risks to her reputation. When he said, during an interview with Tim Lott for the *Daily Mail* in Paris in May 1978, that he and Mary had separated, he said this only to protect her. His statement wasn't true, of course. But it wasn't the journalist's fault for reporting it as such. He could not have known otherwise. Freddie said it to throw his inquisitors off the scent. They never broke up. With that pressure off – no further questions asked about Mary or their relationship – they were free to continue on as they had been doing, and live their private domestic life exactly as they wished. There would be no further risk of the press always trying to expose the scandal of the unfaithful husband cavorting with another man.' He didn't want Mary to have to suffer, she explains, the kind of treatment that Elton John's wife, Renate Blauel, would be subjected to during and after their short-lived union (the couple married on St Valentine's Day 1984 and were divorced four years later); nor did he want Mary to have to put up with gossip of the kind that would later surround Roger

Taylor's marriage to Dominique Beyrand, the mother of two of his children.

'Maybe Freddie and Mary were not legally married,' she says. 'But as he has written, he never considered himself less than her husband. When he was with her, he always behaved like the perfect spouse.'

Contrary to everything written and claimed, Garden Lodge was neither Freddie's exclusive residence nor his private domain. Although it belonged to Freddie legally, as confirmed on paper, their firm understanding was that it belonged to Freddie and Mary equally. This was always accepted between them, and was the reason why it was left lock, stock and barrel to Mary when Freddie died. As the lady and the mistress of the house, 'she could and did contradict Freddie about the way things were done if she felt her way was better,' says B. 'Even if Freddie didn't like it, he always gave in to her. He was accustomed to her saying "No!" or "Enough!" to him whenever he crossed the line and became intolerable. He relied on her to do that. He trusted her judgement. They would argue quite fiercely at times, usually about administrative issues, because Freddie had a short fuse and was easily frustrated. But Mary always stood up to him when she thought it necessary. He loved that – it was one of the many things that he loved about her – because she kept his feet firmly on the ground. But also because he always knew she was right.'

No one else was ever allowed to stand up to him. If his employees at Garden Lodge took the initiative and did something their own way and not according to Freddie's; if they contradicted him, or if ever they objected to anything, they knew that they would be kicked out.

'His servants had to comply with Mary's decisions and obey her orders,' explains B. 'They tended not to like this, of course, because as far as they understood the situation, Mary was of the same status as them. They did not know the truth about Freddie's relationship with her. If any of them behaved negatively towards her, Freddie would explode with anger and rage. To him, acting against Mary was acting against him. He regarded such behaviour as completely unacceptable. If they knew Mary's status, they didn't accept it.'

• • •

'I never once had Dad with me on Christmas Day,' says his daughter, not for the first time, showing that she clearly feels hard done by over it.

'Our Christmas holidays were always spent at the homes of grandparents: either the parents of my mother or those of my stepfather. Traditions were rigorously upheld. My stepfather would never give in about that. Later on, he confessed to me, he regretted that deeply, because he knew he had deprived me of something important.' He admitted to B. that he could and should have found some excuse to tell the 'official' grandparents – her mother's parents and her stepfather's parents – and have allowed her to spend some Christmases with her real father. Those other four grandparents would naturally have queried her absence, and would have demanded to know where she was. Had her stepfather thought about it more carefully, B. suggests, he could have come up with a plausible reason. 'I did hold it against him for a while,' says B., 'but in all honesty that was more rebellion than anything else. Because, due to my stepfather's inflexibility about Christmas, Freddie made up for it by giving me memorable Christmases galore, that lasted from early December all the way into January. We also celebrated Christmas more than once. We'd spend days reading lovely, traditional Christmas tales, which instilled in me a genuine passion for old books with wonderful illustrations and illuminations. I've never liked modern editions with their deformed-looking cartoon characters. There would be dinners, concerts and other live performances; magical evenings spent singing Christmas carols and listening to other Christmas music, such as recordings by French cabaret tenor Tino Rossi, and Frank Sinatra; and almost every day, there would be a delivery. Freddie had his own version of what an Advent calendar should be. He also made up his own rules. Christmas with my father was an even happier and more magical time than all the other happy, magical times with him.'

Freddie, she shares, hosted three parties every Christmas: one at Garden Lodge with his personal staff and a handful of friends; another at Phillimore Gardens with Mary and their own closest friends; and one at the home of his parents.

'Mary was always there,' says B., 'on every single occasion. Presents were extremely important to him, especially the gifts he gave to her. There would always be several of those, of course. At Garden Lodge, in front of everybody else, he would give her a "professional" present, usually something that she would find useful. Behind closed doors at Phillimore Gardens, he would give her his private love gifts.'

Birthdays were every bit as important as Christmas. For his own birthday, Freddie describes in great detail how he always gave four parties. There would be 'the big one' with hundreds of guests; another for his personal staff and a few friends; a private party at Phillimore Gardens co-hosted by Mary, for their closest mutual friends; and, the most private of all, a dinner with only Mary and his parents.

'1987 was the last year that he gave the big party for hundreds of guests,' says B. 'And 1990 was the last time he entertained his personal staff and friends.'

Few people know how incredibly generous Freddie was, nor how much he gave to charity, because he didn't strut about drawing attention to himself and making speeches about it.

'He gave quietly and with complete discretion, through his personal lawyers or one of his companies, to keep his name anonymous,' explains his daughter. 'Not just to those in his own circle but also to family, friends, acquaintances, their acquaintances and many others. He supported official charities enthusiastically, and he loved being able to do it.

'Whenever someone gave *him* a real gift, one that came from the bottom of the heart, he was always surprised. Mary was the best at that. She always gave him thoughtful gifts, taking the time and trouble to find rare and unexpected things. She never picked a present at random and thought that it would do, as did so many who were under the impression that he had everything money could buy, or that he could buy himself whatever he wanted. Mary's gifts were always special and appropriate, and he was so touched by them.

'It's often said that Freddie was a complete spendthrift; that he had no idea about the price of anything, and that he didn't know the value of money. It's not really true. He did spend freely without counting the cost, both on himself and on others, because he could afford to. But he always lived within his means. He invested carefully for the future in flats, houses and artworks. Everything else, he spent.

'He never imagined that a film about him could have made so much money. If anyone ever raised the subject of making a movie of his life, he would always laugh it off. He was very thankful that people bought Queen's records in such vast quantities, thus providing him with his incredible standard of living. He knew how privileged he was, because he was well aware of the cost of living, the minimum wage and the average take-home pay. He never forgot his years spent living hand to mouth with no money in his pockets. Nor did he forget his family's arrival in England, or the many difficulties that went with that. He knew a lot of people with ordinary jobs and lifestyles, and he never hesitated to help them when they needed it. His generosity was in evidence every day. For example, one of his favourite things to do was to buy several of the same item, whether it be a garment, a pen, a lighter, a vase, or even a piece of jewellery – such as the ubiquitous gold Cartier bracelet. He would purchase, say, ten of them, keep one for himself, and give the other nine away to his friends.

'He was very good at spoiling his nearest and dearest, and of course he spoiled me more than anyone else. After he gave me some cat figurines, I started to collect them. With his help, of course, because he couldn't do anything the way ordinary people do. He had to get me every single kind of cat, including soft toys and tiny trinkets, but also imposing bronze ones, delicate porcelain ones and even one made of Baccarat crystal. It was the same thing when I started to collect tortoises, pandas and elephants. Thank God it never occurred to him to bring a live elephant home!'

• • •

The very first time that his daughter saw her father perform live on stage was in 1982, in Zurich, during Queen's *Hot Space* tour. They performed over two nights, 16 and 17 April, at that city's Hallenstadion.

'Although it is a medium-sized venue,' she says, 'it seemed vast and imposing to me. At only five years old, I didn't have a clue. I was used to watching Dad playing the piano and singing, so of course I already knew that he was a musician. But my child's mind expected to see the piano in the middle of the stage, while Freddie's piano was pushed to the side of the stage. And where were the orchestral conductor, and the singers in big stage costumes and formal dress, all making dramatic gestures? There were big flashing lights, and the audience was really loud. I expected to see my dad walk out onto the stage looking very serious, wearing a dinner jacket and bow tie, and bowing to the audience. Instead, there he was gesticulating from one side of the stage to the other and shouting four-letter words!'

• • •

One of the claims that annoys his daughter most is that Freddie did not read; that the only book he ever devoured from cover to cover was *The Spartacus International Gay Guide*, a now-discontinued annual that offered, in several languages, information on gay-friendly hotels, hang-outs, bars, beaches, saunas and restaurants in major cities around the world. The publication was axed following an accusation that it promoted paedophilia.

'Peter Freestone remarked that he couldn't tell you of any other book Freddie had ever read,' B. reminds us. 'Perhaps he simply never saw Freddie reading anything else. But Freddie was a highly intelligent and well-read man. He was passionate about history, art, English literature, French royal history – specifically Louis XIV, the Sun King, Louis XV and of course Louis XVI, the last king before the French Revolution and the fall of the monarchy, and his wife Marie Antoinette. As a royalist, he was fascinated, excited and terrified all at once by the idea of subjects decapitating their king. The India of the Maharajas, mythology, history of art and of course anything to do with Japan were all subjects that enthralled him. He had extensive knowledge of the history of Persia and Mesopotamia, the history of Great Britain and its empire, the ancient Greek and Roman empires, the Egypt of the Pharaohs, Genghis Khan, Alexander the Great, Marco Polo and so on. He adored *The Arabian Nights* and the Persian *Book of Kings*. He had unrivalled knowledge of the Gathas, the Holy Bible and the Sri Guru Granth Sahib, the holy religious scripture of Sikhism. He was passionate about the works of Rudyard Kipling, Hermann Hesse, Robert Browning, D.H. Lawrence, William Blake, T. E. Lawrence, Friedrich Nietzsche, Albert Camus and Johann Wolfgang von Goethe, all of whom he read voraciously. He favoured literature from a wide variety of genres. But he had to be gripped by both topic and content, otherwise he would discard a book without finishing it as a complete waste of time.

In addition to having a wonderful ear, he had a great and eidetic [photographic] memory. Observing him with a book, people tended to think that he was simply skimming through the pages without reading them, but in fact he was speed-reading, absorbing the text incredibly quickly.'

Freddie's vast knowledge, she points out, 'was omnipresent in his lyrics and music with their endless metaphors, symbolism, references, forms, structures, rhythms, melodic and harmonic content'.

In other words, it all had to come from somewhere.

• • •

Talk often returned to privacy, a pet subject of Freddie's. He wanted to make sure that his daughter understood both its meaning and its worth. Because he had been too open about himself and his life at an early stage in the fame game, privacy was of the utmost importance to him. Having given his own away far too easily and having discovered to his immense cost that there was no way of getting it back, he became very cautious about who he shared his inner self with.

'Asked about his privacy,' says B., 'he would respond: "I hate talking to people I don't really know, so they don't really know the real me," as he told Lisa Robinson on *Radio 1990* in March 1984. "There are very few people who actually know the other side of me." "My private life is private, and little bits of it sneak out, and I can come up with outrageous quotes, and that's as far as I go," he also said [as quoted by Brooks and Lupton in 2006]. "I just hate talking to people about myself, basically," he told Simon Bates on BBC Radio 1 in April 1985. "I don't want everyone to know about my real inner feelings, because that's my private life, so I think there are very few people … who actually know the other side of me." Freddie said freely in interviews that he slept with both women and men and admitted to being very promiscuous. So he didn't talk about his male partners or his sex life whenever he talked about "the real him", simply saying that he wanted his privacy to remain private.

'Peter Freestone admits that Freddie never spoke to him about, nor did he witness any conversation between Freddie and any other person about, his childhood, his faith, his religion, his feelings or so many other things that were important to him,' says B. 'Freddie never spoke about such aspects of his life with his day-to-day friends. Those topics belonged to Freddie Bulsara, not to Freddie Mercury. He compartmentalised his life as much as he could, and he was very good at hiding his secrets. Throughout his life, the only person who knew absolutely everything about him, including his undisclosed secrets, was Mary. Definitely not any other friends or employees, whatever they have said or may say in future. Such people only ever knew and saw what Freddie wanted them to see or know about him.'

· · ·

Criticised from all sides, disregarded by members of Freddie's household and scorned by factions of the fandom, poor Mary could not win no matter which way she turned. Her only option was to remain silent and keep her own counsel. For Freddie, her loyalty spoke for itself. When she resumed her rightful place at his right-hand side, she did so as his soulmate.

'With Mary,' explains B., 'Freddie felt understood and accepted. He felt secure. They only had to look at each other to know what each other was thinking, how the other was feeling. In public, for all the reasons, they kept up their charade for appearances' sake. They would arrive side by side at functions and public events, but then she would assume her usual position, standing directly in front of him. That way, she was not in the photographers' field of vision, but was close enough to Freddie that she could easily turn and make eye contact with him and quiet comments to him. He was fine as long as he could see her face. In her eyes, he found the support, encouragement, patience and comfort that he needed.'

He is unequivocal on the subject throughout his diaries: Mary was his one and only love.

'Only she was able to console his wounded heart,' says B. 'He refers to it over and over, and returns to it constantly. Together, they avoided all the usual day-to-day petty misunderstandings and silly quarrels that couples are so often afflicted by, and shared wonderful, life-enhancing marital harmony. He had as many men as he wanted. She put up with that, and turned a blind eye. How hard that must have been for her. Then again, she knew without question that she was the only one in his heart, and that his love for her was the only thing that mattered to him. She alone was party to his otherwise undisclosed thoughts, his deepest and darkest wounds, his secrets and his fears. In return, he knew all of hers. With Mary, Freddie didn't need to play the megastar. He didn't need to hide or pretend. All their pain and emotion, dreams and joy, they felt together. They went through everything as a couple, and she was everything to him:

his confessor and confidante, his guardian angel, his anchor and safe harbour, his haven, his solace, his rock. In return, he was all those things to her. They adored and were bound to each other. They saw something in each other that no one else could. To them, it was very simple: they had always been there for each other, and they always would be. They could be vulnerable with each other without fear or embarrassment, without having to restrain themselves, without worrying what their partner would think of them. They loved, took care of and could trust each other, and knew they would never hurt each other on purpose. They didn't even discuss it. There was no need for words. They just knew, and that was enough.'

'Certain factions of the press have long wanted to portray him as gay,' says B. 'But by the mid-1980s, he no longer wanted to play the game. He was done with posing as a homosexual, and he was no longer scared of doing exactly as he pleased or of being who he really was. He loved Mary and had sex with men. He was fed up with hiding, of living a false image of himself.

'Again, it was Freddie Mercury the outrageous rock star, not Freddie Bulsara, who loved and adored the outrageous German actress Barbara Valentin. The real him, the private man, the musician, the singer and songwriter, loved Mary Austin,' B. explains. 'You see the difference – and we must, because this is the key to him. He wrote that love was his greatest creation, tragically unfinished. He had longed to build on his unconditional, everlasting love for Mary, and on their mutual adoration, and create his own family within a happy and secure home – something that had mostly eluded him as a child – and at the same time to enjoy a beautiful relationship with another man without the violence and abuse that had tended to taint his male partnerships. His ideal was the kind of relationship he'd enjoyed with Joe Fannelli. He dreamed of having both, the best of both worlds. Only then would he have been in a state of blissful love and serenity. Tragically for him, his dream was never realised.'

CHAPTER 11

MONTSERRAT

It has long been accepted, because he has been talking about it for more than thirty years, that his loyal assistant Peter Freestone introduced Freddie to opera. So Freddie surprises us. He writes that, while his boarding school instilled in him his everlasting love of sacred music, it was his aunt, Sheroo Khory – the one who lived in Bombay and with whom he stayed during school holidays – who initiated his passion for opera and classical music. Operatic influences could be identified in his early compositions long before Peter went to work for Queen.

'You only have to listen', says B., 'to the intricate, complex structures and progressions and the melodic and harmonic content of "My Fairy King" [on Queen's 1973 eponymous debut album] and "The March of the Black Queen" [on 1974's *Queen II*]. The latter was also inspired by Mozart's *The Magic Flute*, one of the greatest operas ever written and a special favourite of Freddie's. The wider theme of this fairytale of darkness and light is the struggle to find one's way in the world. Freddie writes about the duality between Soroastre [Zarathustra] and Queen of the Night [the Black Queen]. He liked to amuse himself by singing the opera's aria that is delivered by this queen, "*Der Hölle Rache kocht in meinem Herzen*" [Hell's vengeance boils in my heart], one of the most famous arias in operatic history. It is acknowledged as one of the most difficult to sing of all such pieces.

My dad was always challenging himself to reach that impossible top F-sharp.'

Freddie drew inspiration from *The Magic Flute* for his most celebrated creation.

'We find it in "Bohemian Rhapsody"'s first movement,' B. points out. 'You only have to examine the librettist Emanuel Schikaneder's text, which he wrote in German. Phrases such as, "Is this reality?" and "Or is this just imagination?" become "Is this the real life?" and "Is this just fantasy?" If Freddie hadn't acquired such a vast knowledge of classical music and opera over several decades, his most famous songs would have sounded completely different.'

In his own book and in director Rudi Dolezal's documentary *Freddie Mercury: The Untold History*, released in its own right in December 2000 and Grammy-nominated, Peter Freestone talks about Freddie having been 'new to opera' as late as 1983. He relates that their attendance together at a performance of *Un Ballo in Maschera* ('A Masked Ball') at the Royal Opera House was Freddie's first exposure to the live brilliance of Montserrat Caballé. He observes that Freddie had no idea who the singer was. 'He didn't know the name, he didn't know anything about her,' Peter says in the Dolezal interview. Freddie, however, had long known and appreciated the incredible voice and legend of 'La Superba'.

Between 1967 and 1981, as documented by his own hand in his diaries, Freddie attended numerous opera and ballet performances in London, Paris and New York.

'He even took me to my first opera in spring 1980,' says his daughter, 'when I was three years old.'

Which seems impossibly young, until I remember that I started taking my eldest child to see *The Nutcracker* ballet at Covent Garden when she was around the same age. Freddie's fellow opera buffs must have assumed the little girl in the seat beside him to be a niece or a godchild.

'He took me to classical concerts, operas, ballets and recitals,' she says. 'I always wore a beautiful evening dress, and patent leather shoes.'

On 15 January 1981, Freddie received a special invitation to the Royal Opera House to see and hear Montserrat Caballé performing alongside Luciano Pavarotti in Giuseppe Verdi's *Un Ballo in Maschera* under celebrated Dutch conductor and violinist Bernard Haitink.[1]

'It was to take place a few days before Freddie was due to fly to Japan, to perform in a brief *Flash Gordon* tour between 12 and 18 February,' B. explains.

'He had been receiving invitations to major operatic productions since 1979. Unfortunately, he was usually out of the country whenever such opportunities arose, so he was always having to send his regrets. This time, however, he was available to attend the performance, on 3 February … 1981, *not* 1983, as often stated. The concert was also broadcast by the BBC, and Freddie owned a recording of it.'

Because he knew that Peter was also partial to opera, Freddie invited Freestone to accompany him.

'Freddie needed no persuasion to work with the great Montserrat Caballé,' says B. 'It was a long-cherished dream of his to sing with her. The timing was right, and so it happened. Freddie said that he was frightened, nervous and panicked by the prospect – but also totally electrified, thrilled, excited and deeply driven by his desire to do it. It was such a great honour for him that he complied with every single demand of hers. Which was a professional first, for him. *He* adapted to *her*: imagine! This was not the way Freddie did things, yet he yielded willingly to the grande dame.'

This collaboration was down to no one but Freddie himself.

• • •

In New York, Freddie did see Miss Caballé perform that year. Contrary to reports, he did not attend a concert by her in that city the *following* year – although he did purchase tickets.

'He had planned to see her in recital in New York in 1982,' reports B. 'But Montserrat cancelled her three Avery Fisher Hall performances with the New York Philharmonic on 30 September, 1 and 2 October because of health issues. She had suffered from nausea while performing with the San Francisco Opera, and was obliged to withdraw from the rest of her schedule. Freddie was deeply disappointed. But he did see her on stage on several occasions, mainly in New York, London and Paris. Montserrat had made her debut at the French capital's Salle Pleyel in 1966, performing bel canto arias and scenes. After Barcelona, France was her second musical home. She performed regularly in the South of France, and also at the Paris Opera in 1981, in the finale of *Turandot*.'

Montserrat was, declared Freddie, the musical love of his life. The album they went on to record together, *Barcelona*, was the culmination of all that he had ever longed to achieve, and the work of which he was the most proud. It represented, for him, a culmination. It was the sum of everything musical that he adored.

'He let her know through their management and record companies that he would like to work with her,' B. informs us. 'But communication stalled in 1985, because Montsy was dealing privately with a brain tumour and was in hospital for three months. This would not be disclosed to the public until some years later.'

When Queen's 1986 *Magic* tour reached Barcelona, Freddie mentioned during a Spanish television interview how much he admired that city's most famous daughter. Shortly afterwards, Montserrat was invited to record a signature piece for the 1992 Olympic Games, to be hosted by Spain. The committee indicated that they would prefer the music to be non-operatic.

'Her brother Carlos, who was also her manager, suggested that Montsy should work with Freddie,' says B. 'He contacted Queen's manager, Jim Beach. This time, the timing was perfect. Freddie could barely contain himself. A meeting was arranged for later in the year. Freddie, who had already started work on his second solo album with producer Mike Moran, prepared some ideas and developed a piece entitled "Exercises in Free Love" with Montserrat in mind. He even tried to imitate her voice on the demo, mimicking her legendary pianissimo and phrasing.'

For several reasons, the meeting with Montserrat had to be postponed.

'This gave Freddie more time to develop and record his ideas,' says B. 'They eventually met for lunch in March 1987, at the Ritz hotel in Barcelona. Before they came face to face for the first time, Freddie was, he said, as nervous, frightened, scared and panicked as it was possible to be. But within moments, she had made him feel completely at ease. Freddie was thrilled. He was electrified in her presence. They talked, laughed, ate, listened to music and improvised. She was, he said, a very great and funny lady, as well as one of the kindest people he'd ever met. He had her listen to "The Fallen Priest" – originally named "Rachmaninov's Revenge", a piano piece by Mike Moran that then became "The Duet", and which would eventually have lyrics by Tim Rice; as well as "How Can I Go On", "Exercises in Free Love" and an outline of "Barcelona".'

Montserrat left their lunch engagement at around 4 p.m., to attend an orchestral rehearsal. She then returned, four hours later, and they picked up where they had left off.

'A few days later, Montserrat arrived in London for a recital at the Royal Opera House. Freddie attended the performance. During her encore, Montsy sang "Exercises in Free Love" and invited Freddie up on stage to take a bow. Contrary to rumour, this was all pre-planned. Freddie knew she was going to sing the song and was prepared to join her on stage. Afterwards, they went back to Garden Lodge for dinner, then spent the whole night singing, laughing, improvising and talking about what was going to happen with the new Olympic anthem "Barcelona". That crazy night, out of so much laughter and chat, arose the decision to record a whole album together rather than just a single. Only when Montserrat left Garden Lodge early the next morning did the enormity of what he had just promised occur to Freddie. *A whole album!* Even though he hadn't signed anything, he had made a verbal commitment and there could be no backing down. The thought terrified him, but the show must go on.

He turned his attention to the task straight away. He wanted to do something special with her. *For* her. Several sessions took place in May 1987 before the live performance of "Barcelona" in Ibiza at the end of that month.'

During those initial sessions with Montserrat, because *Barcelona* necessitated their collaboration over a long period of time – the Spanish Olympic Games would not be staged for another five years – Freddie felt it was his duty, out of love and respect for her, to inform Montserrat that he was HIV positive and had developed AIDS-related complex (ARC). She, in turn, confided in him about the illness with which she had been dealing privately for several years. Their mutual trust created the strongest bond. Their mortality, Freddie thought, brought them even closer together. The intention was to create something magical, just for the two of them. They developed a great friendship. Each said that they loved the other very much.

'He had to adapt to her way of working,' says B., 'another first, for him. Writing the songs was very different from what he knew. He had to write scores, which he hadn't done previously, to adapt his ideas to her voice. Until then, he had only written music for his own voice. Because of her loaded schedule, everything had to be ready to record the minute she arrived. Because he adored and respected her so much, he was hesitant whenever he had to ask her to do another take, or to sing a line in a particular way. How do you instruct a diva? But their sessions were fun. He found ways to communicate what he wanted, and she did the same. Their work together was without question his most thrilling experience. And she said the same, calling it "the most marvellous year of my life".

'Because Montsy was a Prima Donna, because Freddie's assistant Joe Fannelli didn't care for the opera world or those who inhabited it, and because Peter Freestone had previously worked at the Royal Opera House and knew its foibles, habits and customs, it was he and not Joe who was taken along whenever Freddie was due to work in the studio with Montserrat,' says B.

Freddie's ultimate dream was to record *Barcelona* with a full symphony orchestra. But after the problems he had experienced during the recording of *Mr Bad Guy*, he knew that his dream was an ambition too far. He resigned himself to recording with synthesisers, samplers and drum machines.

'He was extremely meticulous,' says B., 'at times ad nauseam, and was virtually incapable of delegating anything to do with his creative work.

'Had he managed to get his way and pulled off the recording of *Barcelona* with a full orchestra, he would have had to control every single note that was played by every single musician. This, even he knew, was a logistical nightmare. It would never have been finished, nor could it have been released within a reasonable timeframe. Jim Beach did an admirable thing when he had the instrumentation of that album re-recorded with a full symphonic orchestra. When that new version was released in September 2012, he made one of Freddie's greatest dreams come true. Freddie would have loved it.'[2]

'Barcelona' the song is not, as one might suppose, a hymn of love to that city. As B. explains, 'It is about Freddie's friendship with Montserrat. She wanted a song about the place of her birth. Instead, he wrote a song about his dream of her, his feelings for her.[3] Similarly, he wrote "Exercises in Free Love" with her in mind and asked her to write the lyrics. That song became "Ensueño", because the lyrics sounded like an echo of "Barcelona". Montserrat then asked Freddie to sing it, with his natural voice. He did so, allowing her to direct him. It was probably the first time in his musical career that such a thing had ever happened. The tracks "How Can I Go On" and "Guide Me Home" are his most autobiographical songs ever, and the most sincere about what he felt at the time of writing. Although the lyrics of "How Can I Go On" are heavy, the music is neither melancholy nor sad.

'Montserrat and Freddie were alike in so many ways,' says B. 'You described her as the musical love of his life, and that is exactly what she was. Without question. The fact that she went all the way and did an entire album with him, even though she didn't really have the time to commit to it, demonstrates their profound feelings for one another. The connection between them was something unique, and unlike anything Freddie had experienced with any other musician in his entire life. Their mutual understanding was not merely musical. It was deeply human too.'[4]

• • •

The *Barcelona* album, according to Peter Freestone, was something that Freddie alone wanted to do. 'It was done purely for his own delectation,' Peter explained, 'and where it led, he didn't care.'

According to Freddie, he 'had a clear picture of the whole album and of what he wanted to achieve on it', B. reveals, 'and he knew exactly where it was going. It is the masterpiece of his entire oeuvre. Through it, he wanted to demonstrate all the complexity and creativity of which he was capable. Peter said, "Freddie really enjoyed this collaboration because the end results were achieved without confrontation; whereas so much of Queen's work, although superb, was coloured with the memories of confrontation and conflict. It was because of the prospect of argument and disharmony that on occasion Freddie would refuse to go to the studio."

'But during the recording of *Barcelona*, Freddie knew that his days were numbered. He didn't want to fight or argue anymore. He just wanted to write wonderful music and sing with Montsy. That is precisely what they did. But Montserrat almost didn't participate in the writing process. It was, for Freddie, a totally different way of working. When she was in the studio, nothing else mattered. Arguments and friction had always been a part of Queen's creativity, and they thrived on it. But from their *The Miracle* album onwards, Queen's infighting ceased, because Freddie's state of mind had changed due to his HIV status. He was the peacemaker of the band more than ever before, containing tension, mollifying the mood and preventing egos from running wild. All he wanted was serenity and calm. But he didn't have to spell it out. Without him saying a word to anyone about it, the ambience and the atmosphere within the studio changed. When Freddie told the rest of the band that he had full-blown AIDS, they closed ranks. They built a safe and secure environment around him, and he was so grateful for that.'

Second only to Mary, the band was Freddie's family. As Roger's roadie Crystal Taylor said, 'They were always a unit, right to the end. Even though they argued amongst themselves, heaven forbid that an outsider said anything about the family. Just like a marriage, a few squabbles during the day but then a f...ing good time at night.'

But Roger, John and Brian were not the first to be informed of Freddie's grave health status. The first person to whom Freddie turned to announce his seropositivity was Montserrat Caballé. That he chose her over his longstanding bandmates to hear the news first demonstrates the great love and respect he had for Montsy. But was she really the first?

'Yes, absolutely the first,' confirms B. 'Mary received the bad news from Freddie's GP. She conveyed it directly to Freddie. As he and Montsy were working closely together at the time on the album, Freddie felt it was his duty to inform her personally. He duly did. Shortly afterwards he shared his HIV status with "Miami", as Freddie always referred to Queen manager Jim Beach. The next person he told was his close friend and personal assistant Joe Fannelli. Eventually, he confided in Jim Hutton. He also told my mother and stepfather. Freddie records that he never told Peter Freestone.'

• • •

It was from 1983 to 1984, we know from Freddie's journals, that Peter Freestone was employed by Freddie exclusively.

'His responsibilities were Freddie's laundry and cleaning up after him, during periods when the band were in Los Angeles, or in Munich, where Peter stayed at the hotel while Freddie was living at Winnie Kirchberger's home or with Barbara Valentin,'

B. says. 'In London, Peter never lived at Stafford Terrace, and visited Phillimore Gardens only rarely, and usually on an errand.

'So I regret to say that it is baffling to hear him say he was with Freddie all the time during that whole period. From early 1985 until the end of the *Magic* tour at Knebworth on 9 August 1986, when Freddie gave his final performance with Queen, Peter was barely with Freddie. It was Joe Fannelli who tended to Freddie at that time. For most of the time that Freddie spent in Munich, at Phillimore Gardens, at Stafford Terrace, or on tour during that period, Peter was the keeper of Garden Lodge, which at that point was still under construction. He was not present for the majority of the recording of the *Mr Bad Guy* album, nor at the filming of the videos. He *was* asked to work the day of *Live Aid* at Wembley Stadium, and at Knebworth Park. And during the *Magic* tour, Peter worked at the fan club, for the whole band. The assumption that he was with Freddie at all times during those nineteen months is erroneous.'

Peter *was* present, however, B. again concedes, during Freddie's encounters and recording with Monserrat.

'Because she was a Prima Donna, and Peter knew her world,' B. reaffirms. 'As I said, he knew its habits, customs and eccentricities, and how to handle a world-class opera star. Montsy's punishing schedule dictated that she had very little time to spend with Freddie in the recording studio. His sessions with her were much shorter than what he was used to with the band. Absolutely everything had to be ready to go the minute Montsy arrived. He would come in, they warmed up their voices, they recorded her part, then she departed and flew back. It was only ever two days here, three days there. All the mixing and so on was done without her. Peter Freestone was present when she was.'

After *Barcelona*, it was Joe Fannelli who attended the recording and video sessions for the albums *The Miracle* and *Innuendo*.

'I'm afraid to say that Freddie didn't always treat Peter very considerately,' B. says. 'It would be, "Phoebe this!" and "Phoebe that!" without the niceties of "could you", "please" or "thank you." Freddie screamed at Peter frequently; he admitted so himself. He hated it whenever anybody crossed professional boundaries, and would always put them in their place. You could step across the line with Freddie once, but never twice ... as people sometimes found to their cost. Freddie was not the easiest boss. He could be very difficult and demanding, but he gave a lot in return. He and Mary always had time and empathy for both their own employees and those who worked for the Queen organisation. They would enquire after their families, their children, their health and circumstances. But it is true to say that Freddie maintained a clear relationship of subordination, and wanted everything and everyone in their place.'

Only the hardest of hearts would fail to feel sympathy for a lovely man like Peter. There he was, homeless but for the use of a maid's room extended to him by his snappy, dismissive master, but with no personal quarters where he could entertain family or friends. Forbidden to invite anyone back to Garden Lodge or to the Mews, he was forced to socialise away from the place he called home. He lived according to Freddie's timetable, abided by his terms and conditions and accepted his decisions without challenge. He was also required to obey the commands of Mary, his mistress. How that must have stuck in the craw, though Peter bore it with dignity.

As well as being strict, Freddie did not care for confrontation. He never liked to have to fight for what he wanted or needed, expecting to reign without feeling obliged to explain himself. A perfectionist in his work with the highest of standards, he had similar expectations of all who worked for him.

'Peter has said that Freddie couldn't even use the microwave, make a cup of tea or clean up his own mess. He could, of course, he just didn't want to do it! As he saw it, he paid people good money to do that kind of thing for him. Why should he do it himself?'

• • •

To the best of his daughter's knowledge, Montserrat Caballé was the only artist in whom Freddie confided openly that he had a child. That Montserrat was Catholic and very religious perhaps had something to do with that?

'That's true,' agrees B., 'but it was a combination of several things that made him confide in her. She was Catholic and very religious, and he was a great believer; he told her that he was HIV positive, and she told him about her own health issues with which she had been dealing for several years; he was a father dealing with a terminal illness, and she was a mother dealing with a potentially fatal illness.

'It shows how special she was, how deeply he felt for her,' says B. 'After he died, she wrote me a very heartfelt letter. It's not a piece of correspondence from "La Superba", nor from a friend of the artist. It's a letter from a mother, a daughter – who lost her own mother a few days after Freddie's forty-first birthday, which they had celebrated so wildly in Ibiza in September 1987 – to a young girl mourning the loss of her father. At no point in the letter does she talk about Freddie the artist, the music they made together, or what more they might have achieved. She paid tribute to Freddie the musician in public, via the media. To me, in a simple and loving note, she talks only about Freddie the man and Freddie the dad. Such sensitivity and kindness are very rare.'

CHAPTER 12

CONDEMNATION

Freddie did not believe in politics, B. confirms.

'He had no time for political parties. He had his own ideas and theories, of course, but no time at all for politicians. As far as he was concerned, they made a lot of fine and worthy promises during election campaigns that they would forget about as soon as the elections were over. He felt that politicians clung to power in their own best interests, and not for the good of the people. This infuriated him. He considered most of them to be liars and cheats, who didn't care about the plight of those who had elected them.'

On the other hand, she says, he adored the Royal Family.

'He liked their tradition, their constancy, and the fact that they are above politics. I'm sure he would have been saddened and disappointed by royal developments in recent years. He would have been devastated by the death of Princess Diana in 1997, the scandals surrounding Prince Andrew, the furore over Prince Harry and Meghan, and by the passing of Her late Majesty the Queen in 2022. Freddie was extremely proud of his British nationality. He saw in the monarchy something permanent, timeless and reassuring. He appreciated it for the way it upheld the unity of the nation, for the ways in which it gave people joy, and for the relief it offered from our increasingly stressful world.

'Ecological challenges were not yet a hot topic during the 1980s, so the environment wasn't one for him. He used both private jets and Concorde because both were practical in terms of organisation. By today's standards, his carbon footprint was catastrophic. Things were very different back then. Given the kind of person Freddie was, I feel sure that, had he lived longer, he would have changed his habits.'

It has been said that Freddie was no linguist: 'I beg to differ,' says his daughter. 'Freddie was naturally multilingual. As well speaking his mother tongue Gujarati fluently with his parents in parallel with English, he learned to read and write it in early childhood. When the family lived in Zanzibar, he was accustomed to hearing both kiUnguja, a dialect of Swahili, and Arabic on a daily basis. In India, he discovered Hindi. He was fascinated by the richness and uniqueness of different languages. While his command of French was fairly basic, he had the most wonderful accent, and loved having fun with French pronunciation. He had been living for extended periods in Montreux, a French-speaking town, since 1978 – when the band first convened there to record their album *Jazz*. He also had some basic German words, just as Winnie had some rudimentary English. They didn't need Barbara as their interpreter in order to communicate on a day-to-day basis.'

It may come as no surprise to learn that Freddie had a wonderful sense of humour. He was naturally funny, B. affirms, 'and was always keen to make people smile. It was almost as though he needed to do so. An example? When I was four years old, I was learning to ride a bike. One day, when I was trying to show him how much progress I'd made, I happened to skid over a little stone on the path, and I fell off. My knees were horribly scraped and bleeding. He dashed over, scooped me up, hugged and consoled me, and wiped away my tears. Then he took me indoors and tended to the wounds himself, taking great care to clean out all the grit and dirt. He then applied some merbromin.[1] When I saw its bright red colour on my knees, I was terrified and burst into tears. My dad looked directly into my eyes, then took the bottle of merbromin and made a line with it on each of his cheeks. Then he smiled at me, and I smiled back. My stepfather later warned him about something to do with the red lines on his face. Freddie retorted that he didn't care, because it had made me smile. He then didn't shave for the next few days, to allow the regrowth to cover up the lines a little bit.

'That's what I miss the most about him: the twinkle in his eyes. The broad smile that would appear on his face just before he did one of the funny things he'd do to make you laugh. You always knew that something was going to happen, something hilarious. Every moment, for my father, was a celebration of life. He was nothing if not a man in constant pursuit of happiness.'

· · ·

In 1983, when something happened to do with work that delayed Freddie's return to the family home until the day after they were expecting him, his then six-year-old daughter was angry and upset. 'I was very happy to see him when he arrived, of course,' B. says, 'but also furious because he was late. He tried to defuse the situation by announcing, the minute he walked in, that he was taking me shopping. I could have asked him for absolutely anything that day and he would have bought it for me, no question. No request would have been too great. But I was a six-year-old in a sulk. I retorted that I didn't want anything. Far from running out of patience and losing his temper with me, he carefully explained the precise reasons why he'd been unable to get to me sooner. He soothed me over and over, repeating that he was really sorry – which I knew he was. He said he understood why I was angry with him, and reassured me that it was my right to be so. But then he said that I had a choice. The day didn't have to be a lost cause, because we could turn it around and do things another way. We could laugh, sing, dance, play and have fun, he said. We could do silly things together, sit and talk to each other and have a good time. In the end, that's exactly what we did. He cancelled a few other commitments and was able to stay with us at home much longer than he'd originally planned. And of course, he couldn't resist getting out his credit card. He spoiled me rotten, because that was what Freddie did.'

. . .

Raised as a Parsee, according to a religion whose tradition had for centuries been exclusively oral, Freddie was blessed with the gift of the gab. He was, says his daughter, a wonderful storyteller and an even better listener.

'He told stories and humorous anecdotes exceptionally well. He had a rare ability to bring stories to life with immense theatricality, in both his gestures and his voice. He as good as staged them right before your eyes, so that you could virtually see the scenes that he was describing. He turned every little tale or routine bedtime story into a fantastic and irresistible epic that excited me, and kept me awake all night rather than calmed me down and put me to sleep! The fantasy land of Rhye and *The Shahnameh* held great importance in our bedtime stories, and were the perfect means via which he could hand down his ancestral culture to me. The "seven seas" to which he referred in his stories and his song, we now know, were not actual seas but the Oxus River in Greater Iran.'[2]

Whenever something was troubling his daughter, Freddie was the first to notice.

'The first time I was really disturbed by press reports about my dad was in 1987, when I was ten years old. A big article was published about him, his partners and AIDS. At that time, I didn't know what AIDS was. I found the newspaper at home, read it, was shocked to the core, but didn't say anything to anyone. The next time I saw my dad, he could tell immediately that something was wrong. He asked me what was up. I told him I'd found and read the newspaper. We sat and had a long discussion about it. As always, whatever it was, he was open and honest. He taught me about AIDS, explaining that it is a communicable disease only in particular situations, and talked about the stigma attached to it. He also told me, in an age-appropriate manner, about the article, his sexuality, his partners, the newspapers, and about how a certain kind of press was not reliable.

'By the end of that discussion, a big part of me had left childhood behind, I think. Years later, when I came to read his notebooks, I discovered that he had been very troubled indeed by our conversation that day. He was extremely worried about the effect the bad press was having on me – more worried than I'd been myself at the time, because I was only a little girl. Now that I had grown up, and he was no longer here to protect me from such things the way he had been when I was a child, the impact of what I read had far greater significance.'

But she stresses that she remembers more positives than negatives. And she says that his guidance and influence continue to shape her to this day.

'He taught me to believe in myself, to follow my feelings and instincts, and to always know that what I feel deeply inside can never be wrong,' she says. 'He was always very patient with me. He never once lost his temper with me. He always wanted the best for me, and was invariably supportive – even when he was not, let's say, the biggest fan of my choices. He would help me with them anyway.

'I would go so far as to say that Freddie was, in fact, the very soul of goodness. He reminded me often that it was my duty to myself to experiment, to make my own mistakes, and even to disobey – but not too often and never too much, because obedience always had to come first. It was the only way to grow up, he insisted. I realised only much later that he was striving for me to have the kind of liberated, supported but unrepressed childhood that he himself had not enjoyed. He promised me he would always be there for me. He did not break that promise either, because in a way, he always has been. His notebooks have always been there to comfort me and give me the answers I'm looking for. It's as if he was able to predict, all those years ago, what I would need at each future stage of my life. He guides me via his journals exactly as though he were still here with me.

'He taught me what happiness is, and how to face difficulties. He made sure I knew that it's vital to do everything with passion, envy and respect. "Do whatever you want," he would say to me. "All jobs are valuable if you are proud of what you do, if you do it with passion and to the best of your ability, and if you always make the best of yourself." He would tell me that I had an obligation to myself. "You have to give *one hundred per cent* of yourself at every turn and all the time," he said. If you gave a hundred per cent of yourself and someone else was better than you, was his point, it is still a success, because it's a victory over yourself. But if you are number one in your field and you don't give the best of yourself, that counts as a failure. You must never compete with others, he'd counsel. The only person to compete with is yourself.'

Contrary to the public image, the private Freddie was much more traditional than most might imagine. Mealtimes and dinners, for example, were extremely important to him, B. affirms.

'The setting of the dining table was a military operation, carried out with great care and "millimetre precision". He actually used a ruler to line up the cutlery, crockery and glassware with their opposites on the other side of the table. I had too much fun watching him do it. Once, when I was about seven years old and he had gone back to the kitchen to retrieve a missing piece, I got up to the kind of mischief that kids can't resist. I couldn't help myself. I wrecked his arrangement ever so slightly, then hid behind a cabinet to observe his reaction. It was the funniest thing. He was so horrified, he almost choked. I couldn't help myself, I burst out laughing. He heard me, knew immediately that I was responsible, and rushed over to pull me out from behind the cabinet. His face was a picture, one of his amazing frowns – you know, the thing he did with his eyebrows that was a cross between disapproval and astonishment. But I was relieved to see that the infinite tenderness in his eyes was still there: the thing that told me I never had to be afraid of him. He demanded to know whether I had sabotaged his beautiful arrangement. That made me laugh even more. I then had to suffer several long minutes of his tickling, which was total torture because he was so good at it. When that was over, he ordered me to put the table arrangement back in order. With his help, of course.

'Another major lesson Dad taught me is that life is everywhere. In human beings, animals, plants, everything. He could never bring himself to take the life of a living thing. So at home during the hot season and when we travelled to places where such precautions were necessary, we would use mosquito nets and lemongrass candles, and would cover ourselves with citronella – the same mosquito-repelling oil he had used when he lived in Zanzibar and India – rather than manufactured chemical insecticides. He did eat meat and fish but maintained that one must do so with both consciousness of and respect for the sacrificed life. Universal love, he believed, is the highest goal of our lifetime, so we should treat all living beings with kindness. He adored his cats and respected their lifestyle and behaviour. It used to drive him crazy when they marked their territory in inappropriate places, scratching and urinating. But he knew very well that it was normal feline behaviour, especially where several cats lived together in the same residence. Not that he cleaned up after them himself. His employees were given that task. For their comfort, litter boxes had to be cleaned out, and the litter changed, as soon as one of the cats had used it. It drove him even crazier when they scratched his furniture, which they did even though he'd provided them with a large cat tower. But again, it was normal cat behaviour, and of course he respected that.'

Freddie also loved swans: 'Because they are the symbol of eternal love and faithfulness. The love between pairs of swans is so strong that when one of the pair disappears, the other can literally die of grief. That made infinite sense to him. He also loved dogs, monkeys, donkeys, koi carp, penguins and all sorts of other animals. It reflected his child-like soul. All children try to pet an animal: it's as though they sense a connection with them that they don't yet get with other humans. Freddie always tried to catch and copy the expressions of animals.

'Whenever one of his own pets was sick, he was distraught. He did whatever it took to get it treated and to try and cure it. Imagine, then, how devastated he was when Jim Hutton agreed, with Freddie's koi carp dealer, to kill one of Freddie's kois because it was very sick and the vet hadn't turned up. Jim took that decision by himself, without asking Freddie or Mary. Neither one of them had given their permission for the fish to be destroyed. Freddie would not have spared any expense had there been the slightest chance that the animal could have been saved. But Jim had it killed, and Freddie was beside himself with fury. Not because he didn't agree to have the fish put out of its misery, thus prolonging its suffering. He would of course have resigned himself to that had there been no alternative; but he would have preferred to have been informed, so that he could prepare himself for that sad eventuality. The vet would have come, and Freddie would have accepted his advice with a heavy heart. As it happened, he wasn't even asked his opinion. Jim made a decision that was not his to make, and Freddie was presented with a fait accompli. If you knew how deeply he loved his cats and his fish, how attentive he was to their well-being and how respectful he was of all living things, you would understand why he was so furious with Jim. Worse, the decision that Jim made did not solve the problem with the pond or the quality of the water. So as far as Freddie was concerned, the poor fish died for nothing.'

Freddie was, all things considered, a good hands-on dad: 'He spent a great deal of time teaching me chess, to play the piano and how to fly my kite,' she says. 'He always carried a particular bag with him that had many compartments and front pockets. As a child, that bag was like Aladdin's cave to me. There was one compartment I was never allowed to open; I never knew what he kept in that one. All the rest were my playground. My tiny hands discovered many interesting things to play with in all those pockets. He would also deposit gifts there for me to find.

'I wouldn't have questioned it at the time, because kids don't, but I believe now that parenting came completely naturally to him. His patience, attentiveness and caring, his ability to show you the way, his ability to teach, his understanding and tenderness, his kindness and goodness, his propensity for creating happiness and joy, his huge capacity for love, for hugging, consoling and cuddling, his gift for opening your eyes to the things that really matter – who else ever had a father as magical as this?'

But he was also very down to earth, she reveals.

'School was extremely important, and I was required to take it seriously. I had a certain amount of freedom, but I had to do school homework before I could do anything else. I also had to get good marks. This was one of the things he was adamant about.'

Might that have related to the fact that he had sabotaged his own considerable academic potential as a schoolboy, hurling studies aside to focus on rock and pop music, failing all his O levels and getting himself removed from the school his parents had sacrificed so much to send him to? It is possible. Although given what we know now, isn't it equally likely that he paused his academic ability in order to escape an environment in which he was being abused by a paedophile? And also that, had he not done so, he might have been destroyed?

•   •   •

Freddie, the whole world knows, lived a life of luxury and opulence.

'But I grew up in luxury and opulence, whereas he had not,' B. points out. 'As we have seen, he liked to spend money, and to give without counting the cost. He was, I will say again, very good at spoiling you. But he also taught me to work hard and to persevere. He taught me the value of work, and of possessions. He said there is no such thing as something for nothing, that nothing good ever comes easily, that you must earn your own living, and that you have no choice but to work hard to earn enough to spend the way you want.'

He taught his only child well. She applied herself throughout school, proceeded to tertiary education and further training, and became a sought-after medical professional.

'I wanted to be an archaeologist,' B. divulges. 'I am passionate about history, civilisations and the arts, all interests that I inherited from my father. I studied Archaeology, History of Art and Ancient History. When I was eighteen, I lost my boyfriend and his brother in a car crash. One of the other passengers in the car was seriously injured, and had to submit to thirty months of rehab, learning to eat, walk and write again. Having lost my father only three years earlier, this was devastating. The two tragedies affected me profoundly. A profession in which I could be more of service to others then became the obvious choice for me. I completed my studies, then took two years out and travelled around the world. I wanted to see with my own eyes all those wonderful, ancient places brimming with history.'

On her return, she committed to studying in her branch of medicine. Did it ever cross her mind to try to become an artist herself, the way so many rock 'n' roll offspring do?

Never, she insists.

'Why do you think no child of a revered artist can match or surpass the achievements of their famous parent? It's because they had the childhood that the mother or father didn't have. Most major artists develop their talent through hardship. It occurs as though in defiance of all that they had to go through. Children who grow up in a safe, secure, loving and healthy environment have no need to fill an emotional void. When they become teenagers, there are only three possible futures for such children. They are so damaged by their connection to this great figure that they fall into addiction or depression, or develop disorders and phobias. *Or* doors open to them far more easily because of who their parents are, so they get the opportunities but can rarely live up to them. They will invariably be compared to the parent, whose talent they cannot match. Because they cannot exist in that field without that connection, they are doomed never to be fully themselves. Alternatively, they take time and trouble to discover what they truly love, what they are destined for, and they find the courage to follow a different path.

'This third option is the one that my dad always encouraged me to choose. He provided the support that enabled me to do it. "Discover as many possibilities as you can," he would urge me. "Do things with envy. Do the things you believe in. Do them for yourself, and not because others want you to." He was right.

'Like all children, Freddie's childhood had a huge impact on his life. His was truly awful. We now know that it's why he set out to become a rock star. It's the reason why he was one, and the reason why I am not one. Yes, I'm a good piano player. But I am not a pianist, still less a composer. I do not regret that. I love and am passionate about the career that I have. I try always to do my best professionally. But once I became a mother, the most important job in my life was to be the best mum I could be.'

She should, she reasons, be the first person to want to dilute, simplify and sanitise Freddie's X-rated promiscuous lifestyle.

'I should also be the first person to try to erase Mary from his history. It's normal for children to want their parents to be together, isn't it? It was no different for me. But were I to try and paint him as something he wasn't, I would be compromising my loyalty to him. He said on many occasions and even in interviews that he was a man of extremes; that he was made from many ingredients, and that he had conflicting sides. Why would I try to deny the real him?'

Freddie was, she says, like thousands of others, a victim of his time and not of his lifestyle.

'Ten years earlier or ten years later and his fate, even without changes to his lifestyle, might have been a completely different one. A decade earlier, HIV was not as prevalent as it was during the period 1977–1985, so maybe he wouldn't have got it. Ten years later, the world had comprehensive knowledge of AIDS. He would have practised safe sex from the start. I am the first person to regret that he didn't call time on his promiscuous life-style long before he did. The first to regret that he didn't rest more often during his final years, so that he would have been less exhausted and might have extended his life expectancy. The first to mourn when he stopped his treatment, even though his physical suffering was something you wouldn't have wished on any living being, because each hour and every day carried him a little closer towards more effective treatment and even the possi-bility of a cure.

'And I must be the first person who longs for him still to be here, talking with me for hours on end and playing with my child-ren – his grandchildren. It's easy to moralise about his lifestyle when the person doing so knows so little about him. Even fellow rock stars who actually "know better" because they live the same kind of "lifestyle" themselves become hypocritical whenever they talk about Freddie. Why are *their* groupies, *their* several sexual partners every night, *their* boozing and cocaine consumption any different from his?

'Bottom line, I want you to know that I am not damaged by who my dad was. Not by his lifestyle, his excesses, his demons, his dark side or anything else. I knew who he really was, and that was enough for me. Nor am I damaged by my anonymity: quite the opposite. I watched him compartmentalise his life very successfully. That's probably why I have been able to do the same.'

• • •

It must have torn at her father's heart, his daughter reflects, that she lived with her mother, her stepfather and later on her half-brothers, but not all the time with him.

'I know that made him feel guilty and powerless. Not because of my birth – he never once, he insisted, regarded his affair with my mother as a mistake – but because I wasn't born into a perfect and secure family situation, the kind that he had dreamed of creating for himself. Because he couldn't do anything to change it, he made the best of it. He made sure that I had the best possible life.

'I know he loved me and liked me just as I am. I knew I could open up and confide in him without restraint, and that I could always be myself. While it's true that I was kept away from the world of showbusiness and shielded from journalists and photographers, I never felt hidden. I was never made to feel like "the illegitimate one", the adulterine child. I didn't have to worry that anyone was ashamed of me. For Freddie, it was out of the question that a child should be exposed to public scrutiny. So he went to great lengths to protect me. For him, that was normal. He was adamant that life on the road and backstage culture were no place for a child. The many receptions that Queen were obliged to attend, even less so.

'He loved performing, but he loathed being on tour. I saw him on stage several times in 1984, when I was seven years old.

Mostly at the end of the week, because their *The Works* tour took place during term time; and again in 1986, on the *Magic* tour, when I was nine. But my presence made him uncomfortable.'

Not because he worried that someone might join the dots, perceive a likeness and work out that she must be his progeny – although he did fear some of this too, she says.

'He didn't want his public life to affect the privacy of his loved ones, nor for us to suffer harassment from the press. He was also convinced that the rock 'n' roll environment was inappropriate for children. So I would be escorted to the concert, then taken straight back to the hotel. There I would sit patiently, waiting for him to come back. He would never have taken me with him to an album launch party, as others did with their children.'

Again, not because she might be recognised, or because those not in on their secret might realise, but because work was work, and a child had no place being there.

• • •

Freddie's daughter knows how fortunate she is to own so many photos, home audio recordings and home videos, even though it now feels strange to her to listen to and watch them, because she is older than he was when he died.

'He had so few photos from his own childhood that he was desperate to keep a record of all our moments together. Most of the time, it was my wonderful, magnanimous stepfather who was on the other side of the camera, while Freddie and I posed and pranced about together. Because he couldn't avoid public scru-tiny and his privacy was often compromised, he really enjoyed the private filming of our time together, secure in the knowledge that the video footage would remain private forever.

'He had a multitrack recording machine at our home, too. He kept others at Phillimore Gardens, Stafford Terrace and Garden Lodge. He always recorded whatever he improvised. If he thought he might be able to make a good song out of it, he would take the tape to the recording studio. Many of his tapes were left at our home, and there they will remain. For two important reasons: firstly, if he didn't take them to work on further in the studio, it was because he considered them not good enough to develop. Secondly, because the only person who could judge, develop and complete his own ideas was Freddie himself.'

CHAPTER 13

NO DOMINION

It is not for us to judge with hindsight, B. insists, the behaviour of the 1980s. Nor must we measure it against modern sexual mores, social politics or woke sensitivities. Her views chime with what Freddie had to say about HIV and AIDS in his diaries, and with his personal experience of the disease.

'No one has the right to say that Freddie paid the price for the life he lived,' she says. 'Nor does anyone have the right to attack him for his sexuality. It was not a crime. He lived the life he wanted to live, believing it could make him happy. He was a victim of his time, when the disease was new and largely unidentified; before the explosion of the HIV/AIDS pandemic, when theories about it clashed, when nothing was certain, when information was contradictory and before the availability of comprehensive treatment. Which would not have cured him of the disease, but could have kept him alive. He was a victim of all that, and not of his lifestyle nor his sexuality.'

When the human immunodeficiency virus (HIV) was first identified in 1983, Freddie was au fait with developments. Formerly referred to as GRID – Gay-Related Immune Deficiency – it was believed to affect only certain groups. 'But as he explained,' says B., 'we didn't know much else. There were two opposing theories. One held that the syndrome developed after long-term exposure to multiple infections and viruses, so prolonged promiscuity was considered extremely dangerous to health. The other theory focused on a single virus, suggesting that even one sexual encounter with an infected person could be enough to lead to the development of AIDS. Until 1984, a segment of the US gay community was proclaiming the following: "No evidence supports the theory of a new or mutant virus, and the speculation regarding a single new virus continues just because there are rumours that a small percentage of gay AIDS victims claim to have had a low number of sexual partners, and because any researches persist in the notion that the same agent is causing the AIDS that is occurring in four very different groups: male homosexuals, Haitians, intravenous drug abusers, and haemophiliacs." They concluded that there had been no evidence to justify a search for a new mutant virus, and that no firm evidence had been produced to support the view that a new virus was the cause of AIDS. It was widely suggested that if you stopped being promiscuous, you would recover from immunosuppression. The internet was not yet in general use. Information was not easily accessible. When he was in New York City, Freddie knew what was going on there and then. But he didn't know the status of the epidemic in Los Angeles. During his time in Munich there were very few cases, so that was somewhere he felt relatively safe.' But understanding of the disease was in its infancy. The medical profession still had much to learn. Freddie was all too aware that the chances of him not having it were near zero, given the risky lifestyle he had lived.'[1]

In the autumn of 1984, when he learned that his former lover Tony Bastin, with whom he had shared a relationship between late 1979 and the summer of 1980 (so not the 'two-year relationship' so often reported) had developed full-blown AIDS, Freddie knew he must be infected with HIV.

'He had taken countless risks. He'd had a lot of unprotected sex with a significant number of partners. There was also the fact that, as a passive male, he faced a higher risk of infection than an active partner.'

The news about Bastin horrified Freddie.

'To begin with,' B. relates, 'he was in denial. He threw himself into even more excessive and destructive behaviour, overdoing the alcohol and drugs and indulging in a furious amount of hard, no-strings sex. This was his "doing everything with every-body" phase of which he spoke to his friend, the broadcaster Paul Gambaccini, at London's Heaven nightclub: the night Paul said he realised that Freddie was going to die. In March 1985, Freddie discovered his first lesion: just above the right armpit, at the edge of where the hair begins. A few months later a second lesion, larger than the first, appeared on the inner surface of his right arm.' In images captured during Queen's iconic perfor-mance at *Live Aid* on 13 July that year, he can be seen wearing a spike-studded amulet high on the bicep of his right arm, to hide the second, larger lesion.'

His HIV infection was entering its active phase, she says.

'He was now developing the first symptoms of ARC, AIDS-related complex. In the autumn of 1985, he gave in and agreed to take a test, the result of which was negative. Unfortunately, it would prove to be a false negative. How that could possibly have happened remains a mystery. I still don't understand it. One thing I am certain of is that Freddie didn't hide it. Nor did he lie about it. Had the first test returned positive, which it ought to have done, he would have adopted the same responsible attitude as he did in 1987, when he knew for sure. He would have told Mary, Joe Fannelli and Jim Hutton immediately. Having had sexual relations with all three, they too would need to be tested. He would then have taken all the necessary and responsible precautions that he started taking from 1987 onwards.

'I suspect the reason why he didn't do another test when the first came back negative, despite feeling sure that he must be positive, was because part of him remained hopeful that he was really negative. He was hoping against hope that all the illnesses and infections he was contracting were due to his excessive consumption of class A drugs, mainly cocaine but also poppers and alcohol, down the years.'

In spring 1986, Winnie Kirchberger in Munich received confirmation of his own positive status. He informed Freddie directly, at the same time ending their relationship. Winnie soon descended into madness, the virus having gone to his brain. Barbara Valentin told me that she found him starving to death in his own apartment, his cat eating its fur to survive. 'I got him into hospital and paid his medical bills,' she said. 'But it was far too late to help him.'

• • •

The thing that really destabilised and destroyed Freddie, his daughter reveals, was that his most precious dream was now dashed.

'He would never be able to create his own family, see his children grow up, or build the unconditional love and bond with them that he needed so much. Yes, he had me. But he wanted more, and to live with his wife and children all the time, not just visit them. He was, at his heart, completely family-oriented. To have his own little clan and to live happily ever after with them was his only remaining aim in life. At long last, Freddie Bulsara had regained the upper hand over Freddie Mercury. He was of course well aware that he could not arrest the course of events. He had no way of stopping what was going to happen to him. Yet still, almost perversely, he refused to give up on his dream of creating a family.' His personal tragedy was not so much that his dream of having children with Mary was now over, more that he was now in deep denial. He still believed that he could somehow control the outcome.

In July 1986, thirty-five-year-old Mary Austin granted an interview to journalist and loyal friend David Wigg, during which she told him she would like to have a baby before it was too late. She knew, given his health status, that the father of her child could not be Freddie. Later that day, during Freddie's part of the interview, David asked him if *he* wanted a child. Freddie responded glibly that he would rather have another cat.

'He said this because he knew already that he was HIV positive, so he could never have any more biological children,' says B. 'That is, he knew, but not officially. He as good as knew because Tony Bastin had developed full-blown AIDS, and they had had a relationship six years earlier. He knew that his chances of being negative were close to zero.

'David, of course, had no idea that Freddie had a child already, so he was never going to ask him anything about me. As so often happens in press interviews, the newspaper misquoted both Mary and Freddie. They sensationalised the interview, as

David explained, in order to increase sales. Freddie was always infuriated by that kind of thing.'

When interior designer, painter and decorator Piers Cameron started work at the Garden Lodge Mews, he and Mary soon caught each other's eye. Mary and Piers started dating and became a couple. Freddie approved, and their first child was soon conceived.

But Cameron had always felt overshadowed by Freddie, B. reveals. He left Phillimore Gardens shortly before his and Mary's second son, Jamie, was born.

• • •

Having called time on his promiscuity months earlier, Freddie now discontinued all sexual activity within his close circle of regular partners and limited himself to safe sex with Jim Hutton.

'But there soon came the time when sex was the furthest thing from his mind, the very last thing he wanted,' says B. 'The "titillation" to which he and Jim resorted was not enough for Jim, who continued to frequent bars and clubs where he would pick up other men. There were times when he would not return to Garden Lodge until dawn. Not only that, but by then, Freddie and Mary were hardly ever spending the night together either. Freddie hated the thought that Jim was out cheating on him and leaving him all alone, the thing he couldn't bear. He was spending most nights by himself, waiting for Jim to come home. He accepted the situation for a while, but then he grew bored of it. He was also extremely tired from the progression of the disease. All he wanted was calm, serenity and peace, and to live out his days comfortably and safely in his own home. He'd had enough of the turbulent situation with Jim. After an argument too many about Jim's reckless and selfish behaviour, Freddie ended the relationship. He now spent all his nights alone, no longer waiting for anyone to come home. For the first time in his life, Freddie preferred loneliness to bad company.'

In 1989, Freddie lost a great deal of weight and developed full-blown AIDS.

'Those still inclined to believe that he'd had it since 1987 would do well to remember that a person with full-blown AIDS in 1983 had a life expectancy of just sixteen months,' says B. 'By 1993, a decade later, life expectancy had increased only to twenty-two months. Had that been Freddie's status since 1987, he would have lived with the disease for fifty-five months: a medical impossibility at that time.'

AZT, zidovudine, was the main treatment for the terminal phase of the disease.

'But it came with terrible side effects,' B. reveals, 'such as loss of appetite, nausea, vomiting, headaches and insomnia. At that time, full-blown AIDS reduced one's life expectancy to less than two years. But it could also be reduced to only a few days. Any small infection could prove fatal. It was the reason why, when Freddie developed full-blown AIDS and his CD4 cell count reached the most critical level, his doctors said he might not be there for Christmas 1989. Many patients died because they could no longer tolerate the brutal treatment. So much of it was about willpower: they had to try and find the will to live. Most of them, including Dad, did decide to stop the treatment in the end. They did so well aware of the fact that any minor infection could kill them within a few days.

'HIV was also developing resistance to the drug. Only mono-therapy (a single type of treatment) would be available until 1995. The clinical trials for triple therapy (a combination of treatments) did not begin until 1992, the year after Freddie's death. So he never got the chance to try anything other than monotherapy.'

. . .

Death didn't scare him, Freddie wrote: '... despite the fact that he didn't accept that his life was being taken away from him until the very last months,' B. says. 'He continued to follow Zarathustra's teachings closely. That is to say, "There are two worlds, the physical and the World of Thoughts. Human beings live and move in these two worlds simultaneously. The physical world is ephemeral and vulnerable, but the spiritual world is eternal. Life is no more than a long preparation for the World of Thoughts, and it continues in the spiritual realm."'

Freddie knew, he said, that he would continue to write and sing songs as long as his body and mind would let him. He had no fears on that score.

. . .

Mary didn't want Freddie to bequeath Garden Lodge to her. She made no bones about telling him so. The crucible of their happiness had long been Phillimore Gardens.

'Until the very last months of Freddie's life,' says B. 'But Freddie clung to his dream of Garden Lodge as a family home, brimming with children and laughter. Mary had one son already and would soon give birth to her second, shortly after Freddie's death. The house, he insisted, must be used for the purpose for which it had been intended. Mary eventually accepted this.'

Garden Lodge was, as she has confirmed, Freddie's and Mary's house. It was never the bachelor pad most fans understand it to have been. Even though other men had lived there throughout Freddie's occupancy, they were all – including Jim Hutton – his employees.

'They were indeed his servants,' says B. 'That was how he regarded them. Whenever Freddie's parents came to visit, Mary was always there with him. Peter and Jim had to leave and go elsewhere. And whenever Freddie visited his parents at their home for tea or lunch, he almost always went there with Mary.

'Freddie's professional world was light years away from Bomi's and Jer's quiet existence. But when Freddie visited his parents, he was never Mercury. He was only Farrokh, a loving son visiting his mum and dad. They understood the strict demarcation that Freddie made between the private life of Farrokh/Freddie Bulsara and the professional life of Freddie Mercury. It has been written, said, and even alluded to in the film *Bohemian Rhapsody* that Bomi disapproved deeply of his son's way of life, and even that he considered Freddie's lifestyle a mortal sin. Had that been true, Bomi would never have gone to Garden Lodge for family lunches or dinners. He would never have received Freddie at his own home in Feltham, Middlesex. And above all, he would never have attended the many events honouring Freddie after his son's death. He never made the excuse that he was too old and ill to go, which the organisers and fellow attendees would have understood and accepted. No, he turned up, rain or shine, come what may. He did so because he could not have been more proud of his son.

'Freddie always came home to spend Christmas with Mary and to visit his parents,' she says. 'New Year, however, was a time for partying with his friends. For some years, he was in the habit of taking the last Concorde flight out of London to spend New Year's Eve in New York. To Munich or anywhere else that took his fancy; it would always be the final flight of the evening.'

Mary enjoyed her own long, loving relationship with Bomi and Jer.

'During Freddie's extended absences, she would visit them frequently and call them regularly,' affirms B. 'They were to become estranged from each other only after Freddie's will was published. Only then did it become apparent that Freddie had left Mary the bulk of his estate. Very sadly, because of bitterness that arose regarding the terms of the will, the relationship between Mary and Freddie's parents fell apart, never to be restored.'

. . .

'I can't believe how some people don't remember when Freddie told them he had AIDS,' his daughter muses. 'Nor how such a story can change multiple times. All I can say is, surely you don't forget something as life-shattering as that. I for one will never forget the spring day in 1990 when he told me to my face that he was very ill. I will never forget his voice, nor the way he looked. He wore a strange expression, one that I'd never seen before. Nor will I forget the day, fifteen months later, when he told me that he was dying. The state of the sky, the weather, the colours and sounds of nature, every detail about that day is imprinted on my memory. I realised only much later that he had been preparing me slowly for this outcome. It was a few days after the second conversation that he gave me the notebooks. Three months after that, he finally admitted to me that he had AIDS. Four weeks later, he was gone.'

As one might expect, Freddie spent his final years in denial.

'Firstly,' says B., 'he denied to himself that he was probably HIV positive. When there was no longer doubt about that, he sought to deny that he was ill. When he knew black on white that he was sick, he began to deny that he was going to die. When at last he accepted that he was dying, he wanted, most desperately, to live. When his life was no longer a life – such as when you hear the crackling of a record player needle when the record has finished playing, which was his way of describing it – it was only then that he agreed to let go.

'AIDS is a terrible disease. It makes a living corpse of the human being, wasting the muscles and draining the body of energy. At only forty-five, my dad was a geriatric. His condition got worse and worse, until he could no longer bring himself to look in the mirror.

'Perhaps the cruellest thing is the way it creeps up on its victim. In the beginning, it's easy to kid yourself that there's nothing wrong. Then the virus activates and begins causing random infections. You start to lose weight and suffer desperately from weakness and fatigue. He could work for only a few hours each day before becoming overwhelmed with tiredness. He made himself take long siestas, believing that they would revive him. But the more he rested, the more exhausted he became. The remainder of his day was punctuated by loss of appetite and nausea, stomach cramps, limb cramps and all-over aches and pains, insomnia, headaches and all sorts of other disorders. It soon became virtually impossible for him to eat or to swallow. He struggled to go to the bathroom. Standing up, sitting, lying down – everything was now painful for him. This process happened incredibly quickly. He was given gym exercises to prevent his muscles from becoming atrophied. He did manage, and he enjoyed, short walks. Then he became contemplative, which he had not been for quite a long time. It was a revelation. He started finding everything he looked at – mountains, nature, sky, the light – magnificent and beautiful.

'His CD4 cell count tests, which are used to monitor HIV, had been lending rhythm to his life since 1987. Their ups and downs corresponded to his hopes and dark despairs; to his bright recoveries and his abysmal collapses. There came the time when he no longer wanted to know what his weight was, nor to be told the result of his latest CD4 count. He continued to do all the tests his doctors encouraged him to do, including the most brutal, but he didn't want to know the outcome. By then, he was well versed in the different stages of the disease. Eventually, he felt himself falling, and realised he must be close to death. It was now a question of weeks, not months. At last, he accepted that nothing more could be done for him.'

There were still things he had to sort out, and plenty of things to put in order.

'He also wanted to prepare for several Christmases ahead, and the next few birthdays to come, for his loved ones. That the last activity in life that brought him pleasure was the buying of presents to please us all in his absence is utterly heartbreaking to me. I received gifts from him for years after his death: not only for Christmas and birthdays, but for my final university exams too. You know, all that giving was very Freddie. But I don't think he can have anticipated how painful for us the receiving would be.

'He dealt with the last remaining demands. He tied up loose ends. He carried on buying Mary paintings almost until the end, always keen to keep the tax bill down. Then, when all was said and done; when the painkillers were killing the little strength he had left but not the pain itself; and when he was suffocating except under dosages heavy enough to sedate him, he was at last ready to die. He decided it was time to stop taking his medication, to say goodbye – which he had never been able to say but could at last bring himself to do – and simply let go. When he returned to London from Switzerland that final time, the decision had already been taken. Having stopped his treatment, he knew that his condition would deteriorate very quickly, and that his final few days would be extremely painful for him.'

• • •

Freddie did not consider Queen's manager a friend, his daughter reveals.

'Jim Beach was the band's lawyer before he became the manager of both the band and Freddie independently, and he was the executor of Freddie's will. But he was not Freddie's lawyer,' B. says. 'He didn't have control over Freddie's money, nor over how Freddie spent it. As his executor, he has responsibilities. Were he to manage the trust incorrectly, he would have the court to answer to. His role was only ever about business. Freddie makes clear that he did not regard their relationship as a friendship. Beach simply did whatever Freddie told him to do.

'To be clear,' his daughter adds, 'those who care to go looking will find no mention of me in Freddie's will, because I am not, nor have I ever been, the beneficiary of a trust fund. I received, by other means, enough money to live comfortably for the rest of my life. Freddie had fifteen years to arrange that. In those days, exclusive Swiss banks and their numbered accounts facilitated private transactions with total discretion. Works of art, gold, jewels and bearer bonds, providing fixed-income security for their holder, were other means by which to bequeath wealth. Even though my dad left me very well provided for, you will not find any trace of me anywhere. He did not make "official" provision for me. This was all to ensure that I could retain my privacy.'

To this day, she laments, 'People often confuse HIV and AIDS. AIDS is what the HIV infection develops into, when the CD4 cells have dropped to a very low level. Freddie had been diagnosed HIV positive in 1987, and he developed full-blown AIDS in 1989. As I have said, because he was working on the *Barcelona* album with Montsy, whom he loved and respected, he felt it was his duty to tell her. Because he was not working with the band at that time, he didn't tell Roger, John or Brian. They did not hear about it from Freddie until much later.'

Even though there was strong public support and outpourings of love for Freddie during that period, she says, he was also subjected to 'an avalanche of hatred. People who didn't know him said that he got what he deserved. They jeered that his whole life had been about debauchery. Some called him a predator, a pervert, a deviant, even a criminal. The wave of hatred and aggression was horrible. This kind of thing still happens, even now. Freddie hated the verbal violence, lies and betrayals with every shred of energy he had left.

'Despite the fact that Freddie did not regard him as a close personal friend, it was Jim Beach who went to Garden Lodge to take Freddie's final instructions, prepare his statement and agree when it should be published,' she says. 'Mary, even though she was heavily pregnant, stayed with Freddie much of the time, and was relieved regularly by his close friend Dave Clark. Joe Fannelli was in charge of Freddie's painkillers. Joe and Peter Freestone took it in turns to respond to his personal needs. The publication of this statement, when it happened, was Freddie's decision and his alone.'

Following the enormous conjecture in the press over the last two weeks [it read], I wish to confirm that I have been tested HIV positive and have AIDS. I felt it correct to keep this information private to date to protect the privacy of those around me. However, the time has come now for my friends and fans around the world to know the truth, and I hope that everyone will join with me, my doctors and all those worldwide in the fight against this terrible disease. My privacy has always been very special to me, and I am famous for my lack of interviews. Please understand this policy will continue.

Freddie died in his own bed, under his own roof, with only his close friend Dave Clark at his side. Mary could not be there because of her condition. The stress of watching her partner die could have put her and her baby at risk. She would give birth to her second son soon afterwards.

• • •

The day Freddie died is very difficult for B. to recall.

'I have such terrible memories of it,' she says. 'It is well known that some of the media's representatives behaved abominably. A number of journalists and photographers camped outside Garden Lodge for the duration. Some behaved like vultures, waiting for him to expire so that they could consume him. Those people deprived him of his last days, his final precious hours. To them, he was no longer a human being. He was just a headline. I found their cruelty towards their fellow human hideous.

'Some who have written since his death about the last days of his life seek to justify their revelations and opinions with the excuse that Freddie isn't here to tell the truth for himself. "And as you know, he would have said, the truth, warts and all," they protest. But that should not give them free rein to act without respect, or to deprive him of his dignity. Whenever a so-called friend spoke indiscreetly about how well endowed he was, or revealed details about the final moments of his life, describing how nature took its course and what kind of underwear they changed him into, they stole Freddie's dignity. The world did not need to know these things.

'I am so grateful to my father for the notebooks; for being so intimate and for letting his guard down. I'm so glad that he left this complete record of his life, and that I am able to share a little of it here with the many who care. Otherwise, the Freddie I knew so well and loved so deeply would by now have been swallowed up by all that hatred and all those lies. He always did everything right, with so much love, attention and care. Certain people benefitted hugely from having known him. He did not deserve the way he has been treated since.

'I remain grateful for small mercies. One of which is that Freddie is still around. I feel his presence everywhere. There are aromas, perfumes and pieces of music that pull me towards him every day, even after all these years. It's as if he's right here with me, in the room. Not that this is always the comfort I want and need it to be.'

As the Japanese writer Haruki Murakami said, 'Memories warm you up from the inside, but they also tear you apart.'[2]

• • •

From the moment there was no doubt in Freddie's mind that he was HIV positive, Mary was, as she had always been, his fortress.

'She endured everything with him,' says B. 'As ever, she saw everything. Knew everything. He never had to hide a single thing from her. If anything, and if that were possible, his illness drew them closer together. She had always accepted everything that Freddie was. She had given him both freedom and stability. He gave her those things in return. He would never have sacrificed their love for any other relationship. He was unfaithful to her over and over in a sexual context, yes – but he never betrayed her in his heart or his thoughts. He knew that the way they lived was something most people would never be able to accept or understand. That was the reason why they never went public about it. Why should they? Their relationship was for them and them alone.'

CHAPTER 14

A FEATHER ON THE BREEZE

In 2005, fourteen years after Freddie's death, Brian May was appointed Commander of the Most Excellent Order of the British Empire (CBE), the third class in order of appointment in the British Honours system, for services to the music industry. Seventeen years later, in 2022, Roger Taylor was appointed Officer (OBE), the fourth rank of five.

'What about John Deacon?' asks B. 'And how about Freddie? John should have been awarded too, while Freddie should have been recognised posthumously. All four of them, after all, were major contributors to the Queen oeuvre.'

On the subject of John, there is something else she wishes to make clear for the record: 'Freddie was the one who encouraged John to write songs,' she says, 'and who helped him to do so. There are songs, such as "Friends Will Be Friends" from the *A Kind of Magic* album, that Freddie and John wrote together. Are there any written by John and Roger together, or by John and Brian together? Freddie – Bulsara, I mean, the real him, not Mercury – and John were close friends. Both were deeply scarred and equally reserved. John regarded Freddie more as an older brother than a father figure, as Freddie has sometimes been described. There were several occasions when John wanted to leave the band. He was sick of living away from his family, he missed his wife and children dreadfully, and when problems arose among the members of Queen, he simply couldn't see the point of being there any longer. Freddie cared for John, and was always mindful of the effect such tense situations were having on him. He would always try to find the right words with which to smooth things over.'

In her humble opinion, while acknowledging that Brian and Roger can be credited for having kept the Queen legacy alive all these years, she does not regard the two of them without Freddie and John as 'Queen'.

'They sing and perform Queen songs, but there is no new material.'

She finds difficult the endless remastering, reworking and repackaging of old songs: 'Because Freddie would never have done this. He always looked at the new musical project, what he could inject into a new concept, what could feed him creatively. As I mentioned to you about the new *Queen I* album, Freddie would NEVER have said, "I'm not satisfied with what we did fifty-one years ago, so we have to rework it." What is done is done, so let's go to the next one, was his attitude. The phoenix is always reborn. It is not consumed by its regrets half a century later.'

She does not like the idea of the fans being sold what they own already:

'As for Queen + Adam Lambert, that was never a legitimate name. Without Freddie and John, that's actually "Half of Queen + Adam Lambert". It's really Roger and Brian plus Adam Lambert, isn't it? As such, isn't that line-up actually a covers band?'

• • •

B. reflects again on comments made by Brian May about Freddie's sexuality and image. It is clearly a theme that preoccupies her. 'I shared rooms with Fred on the first couple of tours,' Brian May told the *Daily Express* in 2006, repeated in 2008. 'I knew a lot of his girlfriends and he certainly didn't have boyfriends, that's for sure. In those days it was the fashion to be kind of dandyish, and I suppose we had a hand in creating the fashion, so there was this doubt in people's minds as to whether you might be gay or not. It was a convenient little place to be. I remember Freddie being asked if he was gay in one of his early interviews, and he said, "Yes, darling, of course I am. I am as gay as a daffodil." It was a neat way of sidestepping the issue because actually, Fred was no fool. I know that all through his life, Fred didn't think that whether he was gay or not was important. He loved music, he loved his work, and he didn't want anything to get in the way. Anyone who portrays Fred as purely a gay story is missing a lot of the point.'

And again, during November 2021, in a BBC documentary entitled *The Final Act*, Brian said of Freddie declaring himself to be 'as gay as a daffodil' in a '1978 interview' with the *NME*, 'That is not a man denying his sexuality.'

'To be clear,' says B., 'the interview, with Julie Webb, took place in March 1974, before *Queen II* was released. And it changed everything. The band had experienced a lot of problems with their debut album *Queen*, and its release was postponed for several months. It was released when *Queen II* was almost finished, and while their third album, *Sheer Heart Attack*, was being written. Their first single, "Keep Yourself Alive", was not successful. "Seven Seas of Rhye" wasn't out yet, "Killer Queen" was still a long way off, and "Bohemian Rhapsody" even further. They needed their second album to be a hit, they needed exposure and they needed to be making headlines. In 1974, androgyny and bisexuality were widespread in the artistic world. So in some ways, Freddie had nothing to fear in being open about his orientation and behaviour. But he had just proposed marriage to Mary. His response during the *NME* interview, therefore, was as Freddie Mercury and not as Freddie Bulsara. It was entirely in keeping with his stage persona. He said it in a camp, provocative way, just ahead of the release of *Queen II*, and during a period of time when all four members of Queen were wearing women's blouses. But by 1978, Freddie and Mary had redefined their partnership, Paul Prenter was now working for Queen, and Freddie was exploring other facets of his sexuality. Brian must have full access to the Queen archives. It would have been easy to look it up and check.'

The same goes, she says, for the song 'Don't Stop Me Now':

'Brian said that this song is Freddie's expression of his gayness. He overlooks the fact that Freddie sings not only about wanting to make a supersonic man of someone, but about doing the same to a woman. The lyrics of this song are in fact bisexual rather than gay. When someone says that Freddie was bisexual, they are accused of being homophobic because they are not saying that he was gay.'

. . .

Freddie wrote his final entry in the last notebook on 31 July 1991, three months and twenty-four days before he died. Not only was his eyesight failing by then, but his strength was deserting him rapidly.

'There are two periods,' says B. 'The one before he told me that he was very ill, and the one after that moment. For several months I had known, inside me, that something was wrong. When you see someone regularly, you don't immediately notice changes. You detect things only when they are particularly pronounced. But I felt it inside. About a year earlier, Dad had started changing physically. The process had speeded up over recent months. I was going through a rebellious phase at that time, so I was in turmoil. I didn't know what was happening. No one said a word to me. I couldn't find the courage, the right words nor the appropriate moment to ask. I'd open my mouth to speak but nothing came out. When at last he sat me down and told me how ill he was, in a way it was a relief. At least, at last, I knew. I no longer needed to torment myself with unspoken questions for which there appeared to be no answers.

'The next sixteen months were more intense than ever, until we left London in early September 1991 and moved abroad again. He told me that he was dying, fifteen months after having told me that he was ill.

'A few days later, after a very odd conversation, he gave me the notebooks. He asked me if I wanted us to talk about them. But after the devastating shock of his announcement that he was dying, I didn't want to talk about any such thing. I was fourteen and a half years old. It was summer. The last thing I wanted to do was to read and discuss my dying dad's writings.'

The final three months were indescribably hard.

'Dad had already planned everything. We still had our daily phone call, every single day, but we could no longer see each other as often as we were used to. He was either in London or

Montreux. I was in neither place. The time left to us amounted to only a few weekends and my school holidays. He had changed so much physically that each time I saw him, he looked like a stranger to me.'

Does she regret not having read the diaries at that time, while he was still alive?

'Not at all. Nor do I regret that we didn't talk about them. We would have talked obsessively about everything that was in them, and in the end it wouldn't have made a bit of difference. What mattered was that we got to enjoy together the little time that we had left. Which is what we did.

'The day he told me he was dying of AIDS was a strangely sunny morning. I was with him in Montreux, in his penthouse apartment at Territet: a suburb of Montreux about a twenty-minute walk along the shore of Lac Léman from where the famous Freddie Mercury statue now stands. The light was very beautiful above the morning mist over the lake. Time, as it tends to when solemn things happen, stood still. What he was telling me didn't seem real, although I knew in my heart that it was true.

'A few days later, the day I saw him for the very last time, it was raining heavily and the sky was menacing and dark. I think he probably knew that day that we would never see each other again … or maybe one day, God willing, in Heaven. I had no idea at the time that it would be the very last time. Did I? Either I didn't realise, or I knew but I was in denial. Either way, I didn't *want* to know about it. Nor have I ever wanted to remember it. Less than four weeks later, he would be dead and gone.

'We continued to speak on the phone every day after that. But our conversations grew shorter and shorter, because he was so fatigued and was suffering so badly.

'Some people have said and written that he didn't care about what happened to him after his death. Had that been the case, he would not have made his final statement that Jim Beach read out to the press, nor would there have been all the secrecy surrounding his final resting place. Dad cared, I can tell you. He cared very much.

'His lack of privacy had been his greatest regret. He had felt imprisoned for many years by his fame and his lifestyle. Again, all he ever wanted was to live a family life. Tragically, he had been able to live only partially away from the "Queen Circus", as he called it, and the "Gay Zoo". At the end of his life, he found himself trapped in his own home, surrounded by all his possessions – like Tutankhamun, he complained – and by people, most of them strangers, who were hanging around outside and waiting for him to die.'

• • •

November has been the saddest month of the year ever since, she tells me.

'Much more than just very difficult to cope with, and not only the twenty-fourth, the day of his death. But there are so many "last times" I wasn't aware at the time would be the "last time". The last photo we had taken together. The last time we walked together along the shore of the lake. The last time we met, the last time he hugged me, the last glance, the last time we talked on the phone – which was a Friday – and his final "*à demain*". Only

355

this time there would never be another tomorrow. He didn't call on the Saturday, nor on the Sunday. But the phone did ring that day: to bring us the news of his death. I do remember who told me; it's not something you can forget. You never do forget such moments. After that, life was a blur. Then came the many tributes. Some of which were very beautiful. Others delivered words worse than any I could have imagined.

'Obviously I can't watch the last videos: his last with Queen, the final home footage of just the two of us together. Nor can I look at the very last photographs. He had changed so much physically that he doesn't look like Dad in them. In every other way he still was my dad. He was still the same thoughtful, loving and caring father I had known and adored since shortly after my birth.'

If she forces herself to recall the last time they saw each other, she says, 'I can tell you the one thing that had not yet changed about him was the intensity of his gaze. Despite his extreme thinness, the huge Kaposi's sarcoma lesions on his forehead, cheek and lower lip, and despite the horrendous fatigue, the incredible power of that stare had not diminished, at least not the last time I saw him. The disease had not yet deprived him of it. That was such a relief to me. Freddie had always communicated as much with his eyes and gestures as he had with his voice. His eyes were one of the last things he had left. But it wasn't to last, as he began to lose his sight over the final days.'

It was another reason why she was so upset by their failure to get Freddie's eyes right in the film.

• • •

Mary phoned Freddie's parents to let them know that their son had died.

'They removed him from Garden Lodge to the funeral parlour, but they did not embalm his body there. Not because he had died of an infectious disease, as has been said repeatedly, but because of Zoroastrian funeral rites and customs. Even though no one should have touched his body because it was disease-ridden, it was thanks to the understanding of the funeral directors, one of whom was a relative of Peter Freestone's, that Freddie's body was prepared in keeping with the rites of his faith.

It was not legal to touch Freddie's body. So I sincerely, deeply and profoundly thank Peter Freestone for his intervention, so that Dad's body could be prepared according to the funeral rites. I know I am sometimes harsh towards Peter because of all that he has said and done since Freddie's death. But on this point, I deeply thank him.'

Such preparation was essential in order for Freddie to reach the World of Thoughts. In fact, according to the religion, every case of death should be supposed to be infectious. There are consequently many rites that those who touch the bodies of the deceased have to adhere to. According to their beliefs, this keeps them safe from disease themselves.

'All his clothes were removed, to leave his body completely naked. If he was still wearing the ring that Jim had given him, that also would have been removed, and later returned to Jim. What would Jim have done with it? I have no idea. But I can't be sure that Freddie was still wearing it at that time. Anything else that might have been placed inside the funeral bag in which he was carried to the mortuary would also have been removed: the soul must go alone into the World of Thoughts. His body was washed with water and placed on a clean, white cotton sheet. The kusti – the cord that Parsees wear around the waist and which consists of seventy-two threads representing the chapters of part of the Zend-Avesta – was knotted around his body. The threads of the cord, incidentally, are interwoven to represent the chapters of the Yasna, the chapters of the Visperad, the twenty-four hours of the day, the twelve months of the calendar and the religious feasts. He was dressed in a clean white cotton suit. His whole body was covered, but not his face. Prayers were offered throughout this preparation ritual, and then his family, but only the Zoroastrian members, were permitted to see him. After three nights – one for his good and evil thoughts, one for his good and evil words, and the final night for his good and evil deeds – he was cremated. Despite what those supposedly in the know have claimed, Freddie did not reject his religion.'

It has often been said that Freddie had a Zoroastrian funeral for the sake of his parents, Bomi and Jer. 'This is totally wrong,' B. informs us. 'It was Freddie's choice, and his alone. It is important to understand that, in Zoroastrianism, nobody can intercede for the salvation of our soul, only we ourselves. The individual and no one else is responsible for his own behaviour, his own sins. No one can save you or absolve you except you yourself. The fact that he was Freddie Mercury did not give him preferential treatment or absolution. If Freddie had not been a worshipper of Ahura Mazda, if he had rejected his religion, if his way of life had been a mortal sin, if his thoughts, words, acts and deeds had not been in harmony with the Zoroastrian faith, his funeral would not have followed the Zoroastrian funeral rites, and no priest would have agreed to conduct the funeral.'

The ceremony, presided over by two Zoroastrian priests, was held at West London Crematorium on 27 November 1991. The service was attended by his family and around thirty-five close friends, including Elton John and Freddie's Queen band-mates. Freddie's coffin was carried into the chapel bearing a single red rose, to Aretha Franklin's rendition of the gospel song 'Precious Lord Take My Hand'. His funeral ended to the strains of Montserrat Caballé's voice singing Freddie's favourite recording of hers, the most demanding and beautiful bel canto aria ever written for the soprano voice: '*D'amor sull'ali rosee*' from the fourth act of Giuseppe Verdi's opera *Il Trovatore*. His body was later cremated at Kensal Green Cemetery. But the commemorative plinth there which bears his birth name does not mark the spot where his ashes are buried. These were entrusted to Mary Austin for burial at a private location. I have visited that location and have seen Mary there. The reason why I know of its whereabouts is because I am a friend of the family who owned the land at that time.

His daughter did not attend his funeral.

'He didn't want me to,' she says. 'He had his reasons, and I maintain that he was right. If he had wanted me to attend, I would have done so. Anyone who might criticise me for that should remember two things: firstly that, at not yet fifteen, I was still a child; and secondly, that I didn't need to go to his funeral to say goodbye. Because Dad and I never said "Goodbye" to each other. Not just because he couldn't stand goodbyes, but because he never said it. Not to me.'

During the days following his cremation at Kensal Green Cemetery, in accordance with Parsee tradition, the clothes that Freddie had been wearing when he left home for the final time were destroyed, along with his personal effects.

'This concept can be difficult to understand,' says B. 'Belongings considered to be "personal" are correspondence, private papers, anything that the deceased has written, drawn or made, his clothes, and anything that he used on a daily basis such as his comb, razor and soap. Things like that. Decorative items that had been purchased, such as ornaments, are not classed as personal belongings – but homemade items are. Gifts he had given, such as drawings from his childhood or artworks gifted during adulthood, do not fall into this category. Nor do gifts received. Anything that you leave behind in a place other than your own home is considered a "gift" to those who remain and is no longer classed as a personal effect. For example, Freddie's album containing his collection of postage stamps had originally belonged to his father, so was not considered to be Freddie's own possession.

'Most of Freddie's personal effects owned by his parents that had not been gifts were burned at the time of his death. Being Parsees of India, Jer and Bomi were devoted traditionalists. They were, however, more progressive when it came to their children. This was because Freddie and Kashmira had grown up in England, where Zoroastrianism follows a rather different path from the one followed by Parsees of India like them.

'Because Mary is not Zoroastrian, she was not required to destroy anything of Freddie's in her possession. As for Kashmira, because gifts do not fall into the personal effects category, his sister had little to burn,' says B.

'I didn't burn Freddie's effects that he kept at our home. I did ask myself whether I should. Many times. But Freddie had made me make that promise to him, the one forbidding me to read some of the notebooks before I turned twenty-five. My stepfather advised me that I should perhaps wait until then to decide. Ten years hence, I could at last read the remaining notebooks and then make my final decision. It was good advice. It made sense. Had I chosen to burn my dad's things straight after his death when I was not yet fifteen years old and couldn't have understood the implications of what I was doing, I may have regretted it bitterly later on.'

• • •

Freddie gave Mary Garden Lodge and the Mews together with all of their contents, all his personal possessions, fifty per cent of his residuary estate and fifty per cent of his future incomes.

'He could never have imagined that one day the *Bohemian Rhapsody* movie would bring in so much money,' she repeats, 'nor that Queen's back catalogue would sell for such a vast sum. When his father, Bomi, died, Jer got his share, twelve and a half per cent of the estate. When his mother, Jer, died, Freddie's sister, Kash, received her share (twelve and a half per cent of Jer's share and twelve and a half per cent of Bomi's share). Until the sale of Queen's catalogue, Mary had fifty per cent of Freddie's shares and twelve and a half per cent of Queen Productions. Kash did too.'

• • •

Freddie Mercury no longer exists, says his daughter.

'He has been twisted, disguised and erased. His words have been distorted and often taken out of context. His songs have been deployed in multiple ways for which they were never intended. There are times when it feels as though his whole life has been rewritten to serve the interests of others.

'Until his death, I never saw him as a "celebrity" or a "superstar". I only realised what Queen was, how big they were, and took in all the stardom and adulation, when I started going to rock gigs myself. Not before.

'Had things been different, Farrokh Bulsara would never have needed to create Freddie Mercury. Had things been different, and had he lived, he would now have been retired for decades from the Queen Circus and from "The Show". He would have stopped touring long ago. For many years, he really enjoyed being on stage. But he hated touring and life on the road more than anything. At forty-five, fifty and beyond, he would have wanted to take time to explore other disciplines that he loved and was fascinated by. He had other aspirations beyond Queen and rock 'n' roll. When it came to songwriting, he was by far the most versatile member of the band, and the one who wrote the most eclectic songs. He would have continued to write songs with the others, and to make albums with Queen. He would even have given occasional one-off concerts here and there. But he most definitely would have stopped touring. He said so himself. This was partly because he was the consummate showman. He gave every single performance his all. He could never have fobbed off the fans with a half-hearted effort, he said. Rock gigs cost the performer a huge amount of energy. He believed that there comes a time when a frontman has to throw in the towel and stop, before he begins to look ridiculous on stage.'

She agrees with him.

'Some bands carry on performing into their sixties, seventies and even eighties, but we all know that they have lost their magic and their glow. They try to camouflage it, often by mechanical means. They augment the performance with big lights and huge visuals. But none of that changes the fact that they are no longer what they once were. Freddie was adamant he would never show on stage that he was no longer what he had been. He resisted the idea of that comparison ever being made. He never wanted to be regarded as a has-been. So he would have given his music and career a new direction. He would have divided his time between the band and other artforms that he wanted to explore, such as opera and ballet, *la tentation* – the opera-ballet hybrid in which both singers and dancers perform leading roles – and musical theatre. He was interested in all fields in which music, dance, costumes, visuals, lights, choreography and theatrics come together.

'Had things been different, the time would have come when he would have started to set limits on me to mark the path of my adolescence, thus enabling him to watch over me while giving me the space to grow up and experiment for myself. But of course, I would have rejected any such limits, and we would have fought. And he would have understood the necessity for that, and would have allowed me a long leash, because he could remember so clearly how things had been with his parents during his own adolescence. He had very strict principles, rules and ideas. He could be fierce, and of course he was extremely protective.

He would not, for example, have allowed me to wear certain clothes or make-up. He would have been firmly against me going out, and all that goes with that, all the things we want to try when we are teenagers. He was all too aware that there is a difference between letting your daughter do mostly what she wants and being supportive of her choices even when you don't approve of them and letting her do whatever she likes and going too far. Given the kind of dad he was, his opinion would have been that I was doing too much and going too far for my age and my own good, even if that wasn't really the case. We would have discussed everything at length, as we always did. Our long discussions were both the basis of our father–daughter relationship and the foundation of his way of being a dad.

'I would still have loved and respected him with all my heart, of course. But I would also have known how to push his buttons. I would have been, in his eyes, a difficult and moody teenager. I would have rebelled. I would have split hairs, I would have challenged him on words and facts, and I would have provoked and maddened, defied and disobeyed him. And he, with all his love and paternal affection, all his tenderness, thoughtfulness, patience and forbearance, his infinite kindness, goodness, cheerfulness and the immense understanding that he was able to bring to being a loving and caring father … he would have won.

'Had things been different, he would have one day walked me up the aisle on my wedding day.

'Had things been different and he were here today, he would have the same love, tenderness, thoughtfulness, patience, kindness, cheerfulness and understanding for his grandchildren as he had for me, his only child. They would not need to listen to recordings of the bedtime stories he used to tell me, to tapes of our conversations, nor to watch our private films, in order to hear his voice and see what he looked like. He would be right here with them, seated among them, his arms around them, telling them and reading them his stories himself. He would be having real conversations with them, drawing them wonderful pictures, playing joyful games and doing all kinds of other activities with them.

'But things are as they are. We cannot change the course of his life.

'He was one of the most important people in my life, if not *the* most important, until I gave birth myself. He was certainly my most significant male figure. He taught me so much, and he continues to teach me. The most important lesson I ever learned from him, and the lesson I am still learning, is how to be a mother. The dad that he was helps me to be the mum that I am.

'During his final years, because he knew that he would soon be gone and how difficult I would find life without him – especially given my tender age – he wrote the most special of his notebooks for me. He would not be at my side during that vulnerable period when we still desperately need our fathers. He would not be there to tell me all the things he hadn't yet had the chance to tell me about himself, because I was not yet old enough to hear them. He wouldn't be there to guide me through the maelstrom and turbulence of his fame, nor to help me recognise and separate truth from lies. He tried to warn me, because he knew that after his death some beasts would be unleashed. He wanted to make sure that, in those moments, I would never doubt the truth nor forget who he was, nor what was really and truly important.

Everything he gave me, wrote to me, drew for me and made for me was from a father to his daughter, the most important being in his life. It was all purely and simply from a dad to his child, and never from a rock superstar to the world.

'I realise now that I should never have read the press cuttings, the features or many of the countless books published after his death. I should not have watched the documentaries, nor the *Bohemian Rhapsody* film. Most of all of this is so offensive to me, but it's primarily a violation against Freddie, a massive insult to him. Without the incredible gift of his notebooks, which give me the true side of the story, what impression would I have had of my father and his life?

'And I say again, he told his story warts and all. He hid absolutely nothing from me. Some people may be shocked by this. They will find such an act unacceptable, even deplorable. They will get on their high horses and seek to moralise and judge. They will vehemently disapprove of a father writing such sordid revelations to his daughter, just as they judged him for the way he lived his life. For the record, I am neither upset nor offended by any of what he revealed to me. That was his truth. He told me everything about who he was and all that he had done. To me, it was the most beautiful thing he ever did for me.

'I have come to believe that meeting someone in person and truly knowing them are two completely different things. I say for the record that many, many people met Freddie face to face during his lifetime, but only a small handful of people ever really knew him.

'Freddie was surrounded by many people who didn't care about all that had made him the man he was. Who couldn't have cared less about his childhood, his roots, his culture, his family, his faith. Who had no interest in the traumatic experiences he had suffered, or how deeply those things had hurt and damaged him: his years confined to boarding school, the Zanzibar genocide, the shadows of his past that prevented him from sleeping, and the recurring nightmares that were the reason why he lived for years, for most of his life in fact, a nocturnal lifestyle. Throughout his life, he never stopped needing a safe and secure place to sleep, where he would not be trapped and terrified by darkness. His many sleepless nights at boarding school led to a fear of the night that never left him. He never stopped thinking about the last time he had seen his closest friends in Zanzibar, their night on the beach, the laughter, the music, then the horror that unfolded, or the interminable torment of never finding out what had happened to them.

'Many of the people around him seem not to have cared about Freddie's essence, his soul, his spirit, nor about his thoughts, his heart, his passion, his inner fire. Many were dismissive of his beautiful love life with Mary. They couldn't be bothered to try to understand his philosophy on love and sex, or his polygamous bisexuality. They disregarded his relationship with his parents and with his truest friends. They were careless about his music, his songwriting, his art. They didn't pay attention to the impact of his disease, nor how he faced the devastation it caused in his own life and in the lives of his nearest and dearest. They didn't take on board how hard it must have been for him to face his own death at the age of only forty-five. And after he was gone, they didn't take the time and trouble to honour his memory and publish his truth, once and for all, or put right the misconceptions, misunderstandings and barefaced lies. On the contrary, some of them perpetuated and embellished those abominations. Some exploited him mercilessly beyond his death. Some even appear to continue to profit from it.

'Few people really care about the truth. It tends not to be lucrative. But Freddie cared. His truth was who he was. He would never have been the dad he was, nor would he have been the brilliant artist he was, without everything that had damaged Freddie the child, Freddie the teenager and Freddie the younger man.'

He was only human, she reminds us. He had his faults.

'As a result of everything that had happened to him, forgiveness was not his best quality,' she admits. 'He did know the difference between forgiving and excusing, and he conveyed that difference to me at an early age. When he found something inexcusable, or when he felt deeply hurt and betrayed, it was sometimes impossible for him to forgive. I don't find that he was particularly bad at it. There is always a point of no return, and for Freddie that point was placed quite far. But once it had been reached, he never forgave, nor did he forget. Once he had made his decision, it was irrevocable. He would simply cut the person off and wipe them out of his life.'

Freddie was, then, an artist like no other. He was all too aware that an artist can only exist in the eyes of the public who appreciate him. Without stage, audience or recognition, it is possible that Freddie the artist would never have emerged at all.

'The public eye was one thing,' says B. 'Sadly, during his lifetime, the scrutiny of some sections of the press was dominant. Because he did everything he could to protect me from it, it didn't affect me much. He was the one who carried the burden of

Mercury. He went to great lengths to ensure that its weight had no impact, or only minimal impact, on those he loved. I imagine there's not a single atom of Mercury that hasn't been probed by the media. But his personal, inner, private self has been largely unknown. Until now.

'Ironically, and so tragically, it was the disease that liberated him from the worst of the intrusion into his private life. It afforded him the opportunity to withdraw from the limelight. It allowed him to free himself from the weight of being Mercury. He no longer needed to stand in front of his audience while enduring assaults in the press. There would be no further tours, no more road, no more press conferences, no more after-shows or everything else that he came to find so tedious. He found refuge in his work, in simply writing and singing. All he wanted, towards the end, was to continue to create while he still could.'

What, I ask her, would she like his millions of fans to take away from her revelations, as a lasting memory of the artist they adored?

'That the character called Mercury was no more than a role,' B. responds. 'I think that all people who endure the kind of thing he went through create a double of themselves, simply for the sake of self-protection. It's no accident that so many damaged and dysfunctional people become artists. Dig only a little into their lives and you will find, almost without exception, that they suffered trauma at some point in their past. It's probably true that Freddie took his double self on stage, off stage and well beyond, much higher and further than almost anyone else. He was, after all, a man of extremes. The Mercury element, however, was still nothing more than a construct. Just a character that Freddie created, whom he used to conceal and protect his inner self.

'He was never Mercury for me. Never Mercury with me. At home, he was never anyone but Dad. The handkerchiefs, bathrobes, towels and dressing gowns that he kept at our home, and which I have to this day, are not embroidered with the initials "FM". They are personalised simply with an "F", or with "FB". The "B" being for "Bulsara". Freddie was just a father like any father. At least, as any father should be.'

Of course, she says, she was damaged too.

'I still am, thanks to those who betrayed Freddie, and to those factions of the tabloid press who hurt and exposed him. But I am not at all damaged by who *he* was. Not by his excesses, his demons, his dark side or anything else. I am not haunted by Freddie Mercury, because the man I know and love is Freddie Bulsara. Nor am I damaged by my anonymity. Quite the opposite. The level to which I was protected may have saved my life. The three parents tried to do their best in this strange triangle, this odd equation, purely for *my* sake. They put *me* first. How many relatives – a child, a sibling, a spouse – are damaged or even destroyed by their connection to someone who is too huge and too famous, or by the public exposure of that relationship? We know how deeply damaged by his childhood and teenage years Freddie was. We know it was the reason why he became a rock star in the first place. We know he was then consumed by all that goes with the territory. "For each step that you go up the ladder of success," he would say, "you have to leave behind something that you love. You will lose friends, you will maybe even lose family. That's the price you have to pay."[1] He compartmentalised his life as much as he could. That, too, probably saved me.'

Freddie's words echo what he told our friend David Wigg during an interview ahead of the British leg of Queen's *The Works* tour in 1984, later quoted in the *Daily Express*: 'I don't trust anybody because they've let me down so many times ... I find it very hard to open up to people, because I don't trust others. I'm disillusioned ... having really true friends in this business is very hard.'

'What I am doing now,' says B., '– building a happy family in a loving home – was the only thing Freddie was looking for. I am able to have this most special of all things because he could not.'

• • •

There will still be people out there who think all this is a hoax, she finishes.

'But why would I do such a thing? It wouldn't make sense. Part of me understands the inclination to doubt Freddie's true story. I have seen, over the years, cards he never wrote, items he'd never possessed and autographs he'd never signed being sold at serious auction houses for significant amounts of money. We are surrounded, today, by fake news, fake videos, fake photographs, deepfakes, and so-called artificial intelligence. Social media is all-pervading. Bullying on social networks has become the norm. What kind of world and society have we created for our children? All of it frightens me.

'I have been emotional over many developments in recent times. The death of my nanny, the huge auction of Mercury's belongings, the sale of Garden Lodge, the offloading of Queen's music catalogue for an extraordinary sum – which will allow any and every kind of exploitation of Freddie's music going forward. There have been major changes in my private life, too. All this over a span of two years. It has been a lot to take in, process and cope with. It's the end of an era. A chapter has been closed. But in spite of everything, I can deal with it because only Mercury left us forever. It is Dad, and he alone, who remains.'

• • •

To those who tried but failed to snap up a piece of him at the auction of his possessions in 2023, his daughter would like them to know this: 'Sotheby's sold items that related to Freddie Mercury the musician, the entertainer, the artist, the cat lover, the aesthete and the connoisseur of art. It was not an auction of the private belongings of Freddie Bulsara, the man behind Mercury. Among the items for sale were stage costumes and clothes that he wore during the promotion of albums or at press conferences. But you were not going to find there the tracksuits that he wore all day long at home. The gorgeous kimonos and valuable antique furisodes that he collected were put up for sale – but not those he wore around the house as dressing gowns.[2] Images taken on tour or during recording sessions of Freddie the entertainer, and the many characters that he projected, were included in the sale – but not photographs depicting the private man, captured during off-duty moments or spending leisure time with his loved ones. They really haven't missed out on all that much.'

Mary Austin's auction barely bothered her at all, she says now, 'because the items that were sold spoke very little to me.

They revived virtually nothing of my father, the real Freddie who was known to so few of us. The sale stirred certain emotions, of course, as anything that marks the end of an era is bound to. I am not insensitive. I was moved by the thought that this was somehow closing a door on Freddie. But it was Mary's right to free herself from most of what he left her; her right to do exactly as she pleased with it all. I respect her for doing it, and I feel no animosity towards her. On the contrary. As I have always said to you, I will never accept, approve or endorse the slightest attack against Mary. She has my wholehearted support.'

The real Freddie was never to be found in any of that stuff anyway. Nor did he lurk in the house where he died. His memory resides elsewhere. As for Jim Hutton's insistence that Freddie was buried under a cherry tree at Garden Lodge, there is the most simple explanation: 'There is indeed a grave beneath a tree in that garden,' B. confirms. 'Jim Hutton talked about a cherry tree, but it is in fact a beautiful magnolia. My father's cats are buried there.'

• • •

'A number of his so-called friends sold things he had given them only a few months after his death,' B. says ruefully. 'And not to donate the proceeds to a charity or a fund, either, but for their own personal gain. Others even sold personal items that had allegedly belonged to him. Many of the clothes he wore on stage ended up in the trunks Queen used on tour, which were then deposited in one of their buildings. In particular, those from the *Hot Space* tour and *The Works* tour. During the *Hot Space* outing,

Freddie was wild. He didn't bring his stage costumes back to Stafford Terrace at the end of the tour. By the end of their *The Works* tour in 1985, he was already planning his move to Garden Lodge. As space at Phillimore Gardens and Stafford Terrace was running out, his costumes ended up in one of the Queen buildings. At the end of the *Magic* tour in 1986, for the same reason, his costumes were stored in one of their buildings. Freddie was about to move, and an arrangement that was supposed to be temporary ended up being permanent. Only his cloak and the crown were brought back to Garden Lodge, after a photo shoot with roadie Peter Hince; also, his yellow jacket and a pair of his stage trousers, after the making of the video for "The Miracle".

'For many of the items that are alleged to have belonged to Freddie and that have gone on sale around the world, there is often no provenance, no proof of ownership. As for the people who buy and sell towels he is supposed to have used on stage and that still contain his "sweat", what can I say?

'As you might imagine, I have kept everything. I now have my own "museum", my personal "collection". It consists of absolutely everything he ever gave me or bought for me. It also has every item he kept and left at the family homes I shared with my mother, stepfather and siblings in England, Switzerland and France: his shaving soap, his razor, his perfume bottle, his toothbrush. I still have his clothes and shoes, his handkerchiefs and bed linen, his pens, pads and scores, his books, his cigarette lighter. All the collections he helped me to accumulate are there, as are his other personal effects, including the chest of drawers from his bedroom with all that was in it, all the items inside still laid out exactly as he kept them; the huge, soft couch where he would sit cross-legged with me on his lap when I was little, where we used to look at books or watch a cartoon or a movie. The video tapes, audio tapes, boxes crammed with photos, books, cards and little notes in lacquered boxes are all there, everything stored carefully behind closed doors to protect them from light and dust. I still have his imposing antique globe. I have the canvas we painted together with lots of bright colours to make a piece of abstract art – I was very young when we did it. And all around the house are his vases, chandeliers and decorative objects. His valuable Old Master paintings share the walls with our children's primitive drawings.

'My beautiful rocking horse and countless cuddly toys were once in the museum room too. Today, these things are in the children's bedrooms and in their playroom. The beautiful board games, the chessboard, the chequers, the Scrabble set with its gold-plated tiles, and the Solitaire game with natural gemstones, all works of art, now reside in our sitting room ... as does the Bösendorfer semi-concert grand piano, which sits proudly in the middle of the room. Before I had that, I owned a Yamaha baby grand that he had given me. Then one day, after I had attended a piano exhibition and had been deeply impressed by the sound and timbre of the Bösendorfer, I happened to tell Dad about it. A few weeks later, that piano was delivered to me! I could have continued to do my scales for years on the Yamaha, but no: Freddie had decided otherwise. My old piano was donated to a local not-for-profit music school. So lots of budding pianists learned to play the piano on an instrument Freddie Mercury himself had played, without knowing anything about it.'

Not a single item in her possession will ever be sold, she says.

'Never in my lifetime will that happen. I will leave it all to my children. They will decide what they want to do with it after I'm gone. There will come a time when Freddie Mercury and Queen will have faded into the past and will have become a distant memory, or even no memory at all. When that happens, maybe no one on Earth will remember Freddie, other than his descendants. None of us can manipulate how they will regard us once we are gone.'

. . .

She has mixed feelings today about Montreux, B. reflects:

'It's not a place where I can now stay for very long. It is peaceful there, yes, and it is still very beautiful. It's where my dad and I shared many happy times. But it is also the repository of my saddest memories. I rarely go back there these days. My father really loved it there, even during his wildest, darkest years. Perhaps he saw it as an antidote to the madness. It was far too peaceful for him in those days for him to remain there for any length of time. But he always enjoyed being there. The anonymity and tranquillity that Montreux afforded him were things he couldn't find anywhere else. Yet again, people exaggerate and misinterpret his words. He never once said that he didn't like it there. He did say that he didn't care for the Mountain recording studio. It was small, and the configuration didn't suit him, but he loved the sound it captured. So he made do with it. Much later, of course, the town became his haven.

'Were he alive today, he would not find Montreux as tranquil as it was in his day. This might sound strange, but I have long believed that the time he lived in was the reason why he died so young. He lived during a period that was perfect for him, when places and things were exactly as he needed them to be. Montreux as it is today would not have suited him at all. We were so fortunate to experience it as it was. The privacy and freedom it offered us then would not be possible now.'

But it is true to say, she agrees, that it became his haven again, right at the end of his life.

'As the disease progressed, he wanted to spend more and more time there. Every six to eight weeks he would go and stay there for two or three weeks at a time, away from London and the harassment of the media.'

• • •

Mythology is alive and kicking. The 2022 updated edition of Jacky Gunn's and Jim Jenkins's Queen biography *As It Began* was authorised and revised with the cooperation of Brian and Roger. But it could never technically be regarded as the official biography of the band, B. argues, because Freddie never gave them an interview for it.

'Before the film came out, I had been protecting my heart and my mind for decades against endless attacks and lies about my father. But there was such a fuss around that movie, and so many people lined up to stab him in the back, that I was forced to suffer it all again from scratch. I had to learn again to detach myself. Things take up, in our lives, the amount of space that we want and allow them to take. Unlike my dad, I didn't have the advantage of an alter ego.

'The person in Freddie's life I feel for the most is Mary. For years, she has been misquoted outrageously and treated dreadfully. She had no choice after Freddie died but to walk away from the circus. From the *We Will Rock You* musical, from Queen + Paul Rodgers, from Queen + Adam Lambert, from the film and everything else. I'm so pleased that she has been able to maintain her privacy and live a different life. That's exactly what Freddie would have wanted for her.'

He would not have minded, she agrees, that Mary married the businessman Nick Holford seven years after Freddie died.

'He would have been sorry that their marriage didn't last. He wasn't here to take care of her himself. All he ever wanted was for people to be happy – especially the love of his life. It was the main reason why he didn't want most people he knew to see him when he was ill. Not because he rejected their pity, but because he didn't want them to be upset by the state he was in. Other people's happiness was always more important to him than his own.'

Mary took a huge amount of criticism for auctioning the contents of Garden Lodge and then putting the house itself up for sale.

'She should have converted it into a museum, a sort of Graceland, they said. Somewhere that the fans could visit to pay their respects. She didn't do it because Freddie didn't want that for the home they created together,' says B. 'What he said was, if he wanted a pyramid in his back garden and could afford to build one, he would have had one. He *could* actually afford it. He didn't have it because he didn't want it. All he wanted of that house was for it to be a happy family home for Mary, himself and their children; to see his children grow up there, and to spend his final years in comfort there. He never in his life wanted a museum.

'After he died, it remained a private house: *Mary's* private house. He wanted her to live peacefully there, away from prying eyes. Fans could visit and stand in silence for a few minutes in front of the famous green door. They could light their candles and pay tribute, no problem. But fans and photographers chasing Mary down the street every time she left the house? Fans ringing her doorbell over and over until somebody came to answer? Intruders climbing the walls to film and take pictures, at a time when her boys were still very young and playing out in the garden? How could anyone regard such behaviour as acceptable? So yes, she had no choice but to increase her security. She installed a video surveillance system and placed a privacy screen above the wall. Who wouldn't resort to such measures in such circumstances? Freddie would have hated having to do all that, but he would have done it without hesitation for her and his family. The many messages and graffiti scrawled all over the wall would have infuriated him. It is ugly and disrespectful. He would have allowed fans to leave pieces of paper bearing their messages at the door. He would also have made clear that they did not have the right to damage the wall.

'If Brian and Roger want a Queen and Freddie museum – and I don't mean the Studio Experience, the little one at the Montreux Casino – then there is nothing to stop them from building one. Most of the material they would need for something like that is stored in Queen's own buildings. They have more than enough stashed away.'

• • •

In recent years, his daughter observes, a great Freddie Mercury craze has flourished in Zanzibar:

'Tourists follow in his footsteps, take city tours, and visit the house he grew up in. Only they don't. They can't, because that house no longer exists. The island fell into extreme poverty after 1964. Only those who collaborated with the new government were safe. The houses of those who had fled were seized by the new regime. But there was no money to maintain or repair them, and the buildings fell into ruin. The beautiful house in which Freddie had grown up, with its parquet floors, wooden balcony and rooftop terrace, suffered the same fate as hundreds of other houses in Stone Town. The same thing happened to the Agiary, the Zoroastrian fire temple. When the island opened eventually for tourism, hotel groups acquired properties there for next to nothing. Barely anything of the Zanzibar of Freddie's childhood remains.

'When tour operators started advertising Freddie-related tours of Zanzibar, I was angry. This was nothing but exploitation, to make people believe they will see the Zanzibar Freddie knew. But the kind of thing they proposed was very far from the reality of Freddie's life there. If he did see the Aldabra tortoises – although they are indigenous to the Seychelles, there is an isolated group of them on Changuu Island in the Zanzibar Channel that had been a gift from the governor of the Seychelles – he certainly never swam with dolphins.'

In other words, it is impossible to tour Freddie Mercury's Zanzibar, because the Zanzibar he knew and loved is no longer there.

'Many people reproached Freddie during his lifetime, and have criticised him since, for having forgotten and turned his back on his birthplace,' she remarks. 'They also castigate him for never having returned. Even members of his own family have said this. They either forget the circumstances, or they fail to understand the situation. Until the mid-1980s, Zanzibar was a hellhole. Hunger raged. Communication with the outside world was virtually non-existent. Zanzibaris had no freedom, and education was completely inadequate. Levels of poverty during the late 1980s were worse than they had been before 1964. Even today, for most who live there, it is a very poor place. The per capita income is only around 1,000 euros per annum and the average monthly salary is 140 euros, with great disparities. Until around 1990, when the island began to open up, it was extremely difficult to obtain a visa to visit. It was even more difficult for Indians, and for those who had, like Freddie's father, worked for the British government. Bomi and his family were blacklisted. They were undesirables. We must also remember that, by the time the island began to welcome tourism, Freddie was already very ill, so could not have made the journey anyway. It is unfair to criticise him for never going back. The truth is, he was never able to.'

• • •

The research and writing of this book has been a long and heartrending process. I have cried myself to sleep countless times. For Freddie, who adored his only child but never got to see her grow up, to give her away at her wedding, nor to meet the grandchildren in whom he lives on. Whose life was redrawn without his permission, as I have often observed, as a grotesque rock 'n' roll panto. Whose nature was never truly understood. I have wept for his beautiful daughter, for her orphanhood, and for the privileged but compromised life she has lived. Guarding their secret, though she stresses that she has never regarded it as a burden, has taken its toll.

'I'm an emotional sponge,' she says, 'but then so was he. I saw him cry sometimes, and not for joy. There were also times when we would sit and cry together.'

Now that she has come clean, delivering his truth as he lived and recorded it, restoring her father's dignity, silencing the speculators and shutting down those who have long peddled lies, I pray that she feels liberated and has found peace. Now, in the manner of someone carrying a bowl of goldfish across Piccadilly Circus, I hand her back her privacy.

'I have always felt his absence,' she says. 'But I also feel his presence. Perhaps I imagine it. Maybe these things are just tricks of the brain or the memory. When you have known someone so intimately that you can tell exactly what they would have thought, said or done in any situation, the absence becomes the presence, embroidered with the memories that remain.

'A few years ago, while I was undergoing minor surgery under mild general anaesthesia, I experienced something strange that I had never felt before. I don't know why, but just as the anaesthetic was being administered, I suddenly remembered a very happy moment with him. The feeling was sublime. The odd thing was that the anaesthetist had difficulty waking me up after the surgery, even though the dose was very low. They couldn't understand what had happened. It might sound ridiculous, but I like to think that maybe I was somehow with him again, if only for a little moment.

'This, too, might sound strange: that whenever I see a squirrel, I always feel that Freddie is nearby. We used to go out and try to spot them high in the trees. He told me that when he was a child in Zanzibar, he and his three best friends, Ahmed, Ibrahim and Mustapha, sometimes went out together on a mission to look for bushbabies. He told me how difficult they were to see in the trees. Just like squirrels. So those little creatures always remind me of him. Perhaps we make these connections to comfort ourselves. But perhaps they are not coincidences. After all, bushbabies are closely related to squirrels.

'Most of all, I love the idea of my dad reaching out from the World of Thoughts, pirouetting about the place and watching over his precious grandchildren.'

CHAPTER NOTES

CHAPTER 1

1 *Love of My Life* by Lesley-Ann Jones published by Coronet/Hodder & Stoughton in hardback, 2021, paperback edition 2022.

2 Kenny Everett died of AIDS on 4 April 1995, four years after his former friend. He was fifty years old.

CHAPTER 2

1 'Time', a song written by Dave Clark and Jeff Daniels for the former's 1986 eponymous musical. The recording featured Mike Moran on keyboards and Ray Russell on guitars. Freddie also recorded the song 'In My Defence', written by the same two songwriters with David Soames. While both tracks appeared on the cast album, Freddie did not perform in the stage production. The promotional video for 'Time' was shot at the Dominion Theatre, Tottenham Court Road, London, where the Queen musical *We Will Rock You* would later be staged.

2 Roger Taylor is the father of Felix Luther Taylor (22 May 1980), an artist, and daughter Rory Eleanor Taylor (29 May 1986), a doctor, by Dominique Beyrand – whom he had met in 1976, and to whom he was later married for just one month in 1988. His other children are Rufus Tiger Taylor (8 March 1991), a drummer; Tigerlily Taylor (10 October 1994), a model, and Lola Daisy May Leng Taylor (2 April 2000), an actor. Their mother is former model Debbie Leng. At the time of writing, Roger is married to South African-born actor Sarina Potgieter.

3 Not that DNA profiling could have been applied in 1976. Such screening was as yet unavailable. DNA fingerprinting was first used in forensic science in the UK in 1986. Before then, doctors relied on blood types and other proteins to establish the likelihood or otherwise of paternity. Results were often inaccurate. By the 1990s, they had become reliable.

4   The prophet Zoroaster, also known as Zarathustra, may have been a contemporary of Cyrus the Great, a king of the Persian Empire in the sixth century BC. Archaeological and linguistic evidence, however, suggests that he lived even earlier, probably between 1500 and 1200 BC.

CHAPTER 3

1   *The Shahnameh* or 'Book of Kings' is an epic poem written in Classical Persian by the poet Ferdowsi between 977 and 1010 CE. Cherished today as the national epic of Greater Iran, it recounts both the history and mythology of Iran from the creation of the world to the seventh-century Muslim conquest.

2   The Indo-Aryan Gujarati, a derivative of Sanskrit (the ancient, sacred language of Hinduism) hails from the Indian state of Gujarat. Spoken today by some 55.5 million people, it is the sixth most common in India. Gujarati is also the fourth most popular in London, behind Bengali – officially the capital's second tongue – then Polish and Turkish.

3   Mr Oswald D. Bason MA was principal of St Peter's School for twenty-seven years, 1947–1974, and was Freddie's headmaster. He was the school's first Indian principal, as well as the first non-British clergyman to hold the position. Bason Hall, a large dormitory at the school, was named in his memory.

4   The Dhom Dam, construction of which took place between 1976 and 1982, many years after Freddie left St Peter's, was built to flood the valley, provide irrigation for agriculture and industry, and to create a water supply for the surrounding towns and villages, including Panchgani-Mahabaleshwar. The dam also generates hydroelectricity.

CHAPTER 4

1   The Holy Bible, Matthew 6: 5–8.

CHAPTER 5

1   Freddie's naturalisation record documents are held by, and are available to view at, the National Archives, Kew, Richmond, Surrey.

CHAPTER 6

1 Joe Fannelli was dubbed 'Liza' because his surname reminded Freddie of the American actress and singer Liza Minnelli. Various other men in his circle were given drag names/cross names: Roger Taylor became 'Liz', after the actress Liz Taylor. Brian May was 'Maggie' (as in the song), Peter Freestone was 'Phoebe', John Reid 'Beryl', Elton John 'Sharon', Rod Stewart 'Phyllis' and Paul Prenter 'Trixie'. Freddie himself was 'Melina', inspired by the Greek actress Melina Mercouri. In a reversal of the gag, Mary Austin was 'Steve': her nickname inspired by 'The Six Million Dollar Man', NASA astronaut Steve Austin, the lead character in a popular US TV series who was played by actor Lee Majors. They had the technology. They could rebuild him ... There is a suggestion, unsubstantiated, that artist Long John Baldry, a pioneer of the British blues-rock scene in the 1960s and who scored a British number one in November 1967 with 'Let the Heartaches Begin', started the trend by renaming Elton and Rod, both of whom he had been in bands with before they hit the big time. As Baldry died in 2005, we can't ask him.

2 *Strange Case of Dr Jekyll and Mr Hyde*, published 1883, is a legendary Gothic horror novella by Robert Louis Stevenson in which good and evil in a single character are explored. Gizmo and Mogwai featured in the 1984 comedy horror film *Gremlins*.

3 In a 2013 filmed interview, Thierry Amsallem says that he was twenty-three years old when he and Claude Nobs met, making the year they got together 1987. Thierry also told some of his stories in a 2023 blick.ch documentary, *Découvrez les chalets de Claude Nobs et leurs secrets* ('Discover the chalets of Claude Nobs and their secrets'), available online in French. Blick is Switzerland's largest Swiss German-language print newspaper and news/features website. He gave a long interview for the Montreux Jazz Festival that year, and has spoken publicly at the Montreux Freddie Mercury events. He is widely commended today for the wonderful job he is doing, preserving the life's work of his later partner Claude Nobs.

4 Vicky Vocat worked for Claude Nobs, and was once manager of Mountain Studios. She later became a spokesperson for the Mercury Phoenix Trust charity for HIV and AIDS awareness and prevention. In the mid-1990s,

engineer and producer David Richards acquired the studio from Queen, and relocated it to Attalens. He owned and ran it there until his death in 2013. The Montreux Casino Barrière building later became the home of a small, permanent Queen exhibition featuring recordings, concert footage, a video about the making of their final album *Made in Heaven*, photos, a few costumes and other items of memorabilia. 'Funky Claude', as Nobs was referenced in the Deep Purple hit 'Smoke on the Water' from their 1972 album *Machine Head*, sustained an accident on Christmas Eve 2012 while out cross-country skiing, fell into a coma and died just over a fortnight later.'

5   Jo Burt later had his own band, the Jo Burt Experience, who now go out under the name Jo Burt and the Lazy Farquhars, playing 'Anglicana' music: 'Nashville rock with an English accent'.

6   '*Repos du guerrier*' is a French expression meaning 'the warrior's rest'. It was the title of a 1962 film by French director Roger Vadim (that title became *Love on a Pillow* for the US market). When a noble warrior returns home after a long absence and challenging battle, he finds quiet, calm, peace and love there, as well as a well-deserved rest beside his beloved.

CHAPTER 9

1   J.J. Grandville's *Un autre monde,* with illustrations and designs by Grandville and text by Taxile Delord, was published in French in 1844.

CHAPTER 11

1   Bernard Haitink (1929–2021) was principal conductor of the London Philharmonic Orchestra from 1967 until 1979, music director at Glyndebourne Opera for ten years from 1978, and music director of the Royal Opera House Covent Garden 1987–2002. His last concert was with the Vienna Philharmonic at KKL Luzern – the Lucerne Culture and Congress Centre – on 6 September 2019, when he was ninety years old. He died in October 2021, aged ninety-two.

2   The 2012 special edition of the Barcelona album features the FILMharmonic Orchestra of Prague, comprising leading members of

the Czech Philharmonic and the Prague Symphony orchestras, and live percussion.

3 The 'Barcelona' single released in 1987 later became that city's anthem for the 1992 Summer Olympic Games, staged in the city between 25 July and 9 August. They commenced almost exactly eight months after Freddie had died. Montserrat sang at the opening ceremony with Spanish tenors Plácido Domingo and José Carreras.

4 Montserrat Caballé's fifty-year career ended in her death at the age of eight-five on 6 October 2018. She survived Freddie by twenty-seven years.

CHAPTER 12

1 Merbromin, an antiseptic that combines mercury and bromine, is poisonous and very harmful if swallowed. In October 1998, the US Food and Drug Administration reclassified merbromin from 'generally recognized as safe' to 'untested', thus effectively ending its distribution throughout America. In the UK, it is still sold in antiseptic solution, liquid plaster and sticking plaster form, under the brand Mercurochrome.

2 The Amu Darya, 1,500 miles/2,400 kilometres long and known historically as the Oxus, is a major Central Asian river that crosses Tajikistan, Turkmenistan, Uzbekistan and Afghanistan. Compare this to the UK's longest, the Severn, at 220 miles/354 kilometres, and the USA's longest, the Missouri, known as 'the Big Muddy', at 2,300 miles/3,767 kilometres. *Daryā* is the Persian word for lake or sea. Medieval Arabic and Islamic texts refer to the river as *Jeyhoun*, which derives from *Gihon*, a Hebrew word meaning 'gushing' or 'bursting forth'. It is the biblical name for one of the four rivers of the Garden of Eden, the others being the Tigris, the Euphrates and Pishon rivers.

CHAPTER 13

1 Richard Berkowitz, Michael Callen, Dr Joseph Sonnabend, *How to Have Sex in an Epidemic* (AIDS Medical Foundation, May1983).
Richard Berkowitz, 'Staying Alive in the Year of the Plague', *Mandate*, November 1983.

The National Gay Health Education Foundation held the First International Lesbian and Gay Health Conference at New York University's Loeb Student Center in June 1984.

How to Have Safe Sex in a Bathhouse, a Florida presentation commissioned by Jack Campbell, CEO and Founder of the Club Bath Chain (CBC), February 1985.

2   Translated from the Japanese by Philip Gabriel, from *Kafka on the Shore*.

CHAPTER 14

1   As quoted by Rudi Dolezal in February 2019.
2   A furisode is a formal Japanese kimono with long, swinging sleeves.

ACKNOWLEDGEMENTS

Writers work in isolation, sustained by insomnia, supplements and biscuits. We depend on small armies to turn our work into books. I am indebted to John Bond, Julia Koppitz, Kiana Palombo, Jess King, Zoila Marenco, Chris Wold and everyone else employed by and associated with Whitefox, not least Nicola Bigwood and Gill Phillips, who had a hand in creating and publishing this one; to the multi-award-winning artist and designer Ahlawat Gunjan, whose vision for the cover captured Freddie perfectly; to the estate of Mick Rock, 'the man who shot the seventies', for granting us the rights to use this beautiful portrait of his close friend; and to Bridie Shine MA, for their painstaking research in sexuality and gender that has informed this book.

For their lifelong friendship and support, I am so grateful to Maureen Ong, Ghee Ong, Jan Moore, Sue Foo, Nelson Foo, Jitna Por, Chye Por, Penny Crosby, Kate Peacock, Julie Ives-Routleff and Karen French; also to Gönül Güney, Lisa Tsang, Tessa Niles, Pauline Cutler, Richard Hughes, Martin Barden, Ed Phillips, Alison Joyce, Suki Yamamoto, Berni Kilmartin, Leo McLoughlin, Fiz Shapur, Aoibheann Greene, Simon Napier-Bell, Yotin Chaijanla, Clem Cattini, Brian Bennett, Gill Cornell, Jaqui Delbaere and Joan Chappell.

With love to Misa, Peter, Ella and Petra; Wendy, Phil and Jess; Gareth, Bev, Cleo and Jesse; Bev, Rob, Nick, Alex and Christian;

and to Sam, Chris, Adam and Matty Boy. Today NASA, tomorrow the universe.

This book is dedicated to my beloved children Mia, Henry and Bridie; to my mother and father, Kathleen and Ken; to Lynn Ashby, whose faith and passion drove the cause and made all things possible; and, not least, to the cherished memory of Norbert Muller. Now cracks a noble heart.

laj

September 2025

INDEX